Norman Van Aken's

FEAST OF SUNLIGHT

200 Inspired Recipes from the Master of New World Cuisine

Norman Van Aken

The Harvard Common Press
Boston, Massachusetts

The Harvard Common Press
535 Albany Street
Boston, Massachusetts 02118

Printed in the United States of America
Printed on acid-free paper

Library of Congress Cataloging-in-Publication Data
Van Aken, Norman.
    Norman Van Aken's feast of sunlight : 200 inspired recipes from the master of New World Cuisine / Norman Van Aken.
        p. cm.
    Originally published: New York : Ballantine Books, c1988.
    Includes bibliographical references and index.
    ISBN 1-55832-136-5 (alk. paper)
    1. Cookery, International. I. Title.
    [TX725.A1.V28 1997]
    641.59—dc21   97-6625

Cover design by Suzanne Noli
Cover photograph by Greg Schneider
Text design by Michaelis/Carpelis Design Associates

Special bulk-order discounts are available on this and other Harvard Common Press books. Companies and organizations may purchase books for premiums or for resale, or may arrange a custom edition, by contacting the Marketing Director at the address above.

10 9 8 7 6 5 4 3 2 1

For our son, Justin.
For my wife, Janet; my mother, Ruth;
my late father, Harold; and
lastly, in loving memory,
for our Nana, Janie Quinn Manderson.

CONTENTS

ACKNOWLEDGMENTS

This book (and the knowledge I have attempted to convey in it) was made possible by thousands of circumstances, and people, as everything that touches us shapes our thoughts. The people I knew but for a moment . . . the short-order cook in an all-night hash house in Honolulu whose rhythm and concentration captivated me and made me curious about the joy he brought to his work fifteen-odd years ago . . . the Mexican laborers who shared their wonderful lunches of warm tortillas, eggs, and fried beans in the heat of a Kansas summer as we broke from the numbing labor of working concrete . . . and the offhand plea of a fellow cook (and my superior at the time) who, exasperated with my constant flow of questions, suggested that I read a cookbook—and magically added, "Beard."

But more than any other, it is quite singularly my editor and now good friend, Risa Kessler, who made this book happen, and I feel deep gratitude, for I have learned much in the process of writing it.

To properly acknowledge everyone else, it is necessary for me to think geographically, so I give thanks as follows:

International: To Roger Vergé, Michel Guérard, Alain Senderens, les frères Troisgros, Giuliano Bugialli, Marcella Hazan, Richard Olney, Paul Bocuse, and Fernand Point, for their superb guidance and inspiration.

National: To James Beard and Alice Waters, perhaps the two most profound influences on my work; while others may have offered as much, the special vision of these two affected me most deeply.

Special thanks to Paula Wolfert, whose passion and intelligence about cuisine is always motivating.

Thanks to M.F.K. Fisher, a voice that sings through time, from Brillat-Savarin to now.

Thanks to Bruce and Barbara Neyers for their generous hospitality and infinite good humor.

Thanks to Jim Harrison, writer and poet, whose company is a banquet for the mind.

For Butchie and Tokio, in memoriam.

Chicago: Very special thanks to Gordon Sinclair, who gave me the chance to try my hand, and to my first crew at Sinclair's Restaurant in Lake Forest, Illinois: Rick Carbaugh, Tom Trieschmann, Carrie Nahabedian, Suzy Crofton, Ed Hale, Pam Hale, Carlos Torres, Kurt Kuss, and Celeste Zeccola.

Thanks to Roy and Bonnie Axelson of Seafood Merchants, Sophia Solomon of Tekla Inc., and Kaye Zubow of Wild Game.

Also thanks to two of the most influential restaurateurs in the country—Jean Banchet of Le Français and Carlos Nieto of Carlos'—who have done more to teach young chefs and waiters than they will probably ever know.

And heartfelt thanks to my *beautiful* sisters, Jane and Bette, and my niece, Cayce.

Lastly, to my late father-in-law, Irvin Amsler, a man who understood the true gift of giving, and my mother-in-law, Millie, who still lives it.

Key West: For the old days at the Pier House with Alan Katz, Annie Donovan, Nino, Betty, and the angelic Drapes.

For friends Warren Sweeney, Danny and Ann, Jeff and Nancy, Pam and Steve, Wade, Rick and Nancy, Joel and Jerrie, and, of course, Susan, Rebecca, and Matthew.

For those who bring the goods: Buco and his staff at Waterfront Markets Produce; the Lobster Man; Croissants de France; the Herb Lady; Ron and Keith from BVM Meats; Big Bobby; George Collins, and many more.

For our truly magical photography team—Jeffrey Cardenas, Katie Truax, and Irene Carpelis.

For my original kitchen staff at Louie's Backyard, my deep gratitude goes to Danny McHugh, Barbara Cantilini, Susan Porter, Alan Baum, Kelle Williams, Larry Teeter, Heidi Nickel, and Sharon Fisher. Thanks to Susan Ferry for her special help with the testing, to Phil Tenney for his wit, and to chef Doug Shook.

Finally, I would like to thank the marvelous Donna Hastie, who typed and helped organize this book more times than you can imagine, yet still manages to smile at me.

And my partner, friend, and brother, Proal Perry.

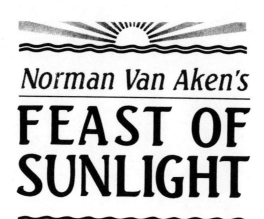

Norman Van Aken's
FEAST OF
SUNLIGHT

Introduction to the Paperback Edition

I was born on a hot and steamy July morning in the little town of Diamond Lake, Illinois. Born on a sunny day, I have, it seems, from that moment on always loved the sun.

When I was a young boy, this love was delightfully reinforced every year at the end of December, when my parents would take me and my two sisters for a vacation to Miami Beach, Florida. We'd leave the day after Christmas and stay for two weeks.

It was the late 1950s and Miami Beach was just then coming into its own as the "Fun and Sun Capital" of America. It was so magical, getting on a Delta plane and trading snow suits for swim suits in the short space of half a day!

The candy-colored Art Deco hotels, the coconut smell of suntan lotion, and the warm, thick, caressing feel of sunlight all hypnotized me. As I write these words many years later, I remember the man who raked the sand to a gleaming whiteness every morning while I swam, the smell of French toast and pork sausages cooking at the drugstore counter we'd go to for breakfast, and the sultry feel of the night air as we cruised in my father's rented convertible down Collins Avenue or Ocean Drive, on our way to some fabulous "big-steaks-and-lobsters" restaurant.

Unlike at home in Illinois, in Florida the term *outdoors* made little sense. So few doors were needed. The breezes and the ocean never left you. The world was wide open, and the warmth and the sound of water were always present. The quality of the Miami Beach light, folded into the rich, salty air, made indoors and out one and the same.

Of course it would end. We would return home and go back to school, our winter tans fading quickly in the decidedly indoor pursuits of a Midwest winter. It was during those long winters that I started to cook, first with my mother and my sisters. When Mom and Dad broke up, my grandmother, Nana, came to live with us, and she taught me even more about cooking and baking.

The boy I was became the teen, and the teen became the man. Things change, and there's the rub. I celebrated my eighteenth birthday four days after Neil Armstrong touched the moon. While we achieved that dream another dream was dying every night on television, in a distant place called Vietnam. Looking back now, I see how it all affected me artistically. To become an artist, you try, in your own way, to remake the world. You hope that you make it a better place.

Out of high school, I didn't know what I wanted to be, so, after a short try at college, I hit the road, to Hawaii, Colorado, California, Key West, and other places. I took all kinds of jobs: construction worker, factory worker, carny, landscaper. I even sold flowers on the streets.

Eventually I came home to Illinois, and I rented a place with a bunch of guys. Looking for a job, I saw an ad in the paper for a short-order cook at a mom-and-pop place called Tom and Jerry's Fireside Inn, in the town of Libertyville. A small place, Tom and Jerry's was made grander by the thirty-foot-tall milk bottle on the roof, which you could see from a long way off. Working-class people, and even some of the upper crust, followed the milk bottle to the inn at all hours of the day.

I tucked my long hair up under my cap and applied. Much to my surprise, they hired me, at $3.75 an hour. Rent would be a snap with that kind of jack! They were surprised to see the hair when I came in the next day, but I shortly proved myself and they even came to like me. I met there the girl I would love for the rest of my life, my Janet, who was working part-time and was still in high school. We were married in 1976 and moved to Key West the next year.

I've since worked in many restaurants, but I never have gone to chef's school and I never did a "stage" with any of the great chefs. No particular genius's vision guided me through the early years. Instead, I read and read. I traveled. I cooked and tasted, burning myself and cutting myself in countless hours in the kitchen, and cooked and tasted more. Sometimes I would leave one job to take another where I could learn more. Slowly the food I was cooking was becoming my *own* food.

Living in Key West as a young cook proved to be the most creative experience of all for me. It helped me find my own identity in cuisine. I acquired a love of Caribbean, Southern, and Latin flavors. Yet, from books as much as from experience, I retained a great respect for classical cooking, particularly French and what was coming to be known as New American. I realized that no chef in our region was doing the kind of regionally inspired but classically informed cooking I wanted to do.

I began to forge together a collection of recipes that would bespeak the fertile culinary culture in which I was living. In this first book of mine you will see the early shoots of what I later termed *New World Cuisine.*

At our restaurant, Norman's, in the Coral Gables section of Miami, the love of the sun and of the flavors of sunlight is still celebrated. As I expressed it when I first wrote this book in Key West, so I would put it today: The cuisine that incites my imagination is clearly born and routinely inspired by the sun. It is a cuisine of the sun on which I focus my attention in this book. Not all of the recipes will be immediately evocative of sand and sea, lush tropical foliage, and tiny winding streets in villages with bars and cafés where ceiling fans push back the midday heat. But my cuisine has much to do with the sun, and whether it is the boot of Southern Italy, the sun-drenched streets of Mexico City, or home here in Florida, it is the passionate theme of heat that fires me on.

For me, this book is like a mirror that reflects an incredibly formative time in my life. Hold it up and see if you find anything that inspires you. I hope it will be a feast—a feast of sunlight.

Coral Gables
Spring 1997

FOOD FOR THOUGHT

The verb *to cook* implies that something is happening; changes are taking place that create a variety of results. To understand where you want to end up, you must first understand how to get there. As you work with food you learn how it changes; and to really learn you need to work with all of your senses. You see, smell, touch, taste and even listen to the food. You are after something specific here—that very special will-o'-the-wisp known as *flavor.*

How is flavor perceived? Certainly the sense of smell is key. Webster's says that we discern flavors by the sense of taste, and goes on to describe taste this way: "The sense that is stimulated by contact of a substance with the taste buds on the surface of the tongue and is capable of distinguishing between sweet, sour, salt, and bitter."

Sweet, sour, salt, and bitter are, in a way, the compass points of taste: the North, South, East, and West, if you will. When you cook, you make decisions about which direction you wish to travel in. The further in any one direction you go, however, the less balanced your food will be. But that's not always bad—who would want salty ice cream?

While teaching myself about wine, I learned another analogy that helps me understand the balance in flavors; when you study the flavor of wine, you find that you can apply the same technique to food. When people speak of wine, they often refer to its *structure.* This idea mystified me until I thought of structure in terms of the human body. The most easily accessible qualities in wine are the fruity and acidic flavors of the grape; so if you imagine the rich fruit as the flesh of man, and the acid as the bone structure, you can easily see their interdependence on one another. Too much richness and you have a heavy, flabby dish; too much acid, and it is brittle and hard. We must balance the structure of flavor by being aware when we cook; analyze your food continuously and taste it for the direction it has taken relative to where you want it to go.

Marcella Hazan, in her brilliant way, has summed it up quite well. She tells us that Italians use the word *insaporire* to describe the process of making something tasty. She goes on to describe the method for making a sauce where finely diced vegetables are sautéed until they are glazed and imbued with flavor before the next step is taken. If you are making a cream sauce, for instance, I would normally advise you to cook the vegetables in butter (the flesh), then add wine or vinegar (the bones), and finish with cream and seasoning (more flesh). With only butter or cream your sauce would be fat and heavy, but the addition of vinegar helps add structure to your sauce, the way your spine adds structure to your body. This knowledge will help you obtain rounded, layered flavors that will move across the palate in waves.

Rather than give you dozens of specific examples of this "body analogy," I am offering the following chart which will serve as a kind of shorthand. Your own imagination can do the rest!

The Body Analogy

Butter *Cream* *Oil*	=	*Flesh*
Wine *Vinegar* *Citrus*	=	*Bones*
Meat *Stock* *Glaze*	=	*Muscle*
Vegetables *Herbs* *Spices* *Fruit/Sugar*	=	*Soul/Personality*

Let's talk about shock and seduction. Shock is the storm trooper's style. He grabs French green beans and plunges them into a pot of furiously boiling water. They cook a few moments, then are scooped out and dropped immediately into icy water. This is shock treatment. Or take a few precisely cut sections of raw filet mignon, as a Japanese chef would, heat a wok to maximum and spin the beef in sizzling peanut oil. This, too, is shock treatment.

Conversely, we have the hand-in-hand stroll of seduction. Consider beef stew: it may have begun on the hot fire of a searing moment, but it went on to enjoy the intimacy of slow cooking where flavors court and exchange back and forth until the characteristics of every component are imbued with the whole.

Time, temperature, and environment.

These three factors have major capacities to affect food. The French speak of *saisissement* and *échange,* sealing and exchange. I call it shock and seduction. When we employ the method of shock alone, we insure that the individual character of a specific item will be sealed and locked within it, waiting until we taste it to reveal its singular flavor and identity. When we cook by seduction, we create an environment whereby we seek to elicit a communion of flavors and textures.

You can purposely utilize both techniques in one dish. For instance, you may sear lamb shanks on high heat to seal in their meaty juices only to go on to an exchange method of braising the lamb in wine and broth with vegetables for several hours to attain the rich, resonating flavors that slow cooking can foster.

The important point is to know that differentiating between the two should be a conscious act. The cook who takes something as delicate as asparagus, lets it sit out in the heat for two hours, cooks it in tepid water and allows it to cool in that same water will end up with a dull-colored, limp victim of poor methodology. By the same token, the cook who boils beef stew at full tilt for forty-five minutes and then pronounces it cooked has robbed it of the time it needs for any exchange of flavors. In each case, the principles of sealing and exchange were confused.

In cooking, some things are done quickly; some take time. Knowing something about shock and seduction can be critical in the kitchen, too.

Ripeness is everything. Foods are not always ready to be eaten when brand new—consider a banana, or a wheel of Camembert. It is obvious that we must give nature time to allow certain foods to come to fullness; yet the flavors of other foods are momentary things and can fade from their newborn perfection at lightning speed. The cook must bring food to the table within its time.

So don't be too rigid with any recipe. I encourage you to read through the book, then put it down and go to the market. It seems to me that we put the cart before the horse when we go down the aisles with a recipe fixed in our minds, trying to match what is on the shelves to words on a printed page. A recipe is a guide, at best, and alterations are certainly acceptable. The raw product should be the first inspiration for excellent cuisine.

If there is to be a lasting renaissance of cooking in this country, it will have to be nurtured in many ways. One way that we can contribute is through the demands we place on the market—when you go to the store and you don't see what you want, *tell* the manager. The law of supply is contingent upon your demand.

There are small purveyors sprouting up all over the country. Many of these people are working on a level that needs the economic support of the public, but they don't have the huge advertising budget of a conglomerate to create this public awareness. As you hear about small, quality-driven suppliers, tell your store manager about them. The more quality choices we have, the better.

Some of you may be daunted by the prospect of attempting many of my dishes yourselves, since you don't have the advantage of a professional staff at your disposal! Rather than tell you in recipe after recipe how you can take various shortcuts at home, I hope you will try to follow the recipes as written. If you choose to substitute water for stock, dried herbs for fresh, that's up to you. But remember that a recipe is like a road map; I've done my best to give accurate instructions on how you can get from point A to point B, but you must realize that there are limitations to recipes. In following a recipe, you are not only given physical directions, you are given time and temperature instructions as well. However, your sauté pan might heat more slowly than mine, your grill may be hotter, your idea of doneness may differ, your sense of spice may be more delicate. Therefore you, as the cook, will have to sense what is right and make judgments on the recipe as you work it. Just a little common sense and the realization that everything is not the same for everyone will make it all work out fine in the end.

FUNDAMENTALS

~~~~~~~~~~~~~~~

Here I include information basic to the use of this book. These notes on ingredients and techniques are intended to simplify your buying and preparation, and to help assure the quality of the finished dishes.

Ingredients

The following specifications apply throughout the book, with any exceptions noted in individual recipes:

• All ingredients such as meat, fish, herbs, fruits, and vegetables are fresh, not dried, frozen, or canned.

• Eggs are extra large.

• All butter is unsalted.

• All citrus juices are freshly squeezed.

• Pepper is freshly cracked black pepper from a peppermill.

• Flour is unbleached all-purpose flour.

• Heavy cream is cream with a 38 percent butterfat content. Avoid the ultrapasteurized type if possible; cream that is not ultrapasteurized is more perishable but vastly preferable in taste, and it whips better, too.

• Parmesan cheese should be true Parmigiano-Reggiano. When a recipe calls for grated cheese, it should be freshly grated.

• When an ingredient is to be diced or chopped, use a medium dice unless the recipe specifies "finely" diced, "coarsely" chopped, or other variations.

Cracklings: The crisply cooked fat from ducks, geese, chicken, and other fowl is splendid in salads, as a soup garnish, or even, salted and peppered, as a snack. You can save the fat from various birds and store it, tightly wrapped, in the freezer until you want to make cracklings. Then chop the fat into medium dice and add it to 1 or 2 cups of water in a heavy pot. Melt the fat, stirring. Gradually the water will evaporate and the fat will crisp and turn deep brown. Carefully strain the contents of the pot through cheesecloth, reserving the oil for cooking if you like.

Mussels and Clams: Cleaning them thoroughly is a fairly tedious but absolutely essential first step. Put them through several changes of cold water, scrubbing them hard with a stiff-bristled brush each time. When the shells seem pristinely clean and the water remains clear, you've done the job. Debeard mussels by removing the ropy protrusions with a sharp paring knife. Proceed with recipe instructions. If these call for heating the mollusks, with or without liquid, until the shells open, be patient. It could take a while. However, it's a good idea to remove those that open first, lest they toughen while the others are taking their time. And if one or two stubbornly refuse to open, discard them.

Peppers and Chiles: The recipes in this book make abundant use of both bell peppers and assorted chiles. By no means do all require that they be peeled, but you do have to remove the seeds and ribs. This is simplicity itself: Simply slit down one side of the clean pepper, open it up, cut out the main seed pod clustered under the stem, and shake out all the loose seeds. Then trim off the interior ribs and prepare the peppers as instructed.

Peeling is another matter. For bell peppers, there are a number of ways to loosen the skins. You can roast very lightly oiled peppers on a grill until the skin is charred, then put them in a bowl and cover them with a towel so they steam. If you have a gas stove, you can char the peppers by holding and turning them with tongs over the flame. Or you can broil them. Again, you want the skin charred all over, and this could take as much as 20 minutes of turning them occasionally under your oven broiler. Then put them in a paper bag to steam until the skins loosen and the peppers are cool enough to handle. Either way, you then peel off the charred skins completely, slit open one side, and remove the seeds and ribs. The beautiful red, yellow, or green flesh is now ready for use in the recipes.

Chiles can be confusing, and in this country a mystique tends to surround them. I encourage you to read about them in *Modern Southwest Cuisine,* by John Sedlar, *Feast of Santa Fe,* by Huntley Dent, or any of Diana Kennedy's books. For the purposes of *this* book, you need to know how to distinguish chiles in the market, so you can buy the ones specified.

Fresh chiles can be dealt with as are bell peppers (noting any special instructions in individual recipes), except that you should probably wear gloves when handling them, especially if your skin is sensitive, and you must utterly avoid rubbing your eyes with a hand that has just touched a chile.

The same cautions apply to dried chiles, but in addition you should know that they benefit from being briefly toasted. The ancho, a dried poblano chile, stars in several of my recipes. It has a seductive, smoky, toasty, earthy flavor. To toast the ancho, you can either use a comal, a flat stone griddlelike device, or you can grasp the stem with tongs and hold the ancho over a gas burner or a grill, turning it frequently. (Take care not to let anchos catch fire; any sauce you use them in will then be bitter.) After they are toasted, soak them in a bowl of liquid (usually water, but sometimes stock or vinegar, depending on the recipe) to soften them. Then remove the stems and seeds.

Tomato Concasse: To prepare tomato concasse (from the French *concasser,* to break up), core a ripe tomato and slash a shallow X on its bottom. Drop the tomato into a pot of rapidly boiling water for 10 seconds, remove with a slotted spoon, and plunge it into a bowl of icy water. When the tomato is just cool, peel it, slice it crosswise, and squeeze and scoop out the seeds. Finally, chop the tomato into medium dice and reserve for its intended purpose. The recipes sometimes specify a given amount of tomato concasse, the dice just described, and sometimes call for a certain number of tomatoes, concassée. The only difference is that in the first case the quantity is finished dice, while in the second it's number of tomatoes.

Zest: The extreme outer layer of various citrus fruits gives an eponymous quality to foods in which it is included. The trick is to remove this layer without taking any of the bitter white pith beneath. You can use a very sharp paring knife or a swivel-bladed peeler. (Be sure the fruit is clean—a quick bath in warm water, followed by thorough drying, is a good idea.) The zest must then be finely minced before measuring. You can do this on a cutting board, but a small electric coffee-bean grinder does a marvelous job, if you have one.

Advice and Techniques

Never cook with a wine you wouldn't enjoy drinking.

I like to keep a variety of vinegars on hand. It is not always necessary to use the exact type specified in a particular recipe, but do try to. Small bottles of specialty vinegars are not too costly, and many interesting ones are available in most good markets.

In many of my dishes, I use a combination of olive oil and butter. I like the rich creaminess of butter and the sunny, fruity taste of excellent olive oil. You will want both virgin and extra virgin olive oil in your larder, and perhaps you will enjoy experimenting with some of the many fine varieties from France, Greece, Italy, and even Spain. Their flavors differ dramatically, some mild and some very intense, so your preference may depend to some extent on how you plan to use them.

When you make stocks, especially those based on meat or poultry, try to prepare them at least a day ahead of time. After being refrigerated overnight, the stock will have settled completely, its flavor will have mellowed, and the fat will have hardened on the surface so that you can easily remove it.

To "reduce" means to cook your sauce or stock long enough to decrease its volume. This concentrates and intensifies the flavor while reducing the liquidity. When a stock is greatly reduced, say from 3 or 4 gallons to 1 or 2 cups, it will, on cooling, become so gelatinous and thick that it will harden like a paste. This is called *glace* in French, or glaze in English, and is caused by protein bonding. (A demiglace is thus a stock reduced halfway.) I feel that it is economical and even practical for the home cook to prepare such glazes. They can be kept for a short period of time in the refrigerator, but it is preferable to freeze them in small containers that are dated, clearly marked, and tightly sealed.

Naturally, you should read any recipe straight through before plunging into preparing it. This is particularly important here. Many of the recipes will appear very complex at first glance, with several elements and a lot of steps. But I think you will find that they break down into easily managed procedures, and that often some portions can be prepared several hours or even a day or two ahead. If you have taken my advice and stocked your larder with some of the basics, so much the better.

BATTERIE

The tools a chef works with are known as the *batterie de cuisine*. As a professional chef, I take for granted the presence of some items a home cook might like some advice on. The following comments are just a broad guide to help you know what to look for when shopping for these tools.

Food Mill: This is an old-fashioned tool that requires a bit of elbow grease to operate, but the results are worth it. There are times when a food processor works too well! When you want a heavier consistency in a purée, a food mill will allow you to achieve it. When you are looking for a silky quality to your seafood mousse, the mill helps remove all sinew and connective tissue. A stainless steel model is ideal because it won't discolor or rust; these mills usually come with three different disks with fine, medium, and relatively large holes.

Meat Grinder: I use an electric meat grinder; KitchenAid makes a very good attachment to its electric mixer. Grinders come with disks of varying sizes that will allow for different textures in the grind.

Pasta Machine: If you plan on making pasta by hand all the time for the next decade, I would recommend a large, commercial, hand-cranked machine such as Imperia R220, which is made in Italy. For more typical (occasional) use, a smaller version available in most cookware shops is fine. I do *not* recommend electric pasta machines.

Smoker: Smoking foods is a very simple process; if you can operate an outdoor grill, you can operate a smoker. For our purposes, an inexpensive *water-smoker* for from $35 to $60 works just fine. They are available in most hardware sections of large department stores.

Tart Pans: The best tart pans are tin-lined. Whether they be fluted or cylindrical, you will always want tart pans with removable bottoms.

Terrine Molds: Heavy porcelain terrine molds are quite durable and readily available. I use a one-quart capacity Le Creuset mold, but they do offer smaller sizes. Le Creuset molds come in vibrant, attractive colors.

Soufflé Molds: Porcelain soufflé molds such as the one used here in the frozen lime soufflé are readily available in cookware shops. There are a multitude of sizes available to suit whatever needs you have. It is important, however, that they be heavy enough to withstand extreme cold and heat.

A FEW THOUGHTS ABOUT WINE

by Proal Perry

~~~~~~~~~~~~~~~~~~~~~~~~~

As I sit writing this, I have before me a collection of restaurant bills from a recent gustatory trip to France. And as I reflect on the meals and the accompanying wine selections, I try to recall the reasons I selected each wine. The particulars of those decisions have become sketchy, but the memories of the occasions remain pristinely clear. This reinforces my belief that the satisfaction in properly paired wine and food is so special it is hard to imagine ever having one without the other; good wine and good food simply have a natural affinity for one another. Yet the choice between a Dry Chenin Blanc or a Vouvray Sec to accompany Norman's Pan-Cooked Whole Yellowtail with Key Lime Butter and Basil, or the selection of the Gigondas over a Chateauneuf de Pape for the Fricassee of Rabbit with Corn Cakes, is not my decision, but yours. My only exhortation to you is to *drink wine* purely for the simple pleasure it brings. Whether the meal is grand or humble, wine has the capacity to enhance the occasion, and to make the simplest repast more enjoyable.

It is important to understand at the outset that there isn't one correct wine for any given meal, but rather a host of appropriate wines, depending on the circumstances. You should adjust the quality level of the wine to complement the importance of the meal as determined by the company, the food, or the occasion. My recommendations should serve only as points of departure or stimulus for your own selections. The object of my suggestions is to help you choose wines that are not only compatible with the various recipes, but are also readily available and reasonably priced. Furthermore, you will notice that most of the selections are for younger, lustier, more aggressive wines. This is not because I don't enjoy older vintages of a more complex, subtle nature, but rather because the recipes included in this anthology are generally quite full-flavored. I feel that assertive wines complement assertive foods; the level of intensity of the wine and food should be more symmetrical.

My only criterion when selecting a wine is that neither the wine nor the particular food overpower the other. In making this determination, I consider not only taste, but the weight and texture of both the wine and the accompanying dish. Beyond this, I believe there are no rules, no taboos, no absolute do's or don'ts. Surely, there are less than ideal pairings; but the appreciation of wine is a very subjective thing, and I encourage you to try many different wines. What becomes most important is that you will accumulate

~~~~~~~~~~~~~~~~

your own wine-tasting memories and their association with particular foods, so that mentally checking for harmonious matchups will become automatic.

In most areas of the world, people grow up drinking the wines of their particular region, without knowing any more about the wines of the world than the average American. The abundance of wines available to us in America is mind-boggling and this has unfortunately contributed to Americans being intimidated by the sheer number of choices available to them. We should treat this as an opportunity, however, not as a threat. It is hard to imagine the pairing of any good quality wine with well-prepared food where one had the capacity to ruin the other; through experimentation you will increase your own palatal memory, so for a particular meal you will not only be able to choose a compatible wine, but you might feel that an Australian Cabernet from Coonwara is more appropriate than a Napa Cabernet from Howell Mountain because of a certain subtlety or nuance in the wine that stuck in your memory. So whether the occasion is a dinner party for friends, a recommendation to a patron in a restaurant, or a bottle shared by a couple on their anniversary, when the wine chosen fits the mood of the moment, you will succeed in winning praise and warming hearts—for wine is a potion that truly can perform magic.

SOUPS

In my house I have a portrait of an old man. He has a thick, gray beard and broad, strong hands and shoulders; he wears the clothes of a laborer. Before him are a bowl of soup and a crust of bread. This painting always conveys to me a feeling of gratitude and hope.

A baby learning to feed itself will grasp a spoon and a cup first; most of us can recall the warmth and comfort we felt as children when we ate the hearty soups our mothers prepared. Yet it seems, at least in our corner of the world, that we have witnessed a vanishing interest in this primal course. The quick fix of fast foods has dulled our appreciation for the deep, sensual release that soups can provide—the experience of being truly hungry and then truly fed. Those of you who still appreciate these feelings when sitting as that old man sits, head bowed in rapt attention, will take pleasure in this section.

BAHAMIAN CONCH CHOWDER

Conch chowder is to Key West what cioppino is to San Francisco. This pretty mollusk was so ubiquitous, so intertwined with the folklore and diet of Key Westers, that the people who were born and raised here became known as Conchs (Konks) back in the late 1800s. I can think of no other place where the populace has taken the name of a gastropod as a nickname for themselves, but we have—and we're proud of it.

Conch meat has a rich, exotic clamlike taste and can be used in various ways. It is made into salads, fritters, and chowders. As for chowders, there are those devotees who favor a creamy version, and I'm beginning to hear of those who even include such refinements as hazelnuts! But my recipe is for those in the tomato-fanciers camp. And this is a dish made for people who like to be within walking distance of a beach. I like to think that suitable condiments are nothing more than a hot splash of Tabasco and the salty smell of the sea.

Serves 12

¼ pound diced slab bacon, rind removed

½ cup olive oil

2 jalapeño peppers, seeds and stems removed, diced medium

1 large Spanish onion, peeled and diced medium

½ bunch celery, cleaned and diced medium

2 carrots, peeled and diced medium

1 green pepper, seeds and stem removed, diced medium

1 yellow pepper, seeds and stem removed, diced medium

2 banana peppers, seeds and stems removed, diced medium

1 tablespoon crushed red pepper

10 small, new-boil type potatoes, peeled, diced medium, and reserved in water

1 quart peeled plum tomatoes, thoroughly crushed

1 quart tomato purée

3 bay leaves

One bunch each of fresh thyme, oregano, marjoram, and basil, tied in cheesecloth.

3¼ quarts Fish Stock (page 244)

2⅔ quarts bottled clam juice

2½ pounds cleaned and ground conch meat (see Note below)

Tabasco to taste

1. In a very large soup pot or dutch oven, render bacon fat with olive oil. When fat is rendered, add jalapeños, followed by all vegetables up to but not including the potatoes. Sauté briskly. Add crushed red pepper.

2. Add potatoes, then the tomatoes and tomato purée, being sure the plum tomatoes are well crushed. Reduce heat and add the bay leaves. Add the bouquet of herbs.

3. In separate large pot, bring fish stock and clam juice to a boil and whisk in conch meat. Allow to boil once and quickly strain the clam and fish stock into the simmering soup, reserving conch meat for later.

4. When potatoes are tender, whisk in reserved conch meat. Add Tabasco to taste, boil once, then serve, or chill for later use.

Note: Conch meat is almost always frozen now. Try to buy Grade A conch and be sure to check for any "freezer burn." Do *not* buy the conch if you see ice crystals on the meat. Conch meat can be extremely tough, even if you dice it very small, so it needs to go through the medium-fine plate of a grinder. Also cut away any orange flaplike meat if that has not already been removed.

FLORIDA LOBSTER TORTELLINI
in Chile and Cilantro Broth

Like the Italians' beautiful pasta in brodo, this soup is both visually sophisticated and soul-satisfying. The broth is a fine essence of seafood, heady and limpid. In some ways the presentation also encompasses an oriental sensibility: Less is more.

Serves 4

BROTH

¼ cup olive oil
6 tablespoons (¾ stick) butter
The reserved lobster shells, roughly chopped
2 leeks, white part only, split, cleaned, and finely chopped
4 ribs celery, cleaned and finely chopped

1 carrot, peeled, cleaned, and finely chopped
4 poblano chiles, stem and seeds removed, finely chopped
2 bunches cilantro, roughly chopped
2 cups white wine
2 quarts Fish Stock (page 244)

FILLING

Approximately 2 cups

6 tablespoons (¾ stick) butter
4 shallots, peeled and sliced
1 pound spiny lobster meat, shells split
and meat removed in two large sections
per tail (reserve shells)

3 tablespoons Spanish sherry wine vinegar
1¾ cups heavy cream
Salt and cracked black pepper, to taste
2 egg yolks, beaten

Basic All-purpose Flour Pasta dough
(page 206)
1 egg, beaten

1 tablespoon water
16 slivers raw poblano chile
16 cilantro leaves

1. Make the broth: Heat a large, heavy pan over gentle heat. Add the olive oil and butter. When the butter melts add the lobster shells and cook 2 minutes.

2. Add the leek, celery, carrots, chiles, and cilantro and cook until vegetables are glazed, about 8 minutes, stirring often. Add the wine and cook until only ½ cup remains. Add the prepared fish stock and cook over low heat about 30 minutes.

3. Strain broth through a fine-mesh strainer and/or cheesecloth. Set aside or chill in the refrigerator until ready to serve. Discard the vegetables.

4. Make the filling: Melt the butter over medium heat until it starts to foam. Add the shallots and stir. Do not allow to brown. Now lay the lobster sections in the pan, treating them as you would large shrimp. Turn them from time to time, for about 2 minutes. While they are still rare, add the vinegar and shake the pan to distribute it.

5. When the vinegar has reduced almost to a glaze, add the cream. Turn the lobster meat over in the cream and, with tongs, remove it to a plate. Continue to reduce the cream until it is thick enough to coat a spoon. Taste and season.

6. Using either a knife or a food processor, finely chop the lobster meat. If you are using a food processor, be careful *not* to purée the meat. The texture should be slightly coarse. Transfer mixture to a clean bowl.

7. Strain the cream through a fine-mesh strainer into the bowl with the lobster meat. Add the egg yolks to the lobster and cream and blend well. Cover and chill until ready to fill the tortellini.

8. Prepare pasta, proceeding to the point where you have rolled out and hung the dough.

9. Remove the lobster mixture from the refrigerator.

10. Cut out circles of dough with a cookie cutter or a wine glass and stack them in short piles so they do not dry out. (Sprinkle with a little flour if they seem too wet.)

11. Spoon a small amount of the lobster mixture onto the dough just below the center of the circle. Brush the dough around the lobster filling with a mixture of 1 whole egg, beaten, and 1 tablespoon water. This helps keep the dough sealed. Fold the circle in half over the lobster mixture and seal the edges. Now put your forefinger in the middle of the flat side and squeeze the two ends of dough around it. (If the lobster mixture oozes out, you have used too much to fill the pocket of dough.) Gently pinch the ends together and fold the top curve over to form the tortellini. (Tortellini are supposedly modeled after the navel of the Venus de Milo, so now you know what to look for.) Lay the tortellini on a cookie sheet and keep covered with a dry towel until you are ready to complete the soup, but refrigerate if it will be more than 45 minutes. (Tortellini do freeze successfully, if well covered.)

12. Heat the fish broth to just below a simmer.

13. Heat a medium-sized pot full of water to boiling and cook 24 tortellini for about 2 minutes. (They should be al dente.) Remove them with a slotted spoon and put 6 tortellini in each of 4 warm bowls. Ladle the broth over the tortellini, add the garnish of slivered fresh chiles and sprigs of cilantro, and serve immediately.

Hot Sausage and Shellfish Gumbo

Gumbo is one of the greats. It can grace the table of a friendly Saturday night poker game or be eaten on New Year's Eve with Champagne in one hand and a smiling companion on the other. It is as American as jazz and heavyweight boxing.

Be sure your prep work is done ahead of time so all ingredients can be added to the soup in order. Gumbo is made in steps. Certain parts need long cooking, but other things, e.g., the oysters, suffer if they cook too long.

Serves 10 to 12

2 cups diced onions	1 cup diced celery stalks
1½ cups diced bell peppers, an equal mixture of red, green, and yellow	2 jalapeño peppers, seeds removed and diced medium

HERB AND SPICE MIX

2 bay leaves
2 teaspoons salt
½ teaspoon black pepper
¼ teaspoon cayenne

1 teaspoon minced fresh thyme leaves
½ teaspoon minced fresh oregano leaves
1 tablespoon minced fresh basil leaves

ROUX

¾ cup oil (see Note 1)
¾ cup flour

1 tablespoon minced garlic
1 cup tomato concasse
1 quart hot rich Shellfish Stock (page 245)
1 pound other seafood as desired, cut into bite-sized pieces

1 pound shellfish, cut into bite-sized pieces
1 pound andouille or chorizo sausage, pan-cooked, oils reserved, cut into bite-sized pieces
1 dozen freshly shucked oysters
Cooked rice and pickled okra, for garnish

1. Prepare the vegetables and toss together in a bowl. Combine the herb and spice mixture.

2. Make the roux: Heat the oil in a very large, heavy-bottomed skillet. When the oil is hot, sift in ¼ cup of the flour and whisk steadily. The roux is absolutely crucial in making gumbo. It's not terribly difficult, but you must have total concentration to avoid the irretrievable mishap of burning it. Continue to add the flour, a little at a time, whisking. For this gumbo I make a black roux (for the definitive guide to roux-making, I suggest Paul Prudhomme's book, *Louisiana Kitchen*). So, cook the flour and oil together until the mixture is just about black, but *not* burned.

3. Now, shift into higher gear and add the vegetable mix a cup at a time. The first cup will nearly ignite upon contact with the heat. A degree of caramelization occurs instantly and turns the mixture a black tarlike color. This is just what is supposed to happen. Continue to add up to ¾ of the vegetables; then add the garlic, then the herb and spice mixture, and then the tomato concasse. Add the rest of the vegetables and cook, stirring with a heavy wooden spoon or paddle.

4. Now slowly ladle in the stock, bit by bit, stirring. Stop adding stock while the soup is still thick and stewlike. (You can always add more if you need to thin it out.) Allow the soup to simmer for about ½ hour.

5. Depending on the nature and size of the fish and shellfish, add them to the soup. Larger, oilier fish can handle a touch more time; smaller, light seafoods only need an instant.

6. Add the sausage pieces. Then add the oysters and cook just a moment longer. Serve at once, garnished with rice and pickled okra.

Note 1: Peanut oil may be used to make the roux, but I use duck fat and some of the oily drippings from the cooked sausage to extend the flavors.

Note 2: If you have smoked duck or chicken, they would be a welcome addition to the combination of seafood and sausage in this one-pot entrée.

BLACK BEAN SOUP
with Jalapeño Sour Cream and Cilantro Salsa

There is a rich history of black bean soup in this country. The one served at the Coach House Restaurant in New York City comes most quickly to mind. But Key West's Black and Cuban folks taught me about their affection for black beans in soups and starches years ago and I immediately came to share in their enjoyment of this earthy, comforting food.

I like to use a smoked stock, but if you must substitute chicken, it's still good. If you are in an area where someone is producing smoked turkey breasts for customers, perhaps you can prevail on him to sell you the carcasses. The smoke of the stock and the sweet taste of the Madeira are my kind of combination.

Serves 10 to 12

1/2 pound smoked slab bacon, rind removed, diced small	1/2 cup ground cumin powder
1/4 cup olive oil	2 smoked pork hocks
4 jalapeño peppers, diced small to medium	2 bay leaves
2 Spanish onions, diced small to medium	2 quarts black turtle beans, soaked in water overnight
6 celery stalks, diced small to medium	1 cup Madeira wine
1 green pepper, diced small to medium	1 gallon Smoked Stock (page 241), or substitute chicken stock and double the amount of smoked pork hocks
4 garlic cloves, minced	Salt and pepper to taste

TOPPING

3 tablespoons coarsely chopped cilantro
leaves

2 jalapeños, stemmed, seeded, and finely
diced

½ cup sour cream

½ red onion, peeled and chopped

1. In a large, heavy pan, cook the slab bacon in the olive oil over medium heat. When the bacon is medium-rare, add the vegetables. Reduce the heat and stir. Add the cumin powder.

2. Add the pork hocks and bay leaves and cook a moment more. Add the beans. Add the Madeira and cook 2 or 3 minutes.

3. Add the stock, being sure that it covers the beans by an inch or two, and cook until the beans are just tender, about 2 hours.

4. Remove the soup from the heat and taste. Adjust seasoning as desired. Remove pork hocks. Purée about ¼ cup of the soup and then mix the purée with the rest of the soup. Keep warm while you prepare the sour cream and red onion salsa.

5. Combine the cilantro leaves and jalapeños with the sour cream. (If you do this ahead of time, keep cold.) Have red onion ready.

6. When serving, ladle the hot soup into bowls (a nice, "peasant"-type bowl befits the style of this soup). Add a dollop of the sour cream salsa and top with chopped onion.

CLAM AND CORN CHOWDER
with Roast Chiles

I love Jeremiah Tower's book, New American Classics, *for many reasons. One is his sense of humor. In commenting on flour-thickened sauces, he remarks that they "have recently gained a bad reputation. Like great courtesans, they seem to come and go."*

When I used to make this soup in the kitchens of our restaurants, I would try to make it before the other cooks came in. I wasn't hiding anything from them, but I wasn't sure they would understand. Roux was an epithet in those days and we needed to escape the gummy hold it had had on cooking five and ten years ago. Those days are, in the main, gone and it's time to reincorporate roux into the lexicon of cuisine. But, with restraint!

Serves 8 to 10

BÉCHAMEL

½ cup clarified butter	1 jalapeño, ribs and seeds removed, diced medium
1 medium onion, diced medium	½ cup flour, sifted
2 stalks celery, diced medium	2 cups Fish Stock (page 244), at room temperature
1 green pepper, ribs and seeds removed, diced medium	1 quart cream
¼ pound smoked slab bacon, rind removed, cut into cubes	1 red onion, skinned and diced
2 leeks, white part only, cleaned and diced	5 new boiling potatoes, scrubbed and diced small
2 stalks celery, cleaned and diced	1 tablespoon thyme leaves, stems discarded
½ red pepper, ribs and seeds removed, diced	3 tablespoons basil leaves, stems discarded
½ green pepper, ribs and seeds removed, diced	2 bay leaves
½ yellow pepper, ribs and seeds removed, diced	1½ cups shucked clams, reserving all available liquid, kept cold
1 jalapeño, ribs and seeds removed, diced	Salt and pepper to taste
	1½ cups fresh corn kernels, cut from the cob (reserve cobs)
	Cream, or fish stock, or half and half, as necessary

GARNISH

1 jalapeño chile, roasted, peeled, and cut into strips	1 banana chile, roasted, peeled, and cut into strips
1 poblano chile, roasted, peeled, and cut into strips	

1. Make the béchamel: In a large, heavy-bottomed pot, heat butter. When it is warm, add the diced onion, celery, green pepper, and jalapeño, and stir. Turn up the heat to almost high. Cook the béchamel vegetables, but do not allow them to brown. When they are fairly soft, whisk in the flour. With a wooden spoon push the flour and vegetables around the pan until well mixed.

2. Now add the fish stock and whisk again. Lower the heat and simmer 10 to 15 minutes, stirring as often as necessary.

(recipe continues)

3. Add the cream and whisk again. Simmer about 20 minutes.

4. Remove from heat, strain liquid into a large bowl, and reserve. Discard vegetables. This is the béchamel; it should be somewhat thicker than double cream.

5. Prepare the soup: In another heavy pan, cook the cubed slab bacon to medium, at the most. (If the bacon does not render sufficient fat to sauté the soup vegetables, add virgin olive oil or butter.)

6. Add the leeks, celery, red, green, yellow, and jalapeño peppers, and onion, and sauté briskly. Then add the potatoes, thyme, basil, and bay leaves and cook for 1 minute.

7. Add the reserved clam juice and cook 3 minutes.

8. Add the reserved béchamel, salt and pepper, and reserved corn cobs. Cook 5 minutes. Add more cream, fish stock, or half and half if needed, and keep warm for service or chill for later use.

9. Roast the chiles as you would bell peppers and reserve for garnish.

10. Remove the corn cobs from the soup. (The cobs distribute a nice, milky sweetness.)

11. If the clams are large, chop them into bite-sized pieces.

12. Quickly sauté the kernels of corn in a little butter and add them to the soup. Bring the soup to a moderately high heat and mix in the raw clams. Stir. Pour the soup into warm bowls and garnish with the chiles.

Note: I like to use as many as 3 different kinds of chiles, but one of any kind will do.

Poached Garlic Soup
with Sausage and St. André Croutons

St. André is a delightfully rich triple cream cheese, and here we have the added pungent flavors of garlic and sausage. This soup, like vichyssoise, gets its body from potatoes, leeks, and cream—but this one is served hot. It is a lusty, warming soup that makes a nice light evening meal when served with a small salad.

≈≈≈≈≈≈≈

30 garlic cloves, peeled
1 quart plus 3 cups Chicken Stock (page 240)
9 leeks, cleaned and cut in medium dice
½ pound (2 sticks) butter
8 new boiling potatoes, peeled, diced, and reserved in clean, cold water
Salt and pepper
1½ quarts cream

¼ pound Milano sausage, or any cooked smoky garlic sausage, cut into small pieces (be sure to remove any inedible casings)
Olive oil to sauté croutons
Sourdough bread cut into ¼-inch thick, wafersize pieces (1 slice per person)
St. André cheese, cut into ¼-inch thick, waferlike pieces (1 slice per person)

1. Put the garlic cloves in 3 cups of the chicken stock and bring to a boil. Poach them until they are soft, approximately 15 minutes. Remove the cloves to a bowl and allow them to cool. Now reduce the remaining stock to a glaze and reserve.

2. On low heat, in a large heavy saucepan, cook the diced leeks in the butter. When leeks are translucent, drain the potatoes, add them to the leeks, and stir. Season with salt and pepper. Now add the remaining 1 quart chicken stock and simmer until the potatoes are softened, approximately 25 minutes.

3. Add the cream, cook 10 minutes, and then add the garlic-chicken glaze.

4. Purée the soup in a blender and strain it into a large bowl or pot.

5. Slice the poached garlic and scatter over the soup. Add the sausage.

6. When ready to serve, get a skillet moderately hot and add the olive oil. Sauté the sourdough croutons, turning them as necessary, and then remove them to paper toweling to drain.

7. Ladle the hot soup into bowls and top each serving with a crouton spread with fairly warm St. André cheese and cracked pepper.

CREAMY MUSSEL SOUP
with Saffron, Orange, and Star Anise

I've never been overly fond of the texture of mussels, but I do enjoy the flavor they impart. When you couple their rich, shellfish taste with the subtle pungency of saffron and the sweet licorice of the star anise, and balance them with the acidity of orange juice and the silkiness of heavy cream, you have a creation that is simply perfect, and utterly delicious.

Serves 4 to 6

1 fennel bulb, core removed, diced medium	2 bay leaves
4 stalks celery, diced medium	4 star anise
2 small onions, diced medium	1 tablespoon cracked black pepper
2 tablespoons butter	1 cup orange juice
2 tablespoons olive oil	Large pinch saffron
30 mussels, scrubbed, debearded, and soaked in several changes of water to rid them of any sand	1 quart cream
	Sea salt to taste

1. In a large, heavy pan, sauté the fennel, celery, and onion in the olive oil and butter. When the vegetables are slightly tender, add the mussels and cover the pan, shaking it or stirring it from time to time. The mussels should throw off a little of their own juices, resulting in a mussel stock. Do not let all the liquid evaporate from your pan. (You can add a small amount of fish stock or water, if you have to.) The mussels will begin to open in approximately 10 minutes.

2. Remove the mussels to a bowl as the shells open. When they have all opened and have been removed, add the bay leaves, star anise, and black pepper to the liquid in the pan. Reduce the liquid down to within 1 inch of the bottom of the pan.

3. Now add the orange juice and saffron and reduce again to 1 inch in the pan. Add the cream and reduce until thick enough to just coat a spoon.

4. Meanwhile, pull the mussels out of the shells and put them in a small bowl.

5. When the cream is reduced, remove from heat and strain soup, and add the mussels.

6. Put the soup into a blender and purée in batches. Then strain it again. Season with salt and pepper to taste. Reheat gently and serve.

COLD AVOCADO, BUTTERMILK, AND GRILLED EGGPLANT SOUP

The flavor of grilled eggplant is soft, smoky, and haunting. With a Caesar salad and grilled bread that has been brushed generously with excellent olive oil, I would be content to call this lunch. Add a bottle of Pinot Grigio and I'd call it dinner.

Serves 10 to 12

- 4 medium eggplants, lightly oiled
- 6 cloves Roast Garlic (page 200), cut into slivers
- 1 jalapeño, stemmed, seeded, and diced
- 4 tablespoons (½ stick) butter
- 4 leeks, white part only, cleaned and diced
- 3 stalks celery, diced

- 1 large Spanish onion, diced
- 10 fresh basil leaves, roughly chopped
- 1 bay leaf
- Salt and pepper to taste
- 1 quart heavy cream
- 4 avocados, skin and seeds removed
- 2 cups buttermilk

1. Preheat the oven to 400 degrees. Pierce the eggplants and stud them all over with slivers of roasted garlic. Bake the eggplants, turning often, for approximately 30 to 40 minutes.

2. In a medium-heavy saucepan, cook the jalapeño in the butter. Do not allow to brown. Add the diced leeks, celery, and onion and cook until glazed. Stir. Add the basil, bay leaf, and some cracked black pepper. Cook 2 minutes.

3. Meanwhile, remove the tops and bottoms from the eggplants. Remove the skin and as many seeds as possible. Discard any excess liquid, chop the eggplant pulp, and add it to the soup. Add the cream and cook just until the cream simmers.

4. Purée the soup with the avocados and strain; add the buttermilk. Chill.

5. Check for seasoning before serving. A chilled soup often needs a bit more salt and pepper.

Note: If you wish, you may garnish this with sour cream or crème fraîche.

CHAR-GRILLED VEGETABLE SOUP
with Summer Salsa

During the early part of 1985, the editors of Cook's Magazine *called and asked me to give them an original recipe for a new column they were introducing featuring leading chefs and restaurants in the United States. I was working extensively with wood-burning grills at that time, so I began to think about a creamy vegetable soup that would enable me to bring the special outdoor flavors of the grill inside. If it is summertime and you would prefer to chill the soup, that's fine.*

Serves 4 to 6

2 leeks, white part only, split and thoroughly washed	1 yellow bell pepper
Salt and black pepper	6 tablespoons (¾ stick) butter
2 small eggplants	4 stalks celery, chopped
Extra virgin olive oil for brushing vegetables	½ Spanish onion, chopped
1 zucchini, cut lengthwise into slices ¼ inch thick	24 fresh basil leaves, chopped
1 yellow squash, cut lengthwise into slices ¼ inch thick	2 small bay leaves
1 red bell pepper	2 cups Chicken Stock
	1 quart heavy cream, and extra cream if necessary to thin the soup
	2 tablespoons red wine vinegar

1. Heat grill.

2. In a saucepan, blanch leeks in salted, boiling water to cover until just tender, about 5 minutes.

3. Halve eggplants lengthwise. Cut one half lengthwise into slices ¼ inch thick. Brush all cut surfaces of eggplant liberally with olive oil. Season leeks, eggplants, zucchini, peppers, and yellow squash with salt and pepper and coat lightly with olive oil.

4. Grill the unsliced eggplant halves until quite soft, about 6 minutes. Remove from grill and cool.

5. Grill eggplant slices, zucchini, yellow squash, and leeks, being careful not to char too much, about 6 minutes for eggplant slices and 4 minutes for squashes and leeks. Put grilled vegetables in a bowl.

6. Grill red and yellow peppers until evenly charred. Then cover them with a towel and cool.

7. Scrape out the flesh of the cooled, grilled eggplant halves and discard skin and as many of the seeds as possible. Chop flesh.

8. In a large pot, heat butter until foamy. Add celery and onion and cook until soft. Add chopped eggplant and basil leaves to pot. Season with salt and pepper and add bay leaves. Cook for 5 minutes over medium heat. Add stock and cook 10 to 12 minutes. Add 2 cups heavy cream and boil. Remove from heat and remove bay leaves.

9. Purée the soup. Return it to a clean pot and simmer 5 minutes.

10. Cut the grilled leeks, zucchini, yellow squash, and eggplant slices crosswise into medium strips. Peel and seed peppers and cut like the eggplant. Return vegetables to bowl and mix gently.

11. Stir ⅔ of the vegetable mixture into the soup. Add the remaining two cups of cream, or less, to desired consistency. Season with salt and pepper. Ladle the soup into bowls. Toss the remaining grilled vegetables in the wine vinegar and divide this as garnish among the bowls of soup.

CHILLED FENNEL SOUP
with Grilled Shrimp

I feel there is a natural affinity between shellfish and Pernod. So do the folks in Marseilles, I guess, because they invented a dish called bouillabaisse to illustrate the relationship. This soup is not, however, like bouillabaisse in any other notable respect.

Serves 4 to 6

MARINADE AND SHRIMP

1 tablespoon olive oil	8 whole black peppercorns
1 tablespoon fennel tops	1 pound shrimp, peeled and deveined
3 tablespoons Pernod	

3 tablespoons olive oil	1 quart Fish Stock (page 244)
3 tablespoons butter	1 bay leaf
1 onion, diced medium	1 tablespoon thyme leaves
2 leeks, white part only, washed and diced medium	1 tablespoon chervil leaves
	1 quart heavy cream
4 stalks celery, diced medium	Salt and pepper to taste
2 fennel bulbs, cores removed, diced medium	⅓ cup Pernod
	Sprigs of fresh fennel tops, for garnish
2 small red potatoes, peeled and diced	

1. Prepare marinade and pour over shrimp. Refrigerate, turning shrimp in marinade occasionally.

2. Now, make the soup: Heat olive oil and butter in a heavy-bottomed pot on moderate heat; add diced onion, leeks, celery, and fennel and stir. Cook 5 to 7 minutes, stirring often. Do not allow to brown.

3. When the vegetables are soft, add the diced potatoes and fish stock. Cook 5 minutes. Add the bay leaf, thyme, and chervil and cook 1 minute. Add the cream and salt and pepper and cook gently until soup is thick. Remove bay leaf.

4. Purée the soup and strain it, if desired, into a bowl set over ice. Stir in the Pernod.

5. Prepare the grill and when it is quite hot, quickly grill the shrimp. Discard the marinade. Chill the cooked shrimp and cut into bite-sized pieces.

6. Ladle the soup into chilled bowls and garnish each serving with shrimp and a sprig of fresh fennel.

WARM TOMATO SOUP
with Pesto Crème Fraîche

The flavors of high summer are evident in the use of perfect sun-ripened tomatoes and the fragrance of the basil in pesto here. This soup can be chilled and served cold, but remember that chilled soups require a bit of extra seasoning at the end. This seasoning can be not only salt and pepper, but perhaps a splash of vinegar. (The crème fraîche must be made in advance, but you can substitute sour cream if you wish.)

Serves 10 to 12

CRÈME FRAÎCHE

2   cups heavy cream
2   tablespoons buttermilk or sour cream

1   cup olive oil
8   tablespoons (1 stick) butter
8   cloves garlic, peeled and sliced
3   leeks, split, washed, and diced
½   bunch celery, diced medium
1   Spanish onion, peeled and diced
2   bay leaves

6   basil leaves
9   tomatoes, skins, seeds, and cores removed, coarsely chopped
1   cup Chicken Stock (page 240)
Salt and pepper
1   recipe Pesto (page 224)

1. Prepare Crème Fraîche: Combine heavy cream in a jar with buttermilk or sour cream. Cover the jar and shake it. Allow the jar to stand, loosely covered, overnight in a warm place. The next day, the crème should be quite thick. It can be kept 1 week in the refrigerator.

2. Make the soup: Heat the oil and butter in a large pan. Slowly sauté the garlic slices, then add the leeks, celery and onions, continuing to stir. Add the bay leaves and basil. When the vegetables are almost translucent, add the prepared tomatoes and cook 18 to 20 minutes. Now add the stock and salt and pepper and cook until the flavors are "married," about 20 minutes. Season more if necessary. Remove from heat. Purée this mixture, but do not strain it.

3. Prepare pesto. To make pesto crème fraîche, spoon in 2 tablespoons pesto per 1 cup crème fraîche (more or less, as you prefer). Reserve the remaining pesto for another use.

4. At serving time, check the soup's seasoning and adjust as needed. Ladle into warm soup bowls and garnish with a dollop of pesto crème fraîche. Crusty French bread with garlic butter is a nice partner.

CURRIED CARROT AND CHICKEN SOUP
with Apples and Coconut

Curry and hot weather go well together. The punch of spice brings on just enough perspiration to help cool the body when the tradewinds sweep over the island.

Serves 8 to 10

¾ cup clarified butter	2 or 3 chicken breasts
1 large onion, thinly sliced	1 tablespoon olive oil
¼ cup Curry Powder (page 212)	½ cup diced zucchini
2 quarts Chicken Stock (page 240)	1 green pepper, cleaned and diced medium
Salt and pepper to taste	1 apple, peeled, cored, and cut into fine
6 sweet carrots, cleaned and sliced	slices
1½ quarts heavy cream	½ cup toasted coconut flakes

1. Put the clarified butter in a large flat saucepan or rondeau. Allow the butter to get golden to golden brown over medium-high heat. Stirring quickly, add the onion; do not brown.

2. Add the curry powder, stirring constantly. Take care that the powder does not stick to the pot; lower the heat if necessary.

3. Whisk the stock into the pan in 3 stages. (This helps incorporate the curry into the stock.) Add the black pepper and salt, if you wish. Add the carrots and simmer until they are just soft. Add the cream and cook for 10 minutes.

4. Purée the soup in a blender or food processor, and strain it into a clean pot.

5. In a sauté pan, briefly cook the chicken breasts skin side down in the olive oil—they should remain pink inside; they will cook a little more in the soup. Remove breasts to a platter to cool.

6. In the same pan, in the rendered chicken fat and olive oil, cook the zucchini and green pepper until still slightly firm. Remove vegetables with a slotted spoon and add them to the puréed soup.

7. Dice the breasts into small pieces and add them to the soup. Heat soup gently to serving temperature, ladle into heated bowls, and garnish with sliced apple and toasted coconut.

BEER-CHEESE SOUP
with Rye Croutons

This soup has also been known as "hair of the dog soup" in our restaurants. It is always served on New Year's Day and I can personally attest to its restorative capacities.

Serves 8 to 10

6 Spanish onions, peeled and cut into medium slices	Two 12-ounce cans beer (I use Heineken or Beck's Light)
1 pound butter	1 quart Chicken Stock (page 240)
4 jalapeño peppers, stems and seeds removed, thinly sliced	1 quart cream
10 cloves Roast Garlic (page 200)	1 pound Monterey Pepper Jack or Cheddar cheese, shredded
1 cup flour	Salt and pepper to taste (see Note)

1. In a deep, heavy-bottomed pot, cook the onions in the butter over medium heat until they begin to become translucent (about 20 minutes). Add the sliced jalapeños and roasted garlic and cook a few minutes more on a gentle, medium heat.

2. Sift the flour over the cooking vegetables and stir evenly with a wooden spoon, being careful not to let the flour scorch. Continue cooking and stirring, allowing the mixture to get thick and somewhat sticky. Add the beer slowly, stirring. Allow this to cook and thicken somewhat, stirring often. Add the stock and cook gently for 15 minutes. Keep stirring. Add the cream and cook 15 minutes more.

3. Now, strain the soup into a large bowl. Whisking the whole time, add the cheese in handfuls. The more cheese, the thicker, so judge accordingly. Season to taste.

4. When ready to serve, warm the soup and garnish with croutons prepared according to the following recipe.

Note: Be careful not to oversalt. The cheese eliminates the need for it.

CROUTONS

1 loaf rye bread
1 cup clarified butter
Salt and pepper to taste

(recipe continues)

1. Cut the rye bread into small cubes.

2. Heat a large skillet and add the butter. Sauté the bread cubes until crisp. Season and drain on paper toweling.

Note: Some freshly chopped thyme leaves added just at the end impart a nice herb flavor.

Acorn squash soup
with Smoked Duck

If you have difficulty finding smoked duck in your area, you can substitute smoked ham. What we're after here is a counterpoint to the naturally sweet flavor of squash. Sweet and smoky are a lovely combination in many things—go ahead, use your imagination!

Serves 10 to 12

6 acorn squash	3 cups Chicken Stock (page 240)
¾ pound (3 sticks) butter	6 cloves Roast Garlic (page 200)
2 tablespoons brown sugar	10 basil leaves
4 teaspoons cracked black pepper	1 quart cream (more as necessary)
4 leeks, white part only, cleaned and diced	Salt and pepper to taste
2 carrots, peeled and diced	1 pound smoked duck, cut into small dice

1. Preheat oven to 350 degrees and split the squash in half. Scoop out and discard the seeds. Scrape the inside of the raw squash halves with the tines of a fork and rub their surfaces with ¼ pound (1 stick) butter. Season with brown sugar and pepper. Invert the squash into a baking pan and bake 30 to 45 minutes. Remove from the oven and turn flesh side up.

2. In a heavy pan over medium heat, cook the leeks and carrots in ½ pound (2 sticks) butter until glazed. Add the chicken stock. Continue cooking until the carrots are easily pierced by a knife. Add the garlic and basil. Cook 1 minute. Add the cream.

3. Scoop the meat out of the squash halves and stir it into the soup. Season with salt and pepper.

4. Purée the soup and strain it. When ready to serve, heat the soup and garnish with the smoked duck.

APPETIZERS

We are living in a changing world. To deny changes would be to deny realities. I'm using the plural on purpose, for I feel that to deny certain realities is the option of intelligence—in other words, being experienced enough to make distinctions. We finally know so much of history that we can bear witness to the vicissitudes of culture, the ebb and flow of civilization, over the course of the past twenty *centuries* and more! Mankind has lived both a pastoral existence and a frenetic one, sometimes side by side. The "art of eating," as Brillat-Savarin termed it, has had to respond to the pace of changing man over this evolutionary parade.

If I hear the message correctly, most people want less food in their lives than did their forefathers. This makes perfect sense. I despise regimentation. I hope that throughout this book, you will be inspired to participate in the creative decision-making process of cooking. The designation *appetizer* would seem to indicate that another course must follow. This does not have to be the case! But I have yet to think of another satisfactory term, so "Appetizers" it will be.

You can develop any appetizer into your main, or only, course. The rather modern term being used in the newspeak of culinary jargon is *modular*. It refers to interchangeable courses—like having a tiny, cold oriental pasta dish with grilled duck breast and a vinaigrette, followed by baked figs stuffed with Gorgonzola cheese. A more refined predecessor to this modular cuisine, born of a similar notion, is the menu degustation that probably evolved as a reaction to the seeming overindulgence of the "grande cuisine" of the late nineteenth and early twentieth centuries. Some of the more notable three-star chefs of France such as Michel Guérard and Joel Robuchon present small, precisely orchestrated "mini" versions of certain of their à la carte menus, executed in a progression that harmonizes the whole experience of dining.

Another interesting new development has been the success of such restaurants as Ménage à Trois in London and Primi in Los Angeles. At these places, the entire menu consists solely of appetizer-sized portions. This allows a much less structured dining experience that fits the life-styles of many people today. Tapas, dim sum, and grazing are all permutations of this global phenomenon. As you read and experiment with the recipes in this chapter, please use them as best suits your pace and appetite.

COLD
APPETIZERS

~~~~~~~~~~~~~~~~

Texas Gulf Shrimp Steamed in Dixie Beer
with Southern Slaw and Creole Rémoulade

Obviously, the title of this dish is supposed to conjure up visions of everything from Scarlett O'Hara to the Preservation Hall Jazz Band. In a way, it's my answer to the ubiquitous red-sauce-and-crushed-ice shrimp presentation I waded through in my youth. I offer this recipe as an appetizer, but you can add two dozen more shrimp and some more slaw and sauce and call it a main course, if you like.

Serves 4

SLAW

4 cups julienned vegetables such as carrots, sweet peppers, red and green cabbage, celery, seedless cucumbers	½ cup sour cream
	½ cup creole mustard
	¼ cup tomato juice
⅜ cup mayonnaise	1 teaspoon cayenne pepper
⅜ cup buttermilk	1 teaspoon paprika
½ teaspoon sea salt	Cracked black pepper, to taste
1 tablespoon chopped fresh basil	

1. Toss the vegetables together in a bowl.

2. Mix all the remaining ingredients. Add just enough of this dressing to the vegetables to coat them. Chill for at least 30 minutes.

CREOLE RÉMOULADE

2 egg yolks	1/2 tablespoon Tabasco
1/4 cup olive oil	1 teaspoon sweet paprika
1 tablespoon fresh lemon juice	1/4 cup finely chopped celery
1 tablespoon creole mustard	1/4 cup finely chopped scallions
1 tablespoon ketchup	1/4 cup washed, minced parsley
1 tablespoon Worcestershire	2 tablespoons peeled and finely
1/2 tablespoon Dijon mustard	grated horseradish
1/2 tablespoon red wine vinegar	1/2 tablespoon minced garlic

1. Put the egg yolks in a food processor and beat in the oil, followed by the remaining ingredients through the sweet paprika.

2. Turn off the processor and add the celery, scallions, parsley, horseradish, and garlic. Pulse once and chill in a clean bowl.

16 large shrimp
1/2 gallon Beer Court Bouillon (page 239)
Lemon and lime wedges, for garnish

1. Boil the shrimp in the court bouillon. (You can save the court bouillon for another use.) Chill.

2. Peel the chilled shrimp, discarding the shells, but leaving the tails on.

3. To assemble the dish, mound some slaw on each plate. Dip the shrimp into the chilled rémoulade to coat all but the tails. Arrange the shrimp near the slaw and serve with lemon and lime wedges.

SHELLFISH SEVICHE
on a Creole Vinaigrette
with Southern Slaw

This refreshing dish is a gustatorial swing through several regions on the southern side of our planet. The Mississippi delta, the Carolina low country, the Caribbean, and South America all come together in this dish.

It is usually necessary to prepare seviche about 12 to 16 hours before serving. You can make excellent seviches with such things as thinly sliced scallops that are marinated only for an hour or so. Texturally, they will be inviting. However, the same cannot be said of half-pickled shrimp.

It is fine to prepare the sauce creole a day or two in advance of making this dish.

Serves 4

1 pound large shrimp, shelled and deveined, cut in half laterally
1 pound snapper fillets, cleaned and cut into strips 2½ inches long by ¾ inch wide
2 tablespoons whole black peppercorns

1 tablespoon whole coriander seeds
1 cup freshly squeezed lemon juice
½ cup freshly squeezed lime juice
½ cup freshly squeezed orange juice
¼ cup extra virgin olive oil
2 or 3 bay leaves

CREOLE VINAIGRETTE

2 cups Sauce Creole (page 226)
½ cup Spanish vinegar
1 cup extra virgin olive oil

1 cup Southern Slaw (page 44)
2 jalapeños, stems and seeds removed, diced
2 red peppers, stems and seeds removed, diced

2 yellow peppers, stems and seeds removed, diced
½ red onion, peeled and diced medium-small
1 tomato, concassée
24 sprigs cilantro

1. Place the shrimp in one glass or stainless steel bowl, and the snapper in another.

2. Toast the whole black peppercorns and coriander seeds by putting them in a dry skillet together and heating a few minutes. Shake the pan occasionally. Cool, then put a mixture of peppercorns and coriander seeds in two cheesecloth bags and tie tightly. Add the cheesecloth bags to the bowls of fish and shrimp.

3. Equally divide the lemon juice, lime juice, orange juice, olive oil, and bay leaves between the two bowls.

4. Refrigerate, gently tossing the seafood around in the marinade periodically to insure even marination. The snapper will "cook" before the shrimp. When it is done, pull it out of the marinade, put it on a plate, and refrigerate.

5. Prepare the basic sauce creole if you have not already done so. Purée the sauce in a food processor, adding the vinegar and oil at the end. Pour into a clean bowl and chill.

6. Prepare the slaw and chill.

7. Remove the shrimp from the marinade, put on a plate, and chill. Discard seviche liquor.

8. When ready to serve, arrange slaw in the center of each plate and spoon the creole vinaigrette around the mound. Alternate the shrimp and snapper evenly around the slaw. Randomly scatter the diced jalapeños, red peppers, yellow peppers, red onion, tomato, and cilantro leaves over the fish. Serve.

COLD LOBSTER TERRINE
with Caviars and Citrus on a
Champagne Yogurt Dressing

To many of the locals, late summer in Key West is, strangely enough, the most peaceful and beautiful time of the year. We take some survivors' satisfaction when the town quiets down and becomes the picturesque, almost funky fishing town it was in the earlier part of the century. The water flattens out and the sun's heat comes on. Folks don't walk as much as drift or glide down the streets. To be in a hurry is to court disaster. Many people speak of "mañanaism"—if they want to see it in real (in)action, they should come down here in late August. The cats and dogs sleep in the streets—right next to each other!

A cooling dish like this was created for these tropical evenings. It is light, refreshing, and the slight saltiness of the caviar is a welcome guest. Note that you must make the terrine far enough in advance so it can chill at least 4 hours.

Serves 8 to 12

3 tablespoons olive oil	1 tablespoon finely chopped thyme leaves
5 tablespoons butter, 2 tablespoons softened	12 basil leaves, finely chopped
1 onion, diced	12 whole black peppercorns, bruised
3 stalks celery, cleaned and diced	2 tablespoons brandy
1 carrot, peeled and diced	3 cups heavy cream
1 tomato, concassée	1¼ pounds lobster meat, shells reserved
4 shells of lobster	¾ pound salmon meat
2 tablespoons finely chopped tarragon leaves	2 whole eggs
	3 egg whites
	Sea salt and cracked black pepper to taste

1. Preheat oven to 375 degrees. Choose a deep pan large enough to hold a ½-quart terrine mold with room to spare all around. Place a folded kitchen towel in the bottom of the pan and fill the pan half full of water.

2. In a large saucepan, heat the olive oil and 3 tablespoons butter until slightly foamy. Add the diced onion, celery, and carrot and cook about 5 minutes. Now add the tomato and the lobster shells. Cook about 1 minute. Add the herbs and black peppercorns.

3. Add the brandy, and carefully ignite, shaking the pan until the flames subside. Reduce this combination to a glaze, and add the heavy cream. Turn the heat up and reduce by almost half.

4. Pass the flavored cream through a fine strainer and chill it down to 40 degrees F. Mixture should measure approximately 1⅔ cups.

5. Evenly process the lobster meat and salmon almost to a purée and force the mixture through a medium-fine strainer or food mill into a bowl.

6. Set the bowl of lobster/salmon mixture in a larger bowl filled with ice, and beat in the whole eggs and then the 2 tablespoons softened butter with a wooden spoon or a stiff wire whisk. Now work in the chilled lobster-stock-enriched heavy cream.

7. Beat the egg whites until they peak and lightly work them into the mousse. Season as desired with salt and freshly cracked black pepper.

8. Set the prepared water bath (bain-marie) in the preheated oven.

9. Prepare a 1½-quart terrine mold by very lightly buttering it. Fill the mold with the mousse mixture and gently smooth the top. Cover it with aluminum foil and put the lid on top of the foil.

10. Place the terrine in the simmering bain-marie. The level of water should reach halfway up the sides of the earthenware terrine mold. If it doesn't, add some more water. Bake for approximately 40 minutes (but check at 30 minutes) and remove terrine from the bain-marie. Put the mold into an empty pan and pack some ice cubes around the mold to arrest the cooking.

11. Chill the terrine at least 4 hours or overnight.

SAUCE

Combine the following:

1   cup plain yogurt
1   cup vanilla yogurt
½   cup freshly squeezed orange juice

½   cup Champagne
Cracked black pepper to taste

GARNISH

Assemble the following ingredients:

1   teaspoon black American sturgeon caviar per person
1   teaspoon golden whitefish roe per person
1   teaspoon salmon roe per person

3   orange sections per person
3   lime sections per person
3   blood orange sections per person (optional)

(recipe continues)

TO SERVE:

1. Unmold the terrine and slice into ½-inch slices. Slice these in half diagonally.
2. Ladle sauce onto plates and top with slices of terrine. Garnish with caviars and citrus sections.

Pepper-Charred Tenderloin,
Chile Mayonnaise, and Grilled Tortillas

You can easily dress up this presentation by using some expensive china and folding the tortillas in the shape of sushi rolls. But I prefer a simpler image: You're standing near a good-sized fiery grill outdoors on a Sunday. While the game blasts away inside, you pull long-necks out of the freezer, toast tortillas, and roll them by hand for a few good friends.

Makes 4
appetizer portions

½ cup Salsa (page 223)
½ cup Red Pepper Mayonnaise (page 233)
1 pound beef tenderloin, totally trimmed, butt and tail removed and saved for other use

¼ cup clarified butter
3 or 4 tablespoons cracked black pepper
12 flour tortillas

1. Prepare the salsa and mayonnaise.
2. Roll the meat in the clarified butter and then coat completely with cracked pepper. Allow to rest.
3. Build a good, blazing fire on the grill. (This can be done inside in a large pan, but I don't recommend it. It is much too smoky inside and could be dangerous.) When the fire is no longer flaming, and the grill is as hot as you can get it, put the meat on the rack and turn it frequently. You are attempting to char it and leave it raw/rare in the center. When that is accomplished, remove the meat to a plate and allow to cool.
4. Slice the tenderloin in thin pieces and cut the strips in half.
5. Grill the tortillas a few seconds on each side; brush with mayonnaise. Add two slices of meat and sprinkle with salsa.
6. Fold in half and then in half again. Serve.

A WILD MUSHROOM TERRINE

This recipe is quite simple, but does involve a little extra cost—unless, of course, you gather your own wild mushrooms! I use two pounds of softer wild mushrooms, such as oyster and trumpet mushrooms, for processing and one pound of sturdier mushrooms, such as shiitakes or chanterelles, for slicing and sautéeing. You will note there is no meat stock in this recipe, so it can be enjoyed by most vegetarians as well as meat-eaters. Serve it cold, or it may be sliced and warmed in a pan and served on buttery brioche.

Serves 8 to 10

¼ pound (1 stick) butter	Kosher or sea salt and cracked black pepper (to taste)
3 pounds assorted wild mushrooms	
2 whole eggs	2 tablespoons chopped basil leaves
6 cloves Roast Garlic (page 200), chopped	2 teaspoons chopped thyme leaves

1. Lightly butter the entire inside surface of a half-quart terrine mold. Preheat oven to 325 degrees and put in a roasting pan ⅓ full of water.

2. Purée ⅔ of the mushrooms in a food processor. Squeeze out all excess liquid and put them in a bowl. Beat the eggs and add.

3. In a large skillet, heat the remaining butter and sauté the remaining pound of mushrooms (evenly sliced). Add the garlic and season with salt and pepper. Add the herbs and cook about 2 minutes over medium heat. Remove the cooked mixture from the skillet with a slotted spoon and add to the raw mushrooms. Mix thoroughly.

4. Pack the mushroom mixture into the terrine mold. Cover with aluminum foil and carefully slip the mold into the water bath (bain-marie) in the oven. Bake for 1 hour and 15 minutes and remove.

5. Allow to cool thoroughly, preferably overnight in the refrigerator.

6. To remove the terrine from the mold, run a thin knife around the outside and invert mold over a plate. Wrap terrine and refrigerate until ready to slice.

CHARRED "RAW" TUNA
with Wasabi and Pickled Onions

This is one way to introduce people to the notion of eating raw fish. The crisp, crunchy exterior leads them to the soft sensuality of the raw fish—in this case, tuna.

Blackfin tuna works very well since the loins are cylindrically narrow, much more so than yellowfin; but yellowfin can be adapted by butchering it correctly. Naturally, the most important factor is the freshness of the fish.

Serves 4 to 6

2 pounds tuna, roughly 4 or 5 inches in diameter, cut into 4-inch lengths	¾ cup red wine vinegar
24 coriander seeds, toasted	⅓ cup sugar
½ cup virgin olive oil	2 red onions, peeled and cut into rings
A 1-inch piece fresh gingerroot, peeled and thinly sliced	2 tablespoons wasabi powder (available in the oriental foods section of most large supermarkets)
½ cup cilantro leaves and stems	Water to bind the powder
3 tablespoons dried Chinese peppers (or 2 sliced jalapeño peppers)	Lime wedges, for garnish

1. Place the tuna sections in a mixture of the coriander seeds, olive oil, gingerroot, cilantro, and dried Chinese peppers. Marinate for at least 2 hours in the refrigerator.

2. Thirty minutes before serving, mix the red wine vinegar and sugar in a stainless steel bowl. Add the onion rings and toss. Fifteen minutes before serving, drain the vinegar and sugar from the onions and refrigerate rings in a bowl.

3. When ready to serve, mix enough water into the wasabi powder to form a paste. Put a small mound of the wasabi on each plate.

4. Remove the tuna from its marinade and scrape off any herbs and spices that may cling to the fish. Heat a skillet and sear the tuna in the pan. (No need to add oil; the oil on the tuna will be sufficient.) Roll the tuna in the pan to char the fish evenly. Remove from the pan and place on a cutting board. Allow the fish to rest a minute and then slice it on a strong bias and fan slices on each plate.

5. Scatter the onions over the plates. Garnish with lime wedges and serve.

KUMAMOTO OYSTERS ON THE HALF SHELL
with Smoked Salmon Slaw and Sauce Mignonette

The smoky saltiness of the rich salmon marries well with the piquant nature of the sauce mignonette.

Serves 4

½ cup Sauce Mignonette (page 228)
½ cup Basic Vinaigrette (page 227)
16 Kumamoto oysters (or other fresh variety)
1 cucumber, skinned, seeded, and sliced into strips
1 red pepper, stem, seeds, and ribs removed, sliced into strips
1 yellow pepper, stem, seeds, and ribs removed, sliced into strips
1 small head radicchio, cut into strips
1 pound smoked salmon, skinned and cut into julienned slices

1. Prepare sauce mignonette and vinaigrette; chill.

2. Open oysters, reserving excess liquid for other uses (or strain, reduce to 2 tablespoons, and mix into the vinaigrette; adjust seasoning).

3. Toss the vegetables and salmon slices in the vinaigrette. Spread this slaw attractively over the plates and arrange the oysters still in their shells around the slaw.

4. Serve each portion with a small cup filled with sauce mignonette.

CHIPOTLE CHILE AND SHRIMP TERRINE

You can use other shellfish, such as lobster, either separately or in combination, to make this terrine. The chipotles can be added to half the terrine and the layers split for a nice presentation. (Chipotles are smoked, dried jalapeños. You can substitute ancho peppers if you wish.)

Serves 10 to 12

2   pounds raw shrimp meat, kept cold
2   whole eggs
1½ cups cream
4 or 5 chipotles, toasted and softened in 1
cup water, then seeds and stems removed
(discard water)

Salt and pepper to taste
½   pound butter (not melted, but quite
    soft)
2   egg whites

1. Preheat oven to 375 degrees and set in the oven a roasting pan half full of water.

2. Purée the shrimp meat in the food processor. With the machine running, add the eggs and cream. Add the chipotles and process the mixture to a fine texture. Taste for seasoning and add salt and pepper if necessary.

3. Scoop the mousse out of the food processor and into a large stainless steel bowl. Beat in the softened butter thoroughly, and transfer to a food mill with the fine plate attachment. Work the mousse through the mill into a bowl. (A food mill is an inexpensive and very useful tool. However, if you do not have one, simply omit this step.)

4. Beat the egg whites to soft peaks and fold them into the mousse.

5. Lightly butter a half-quart terrine mold and add the mousse, filling mold evenly. Cover the terrine with aluminum foil or parchment paper, slip it carefully into the bain-marie, and bake for 30 to 35 minutes.

6. Remove and cool the terrine in an ice bath. Then run a knife between the terrine and the mold and invert. Rap gently all over until the terrine slides out.

Note: This terrine may be served cold with a number of sauces, including aigrelette, or warm with pasta and a butter sauce.

STONE CRAB CLAWS
with Mustard Sauce and Vegetable Chowchow

Stone crab might be called the gourmet's ultimate convenience food, for it is almost always marketed precooked. To enjoy stone crab meat you need only a tool to break through the shell. Stone crab is sweet and has a pleasant texture, and simple condiments such as lemon, butter, or a mustard sauce need be used but sparingly. For this recipe we include a vegetable accompaniment—for color, of course—but the pickled, tart flavor of these vegetables also offers a tasty counterpoint to the rich crab flavor. The vegetables are best made one day in advance.

John Mariani notes in his book The Dictionary of American Food and Drink *that the term* chowchow *"may be from the Chinese Mandarin 'cha' meaning mixed, and dates from the 1840s when Chinese laborers worked on the railroads of the American West."*

Makes 4 appetizer portions

½ cup mayonnaise
¼ cup creole mustard
2 teaspoons sugar
Tabasco sauce to taste
½ red pepper, cut into 1-inch pieces
½ yellow pepper, cut into 1-inch pieces
6 baby carrots, peeled
6 baby golden or baby red beets, peeled and cut in half lengthwise
10 haricorts verts
½ red onion, cut into 1-inch pieces

1½ cups cider vinegar
½ cup sugar
¼ teaspoon cayenne pepper
1 teaspoon crushed red pepper flakes
2 teaspoons coarse salt
1 star anise
1 bay leaf
16 3- to 5-ounce stone crab claws, precooked and chilled
Lemon wedges, for garnish

1. Combine the mayonnaise, mustard, sugar, and Tabasco. Mix thoroughly, and chill.

2. Blanch the peppers, carrots, beets, and haricots verts in a saucepan of lightly salted water until just tender. Do this in batches, according to type of vegetable. Allow the larger, thicker vegetables to cook a bit longer, about 4 or 5 minutes for beets, 1 or 2 minutes or less for carrots and green beans, and 1 minute for peppers.

(recipe continues)

3. Drain the vegetables and plunge into ice water. (Keep the beets separate so their color doesn't run on other vegetables.) Drain again and put all the vegetables except beets in a bowl. Add red onion. Put beets in another bowl.

4. Make vinaigrette: In a small saucepan combine cider vinegar, sugar, cayenne pepper, crushed red pepper flakes, salt, star anise, and bay leaf and simmer over medium heat until reduced by a third. Cool slightly and then pour over the vegetables. Cover tightly and refrigerate overnight.

5. When you are ready to serve, put a thick towel on your work table and crack the crab shells open slightly. The guests can finish the task. (You do not want to smash the shells too hard, or you will destroy the presentation. A firm rap with a small hammer or the back of a large knife works well.)

6. Put a dollop of the mustard sauce on each plate. Scoop up a portion of vegetable chowchow with a slotted spoon and mound attractively near the sauce. Spoon a small amount of the vinaigrette over the vegetables. Arrange the stone crabs on the plates and garnish with lemon wedges. Serve.

Tortilla Paisana

This is a traditional tapas dish and should, according to Spanish custom, be served at room temperature although you can serve it warm, if you prefer. This tortilla is much like a flat omelet and quite similar to a frittata, so the components may vary according to your taste.

The recipe calls for my sweet potato gratin, which is cooked, cooled, cut into thin slices, and placed in the cooking egg mixture in such a way as to offer a dramatic presentation. You can substitute cooked potatoes of another sort, if you wish. The dish is very simple to prepare if you made the sweet potato gratin for dinner the night before and have a fair portion left over.

Makes 4 small portions

½ recipe Sweet Potato Gratin (page 193)	½ cup heavy cream, beaten into eggs
2 tablespoons extra virgin olive oil	Salt and pepper to taste
1 Spanish onion, peeled and diced large	¼ pound cooked chorizo sausage, cut into
2 tablespoons butter	small dice
6 whole eggs, beaten lightly	

1. Prepare the potato gratin if you have not done so already, and set aside to cool. (This should be done at least 4 hours ahead of time).

2. Preheat oven to 425 degrees. Heat a large skillet and add 1½ tablespoons of the olive oil. Add the diced onion and sauté until soft. Remove and set aside.

3. Turn the potato gratin out onto a cutting board and cut into slices 1 inch wide by 2 inches deep. Lay all the strips out on a flat surface (do not stack) and cover them.

4. Heat a large skillet to medium-high heat and add the remaining ½ tablespoon of olive oil and the butter. Allow it to foam slightly and pour in the beaten eggs and cream; add salt and pepper. Quickly lift up the eggs from the bottom of the pan, allowing only a portion of them to set.

5. Add the sautéed onion and diced chorizo. Then quickly arrange 4 to 7 sections of the potato gratin like the numbers on a clock around the surface of the eggs. Place the pan in the oven for a few minutes.

6. Place a heavy plate on your cutting board. Remove the skillet from the oven, put the plate on top of the pan, and quickly and carefully invert the tortilla onto the plate. Now slide the plate into the skillet, put back in the oven, and cook 30 more seconds.

7. Remove the skillet from the oven. Turn the tortilla right side up and allow to cool. Cut into wedges and serve.

SALMON CARPACCIO
with Caviar, Hard-Cooked Eggs, and Brioche

Food historians debate the origin of the term carpaccio; *no one debates its appeal. Of course, in the old days it was only beef that received this treatment—but once again we see the Japanese influence as salmon replaces the meat in this interpretation.*

Serves 4

¾ pound extremely fresh salmon, skin and bones removed	4 slices Cracked Black Pepper Brioche (page 209)
2 hard-cooked eggs	2 tablespoons butter, softened
1 tablespoon extra virgin olive oil	2 tablespoons chopped fresh Italian parsley, squeezed dry and set aside
2 tablespoons caviar (let your budget decide, but it should at least be sturgeon)	1 lemon, cut into 4 wedges, seeds removed

1. Slice the salmon thin, approximately 1 ounce per slice. Put onto a plate and chill, covered.

2. Shell the eggs and finely dice the whites. Set aside, covered. Sieve the yolks and set aside, covered.

3. Lay the slices of salmon, one by one, between two pieces of plastic wrap. Gently pound them with the side of a large knife to make them paper-thin. Arrange three slices on each of 4 cool plates, and lightly brush each slice with olive oil.

4. Arrange the caviar, egg white, and egg yolk in 3 concentric circles over the salmon. Start with the caviar as the outside ring, then egg white, then egg yolk as a "bull's-eye." Set aside in a cool place.

5. Toast the brioche and spread each slice with butter. Cut the toast in half diagonally and tuck toast slices between salmon slices. Scatter the chopped parsley over the salmon. Garnish with lemon wedges and serve.

HOT APPETIZERS

CRILLED MARINATED SHRIMP AND CHORIZO
with Spanish Sherry Vinegar

The inspiration for this dish comes from the Four Seasons restaurant in New York City. I have been serving this version at Louie's since I began. Every week, almost without fail, it is ordered by our customers more than any other hot appetizer. The combination of pork and shellfish works as well here as it does in many dishes, such as clam chowder. I see this preparation as conceptually Spanish in tone, so I use Spanish sherry wine vinegar to splash on the vegetables at the end.

While the recipe is simple to prepare, do note that the shrimp must be marinated overnight.

**Makes 8 appetizer servings
or 4 light entrées**

MARINADE AND SHRIMP

¼ cup minced parsley
¼ cup minced cilantro
3 cloves garlic, minced
Juice of 1 lemon
¼ cup semidry Spanish sherry wine
¼ cup Spanish olive oil
½ cup fresh bread crumbs

1 red bell pepper, stemmed, deribbed, and seeded
1 yellow bell pepper, stemmed, deribbed, and seeded
1 green bell pepper, stemmed, deribbed, and seeded

¼ teaspoon ground mace
¼ teaspoon dried oregano
1 teaspoon Hungarian hot paprika
1 teaspoon kosher salt
Freshly ground black pepper
1 large pinch saffron
24 large shrimp, shelled and deveined

2 cucumbers
One 12-inch length chorizo, cooked and cooled
Peanut oil
Salt and pepper to taste
2 tablespoons Spanish sherry wine vinegar
Lime wedges, for garnish

1. Mix all marinade ingredients in a large stainless steel bowl. Add the shrimp and toss, coating them evenly. Refrigerate overnight.

2. Dice the peppers into ½-inch pieces. Peel the cucumbers; cut them in half lengthwise, remove the seeds, and cut into half rings ¼ inch thick. Combine peppers and cucumbers in a bowl until ready to serve.

3. Slice the cooked and cooled chorizo into sixteen ¾-inch slices.

4. Heat and lightly oil the grill and arrange the shrimp and sausage on the surface. Grill until just done.

5. Meanwhile, heat a large skillet and add enough peanut oil to just coat the bottom. When the pan is hot, toss in the vegetables. Season, and when just cooked, add vinegar. Stir to evenly disperse the vinegar and seasonings.

6. Arrange a line of the vegetables on each plate and arrange the shrimp and sausages over the vegetables. Garnish with wedges of lime.

Note: The root vegetable jicama may be prepared and included for a crunchy, slightly apple flavor and an extension of the Spanish image.

PORK HAVANA "NUEVA"

I was first introduced to Pork Havana in 1972 on a visit to Key West. It was delicious and I especially liked the accompaniments of black beans and fried plantains. Plantains, a variety of banana, are among the principal starches of the West Indies. They are not sweet at all, unless you allow them to ripen almost to the point of blackness, which is the thing to do. You will find them in Spanish markets.

The marinade for the pork includes lime. True Pork Havana is made with a whole pork roast and is marinated with sour oranges, which I encourage you to use if you can locate some.

This recipe is an example of how we take a standard dish and shuffle the components to yield a more modern look, taste, and feel, transforming the solid structure of the classic into a fresh and appealing new version. Note that you must make some preparations a day ahead.

Serves 4

≈≈≈≈

PORK AND MARINADE

  1 orange
  2 limes
  1 cup olive oil
6 to 8 cloves garlic, peeled and cut in half
16 to 20 whole black peppercorns, bruised
  ½ bunch cilantro, cleaned and roughly chopped
  2 bay leaves, crumbled

  2 fresh pork tenderloins (each approximately 1 pound total weight), cleaned of any silverskin and cut in half on lengthwise bias
Freshly ground black pepper
  3 tablespoons peanut or olive oil for sautéeing pork
  2 tablespoons Spanish sherry vinegar

BEAN SAUCE

  ¼ pound slab bacon, diced medium
  ¼ cup peanut oil
  1 red onion, diced medium
  1 jalapeño, diced medium
  2 stalks celery, diced medium

  2 cups black beans, soaked overnight in the refrigerator in water to cover
  3 tablespoons cumin powder
  1 teaspoon cayenne pepper
  8 cups chicken stock
  1 bay leaf
Salt and pepper to taste

PLANTAINS

1 or 2 plantains, depending on size, peeled and cut on an extreme bias into ½-inch-thick slices, to make 12 slices

  1 cup flour, seasoned with salt and pepper and ground cinnamon
  ¼ cup clarified butter
  1 tablespoon butter

GARNISH

  ½ cup sour cream
  4 lime wedges (or sour orange wedges if you have them)

  1 large red onion, cut into medium-thick slices

1. Cut and squeeze orange and limes into a large ceramic or glass bowl. Add the fruit rinds, olive oil, garlic, peppercorns, cilantro, and bay leaves and mix well. Add the pork and marinate overnight in refrigerator.

(recipe continues)

2. The next day, begin by making the sauce: Cook the diced slab bacon in peanut oil in a deep, heavy-bottomed pot, stirring often. When bacon is almost cooked, add the diced vegetables and stir.

3. When the vegetables are soft add the drained beans and cook 1 minute. Add the cumin and cayenne and stir. Add the stock and bay leaf and bring to a boil. Skim stock, then reduce heat to a simmer. Cook beans until just soft and reserve. (It's possible the beans will require more stock as they cook.) Taste for seasoning and adjust to your liking.

4. Dredge plantain slices in seasoned flour. Gently cook floured plantain slices on both sides in ¼ cup clarified butter until golden. Remove plantains to a plate to drain on paper towels until serving time.

5. Shortly before serving time, remove meat from marinade, season with freshly ground pepper, and sauté medium-rare to medium in a hot skillet; keep warm.

6. Refry plantains in 1 tablespoon butter and remove from pan.

7. Ladle the black bean sauce into the same pan that you used to sauté pork, and heat quickly. Add a splash of Spanish vinegar and divide sauce among plates.

8. Slice each of the pork tenderloins into 1-inch slices. Arrange meat and plantains alternately over the sauce. Garnish each serving with sour cream, lime wedges, and red onion slices.

My "SHORT STACK"
—Foie Gras, Parsnip Pancakes, and Savory Caramel Sauce

This is one of the most sensually decadent pleasures I've known, and as Mae West once said, "When I'm asked to choose between two evils, I always pick the one I haven't tried—yet."

Serves 4

½ cup Savory Caramel Sauce (page 246)
1 recipe Little Vegetable Pancakes (page 196) made with parsnips cut into 2-inch lengths before cooking
1 cup clarified butter
½ pound foie gras, sliced ¼ to ½ inch thick and kept covered and chilled

2 tablespoons sliced scallions
¼ cup red wine vinegar
¼ cup sour cream
Cracked black pepper to taste
Edible flowers, such as nasturtiums, roughly chopped, for garnish

1. Prepare caramel sauce. Prepare pancake batter.

2. Make 12 pancakes in the clarified butter, in batches, using 3 tablespoons batter for each pancake. Lightly butter four 2-ounce ramekin molds and set aside.

3. Using a cookie cutter, cut the pancakes into uniform circles. Discard the scraps and set aside the pancake circles.

4. Sauté the foie gras slices about 20 seconds on each side in a fairly hot, ungreased pan. Carefully lift them out and transfer them to a plate. There will be fat from the foie gras left in the pan.

5. Add the scallions to the pan and return the pan to the heat. Cook for about 30 seconds and add the red wine vinegar. Lower the heat and reduce till syrupy. Add the caramel sauce to the pan and allow to cook a few minutes.

6. Arrange the pancakes and foie gras in layers in the buttered ramekins. Turn the pancakes upside down as you do this so that when you invert the molds to present them, they will be right side up. You will need to cut the foie gras so that it fits well in the mold. (You can prepare these hours in advance, up to this point, and refrigerate.)

7. About 20 minutes before you plan to serve, preheat oven to 400 degrees. When it is hot, put the molds in the oven. They will be heated through in just 4 or 5 minutes if they have not been refrigerated.

8. While the molds are baking, strain the caramel sauce and keep very warm.

9. Remove the molds from the oven and invert them onto serving plates. Surround the pancakes with the warm caramel sauce. Top the cakes with sour cream and garnish with the pepper and flowers. Serve.

VEAL RAGOUT IN POBLANO PEPPERS
with Ricotta Cream

This is like an Italian version of chiles relleños. I like the soothing, simple creaminess of ricotta as a counterpoint to the heat of the chiles.

Serves 6

¼ cup olive oil or duck fat
A 1-inch piece slab bacon
2 pounds veal shoulder, cut across the grain into pieces 1 inch long by ½ inch wide
1 onion, peeled and diced
4 cloves garlic, sliced in half
1 cup white wine
2 bay leaves
1 tablespoon cracked black pepper
1 tablespoon butter
5 tablespoons olive oil
1 leek, white part only, cleaned and finely diced

1 carrot, peeled and finely diced
1 fennel bulb, stalk discarded, cleaned and finely diced
½ cup marsala
1½ cups heavy cream
1 tablespoon Dijon mustard
12 basil leaves, roughly chopped
½ cup pine nuts, toasted
½ cup dried currants or raisins, roughly chopped
Salt and pepper to taste
6 large, evenly shaped poblano peppers, roasted, and peeled

RICOTTA CREAM

1½ cups ricotta (see page 211 if you want to make your own)

1 cup cream
½ cup sour cream

1. Preheat oven to 325 degrees. Heat a large, heavy, flat, ovenproof saucepan. Add the olive oil or duck fat and bacon. Working in batches so as not to overcrowd the meat, brown the veal on both sides and remove to a platter.

2. Add the onion to the pan and cook briefly. Add the garlic and cook 1 more minute. Return the veal to the pan and add white wine, bay leaves, and black pepper. Cover the pan and place it in the oven.

3. Stew the veal for approximately 1 hour and 15 minutes or until it is tender. Do not cut any fat off the meat. You will note that veal has very little fat; because of this, it progresses from being tight and tough to almost magically tender when it is done. This is the point at which you should remove the meat from the oven.

4. Lift the meat from the pan and put it into a bowl. Strain the pan drippings through a fine-mesh strainer into a large, clean saucepan and allow to settle.

5. Heat another saucepan over medium heat. Add the butter and olive oil and allow to heat briefly. Add the leek, carrot, and fennel and sauté about 2 minutes. Add the marsala and reduce by three-fourths.

6. Skim any fat off the pan drippings and add them to the working sauce (the veal broth). Add the cream and reduce by half. Add the Dijon mustard and remove from the heat. Add the chopped basil leaves, season with salt and pepper, and pour the sauce into a bowl.

7. Roughly chop up the veal and return it to a bowl. Add the pine nuts and currants, reserving a few for garnish. Now add just enough of the cream sauce to the meat so that it is moist and flavorful. Chill.

8. Prepare the peppers: Make a tiny incision in each pepper and *carefully* remove the "head" of seeds by cutting it off with a thin, sharp knife. If you have a tear in your pepper, make your cut there to minimize the number of holes. Gently dip the peppers in a bowl of water and shake out the remaining seeds.

9. Combine the three ingredients for the ricotta cream. Keep at room temperature.

10. Preheat the oven to 325 degrees. Stuff the peppers with the ragout.

11. Put the stuffed peppers seam sides down on a rimmed baking sheet and bake in the preheated oven for about 8 minutes. (Placing the peppers seam sides down helps keep the ragout inside the peppers.)

12. Spoon the ricotta sauce onto 6 plates. Top with the peppers and serve, garnishing with reserved currants and pine nuts.

LOBSTER AND PASTA
with Mango, Avocado,
and Chardonnay Butter

The presence of vanilla bean in a savory sauce may surprise you at first, but it works marvelously as it restates the vanilla flavor of the Chardonnay.

Serves 4 as an appetizer

SAUCE

6	tablespoons Chardonnay		½	cup heavy cream
3	tablespoons Champagne or Chardonnay wine vinegar		¼	vanilla bean, split in half
¼	cup finely chopped shallots		1	pound butter, cut into small pieces and kept cold
1	teaspoon cracked black pepper			Salt and pepper to taste
1	bay leaf			

1	pound lobster meat, cut into 4 equal portions, seasoned with fine sea salt and freshly cracked black pepper		1	pound fresh fettuccine (see page 206 if you want to make your own)
1	tablespoon virgin olive oil		2	ripe mangos, peeled and cut into thin sections
1	tablespoon butter		1	ripe avocado, peeled and cut into thin sections

1. Begin by making the sauce. Put the Chardonnay, the vinegar, shallots, cracked pepper, and bay leaf in a heavy nonreactive saucepan, and reduce on medium heat until only a few tablespoons remain. Add the cream and vanilla bean and reduce until mixture is thick enough to coat the back of a spoon.

2. Now, whisking constantly, beat the butter into the cream, piece by piece, with the pan still on medium heat.

3. When all of the butter is incorporated, season to taste and then strain the sauce into a clean, warm, stainless steel container and keep warm while preparing the rest of the dish.

4. Preheat oven to 400 degrees. In a pan large enough to accommodate the lobster without crowding, heat the olive oil and butter on medium heat. When the butter is just melted, lay the seasoned lobster in the pan and sauté on all sides.

5. Carefully spoon off any extra butter or oil and put the lobster in the oven for a few minutes (the length of time is determined by the thickness of the lobster). When it is just cooked through, remove the lobster meat to a cutting board.

6. Cook the pasta in plenty of rapidly boiling water until just al dente.

7. Ladle the warm sauce onto the plates. Arrange a nest of drained pasta in the middle of the sauce. Arrange sections of mango and avocado around the pasta. Cut the lobster into sections and nestle them around the pasta. Serve.

LOBSTER FRITTERS
with Conch Tartar Sauce

Conch fritters are one of the signature dishes of the Florida Keys. From mom and pop roadside stands to the pleasure palace hotels, cooks have proffered their versions of the tasty batter-dipped mollusk. Too often you get more batter than seafood, but that won't be the case in this version that employs another delicious crustacean native to our waters—lobster.

Makes 10 to 12 appetizer portions

2 small eggs, lightly beaten	1¼ tablespoons minced yellow pepper
¾ cup milk	1¼ tablespoons minced red pepper
1½ cups sifted flour	6 tablespoons beer
2½ tablespoons baking powder	Tabasco sauce to taste
¾ teaspoon salt	1¼ pounds lobster meat, minced
1¼ tablespoons minced red onion	Oil for deep-frying
1 jalapeño, seed and stem removed, minced	Lemon and lime wedges, for garnish

TARTAR SAUCE (see Note)

2 cups Conch Chowder (page 22), potatoes discarded	¼ cup cornichons, rinsed and chopped small
1½ cups Basic Homemade Mayonnaise (page 232)	Spanish sherry vinegar or lemon juice to taste
¼ cup capers, rinsed and chopped small	Tabasco sauce to taste

1. Beat the eggs in a large bowl and add the milk. Now add the flour, baking powder, salt, vegetables, beer, and a few drops of Tabasco and whisk thoroughly. Fold in the lobster and hold in the refrigerator, covered.

2. Make the sauce: Strain the vegetables and conch from chowder and reserve them. Reduce the strained liquid to ¼ cup, stirring often. Chill this, then combine with the reserved conch and vegetables and fold it into the mayonnaise. Add the capers, cornichons, vinegar or lemon juice, and Tabasco sauce to taste. Reserve.

3. Heat oil in a deep-fry kettle to 350 degrees.

4. Using two soup spoons, scoop up a small ball of lobster fritter batter with one of the spoons and scrape it carefully into the hot fat with the other. (You may fry a number of these at a time, depending on the capacity of your fryer.) As fritters are cooking, turn them over from time to time and then remove to paper toweling to drain.

5. Serve with a small container of the tartar sauce on the side, and garnish with lemon or lime wedges.

Note: Of course, you may substitute plain tartar sauce for the conch tartar sauce, or try adding some tomato concasse to plain tartar sauce.

GINGER RAVIOLI
with Smoked Capon and Chutney, Port Mustard Cream

As you read my recipes, you may notice that many of the appetizers are decidedly intense. I feel that the first course often requires extra intensity because at that point the diner's hunger and his need for flavors are most critical. After these desires are satisfied, we would naturally incline toward more lightness and subtlety.

Serves 8 to 10

FILLING

10 ounces smoked capon meat (or chicken or duck)

⅓ cup cream

1 recipe Basic All-purpose Flour Pasta dough (page 206) with ½ cup minced fresh ginger root added to the dough

½ cup Mango Chutney (page 203)

Salt and pepper to taste

SAUCE

1½ cups *port wine*	2 cups *Chicken Stock (page 240)*
3 *shallots, peeled and chopped medium*	3 cups *cream*
1 *bay leaf*	*Dijon mustard, to taste*
12 *black peppercorns, slightly bruised*	

1. Make the filling: Pulse the meat in a food processor (or mince it by hand) and add the cream. Stop the machine and scrape contents into a bowl. Add ¼ cup chutney. Reserve remainder to garnish the dish. Season to taste. Chill.

2. While the filling chills, make the pasta dough. Roll it out and fill as described on page 208. Chill, covered, until ready to cook.

3. Prepare the sauce: In a medium-sized saucepan, combine the port, shallots, bay leaf, and black peppercorns and reduce until liquid has almost evaporated.

4. Add the stock and reduce to ½ cup. Add the cream and reduce until mixture coats the back of a spoon. Whisk in mustard to taste. Strain sauce through a fine-mesh strainer into a stainless steel pot or bowl and keep warm.

5. When ready to serve, boil ravioli until al dente and drain thoroughly.

6. Spoon the warm sauce onto the plates. Put a dollop of chutney in the middle of each plate and surround it with ravioli. Serve at once.

PAN-FRIED BUFFALO MOZZARELLA
with Smoked Plum Tomato Cream

This is like a very sophisticated, crustless pizza. The edge of vinegar in the sauce gives structure to the richness of the cheese. Buffalo milk is the original milk used for mozzarella, but a fresh cow's milk mozzarella will also taste quite good. Plum tomatoes make a nice sauce, but no matter which variety you use, it is important that the tomatoes be ripe. The notion of smoking tomatoes may seem odd, but it is a revelation to taste them and realize this is still a vegetarian dish.

Serves 4

SMOKED TOMATOES

12 *tomatoes, cut in half crosswise*	1 *small pinch salt, per tomato half*
6 *tablespoons red wine vinegar*	1 *large pinch pepper, per tomato half*

CHEESE

1½	cups extra virgin olive oil, to cover only (the oil may be reused for salad dressings)	8	basil leaves (reserve 4 for garnish)
2	sprigs thyme	12	slices buffalo milk mozzarella (you will need approximately 3 "balls" of cheese)
2	bay leaves		4 to 6 cups fresh bread crumbs
6	whole black peppercorns		Peanut or safflower oil
2	sprigs rosemary		

PLUM TOMATO CREAM

3 shallots, peeled and diced small
3 leeks, cleaned and chopped medium
1 onion, peeled and chopped medium
6 cloves garlic, sliced
½ cup olive oil
Salt, pepper, and sugar to taste

¼ pound (stick) butter
¼ cup balsamic or red wine vinegar
1 bay leaf
1 cup roughly chopped basil
6 cups prepared smoked tomatoes
1 quart cream

1. Prepare the smoked tomatoes: Fire up the smoker. Top each of the tomato halves with vinegar, salt, and pepper. Place the tomatoes on the smoker's racks. Allow them to smoke for thirty to sixty minutes after the smoke has developed in the smoker. It is important to keep the heat as low as possible.

2. Remove the tomatoes, and skin, seed, and chop them. Reserve the drippings, skin, and seeds, and put the tomato pulp in a bowl.

3. Strain the liquid, skin, and seeds into a small, heavy saucepan. Reduce the liquid to a glaze, then add to the tomato pulp in the bowl and reserve.

4. Combine olive oil, thyme sprigs, bay leaves, black peppercorns, rosemary sprigs, and 4 basil leaves. Marinate the sliced cheese in this mixture for at least 2 hours.

5. Make the bread crumbs, using bread no more than 1 day old. (Two loaves of French bread will yield enough crumbs for this recipe.) Remove some of the crust, cut the bread into large cubes, and then pulse in a food processor. Do not process until fine—allow the bread to stay somewhat coarse. Any extra crumbs can be saved in a sealed plastic bag in the refrigerator for a few days.

6. Remove cheese from marinade, allowing most of the oil to drip off the cheese, and coat with the bread crumbs. Then place cheese on a plate and refrigerate.

7. Prepare tomato cream: Cook the shallots, leeks, onion, and garlic in the combination of olive oil and butter over medium heat until just shiny. (If using sugar, put in a pinch

or two now.) Cook 1 minute. Add the vinegar and bay leaf and cook 1 minute more.

8. Now add the basil and a few turns of black pepper; add the smoked tomatoes. Lower the heat and simmer gently 15 to 20 minutes, stirring occasionally. Then add the cream, stirring.

9. Remove sauce from heat, remove bay leaf, and purée mixture. Adjust seasoning and hold for serving.

10. Working in batches, quickly pan-fry cheese "patties" in a minimum of hot peanut or safflower oil. Remove to a warm oven (not over 180 degrees).

11. Ladle the warm sauce onto plates and arrange 3 slices of cheese on each plate over the sauce. Garnish each with a fresh basil leaf.

FISHERMAN'S PAN STEW
with Fettuccine and White Wine Cream

Like you, we who work in professional kitchens are faced with the problem of leftovers, for instance fish products in quantities too small to serve by themselves—things like mussels, lobster, clams, shrimp, oysters, snapper, grouper, smoked salmon, caviar—you know, odds and ends, right? Of course, I'm kidding, but in a smaller way you may have a few steamed clams left over from a party on Saturday night. On Sunday, you can either supplement those clams with some other items, or extend the dish with vegetables, and you have Sunday's supper shaping up rather nicely.

Serves 4 to 6

SAUCE

2	tablespoons butter	6	whole black peppercorns, slightly bruised
3 or 4	shallots, peeled and roughly chopped	1	tablespoon thyme leaves
1	clove garlic, peeled and finely diced	½	cup white wine
12	mushroom stems (reserve caps for later)	3	cups heavy cream
1	bay leaf	1	tablespoon mustard

1 pound fresh fettuccine, homemade or store-bought	1 carrot, cleaned and sliced into very thin julienne
4 tablespoons butter for cooking the fish	1 stalk celery, cleaned and sliced into very thin julienne
1½ pounds assorted fish and/or shellfish meat, cut into ½- to ¾-inch pieces	12 farm or wild mushroom caps, sliced
1 leek, cleaned and sliced into very thin julienne	¼ cup white wine
1 zucchini, cleaned and sliced into very thin julienne	1 tomato, concassée

1. Make the sauce: In a large, heavy saucepan, heat butter until foamy. Add the shallots, garlic, and mushroom stems and cook until soft. Add the bay leaf, peppercorns, and thyme leaves. Stir.

2. Add the wine and reduce until almost a glaze. Add the cream and reduce until thick enough to coat the back of a spoon. Whisk in the mustard and then strain through a fine-mesh strainer. Hold for service.

3. Cook the pasta and drain.

4. In a large skillet, heat the butter and add the raw fish (if you have some cooked fish, for instance smoked salmon or steamed mussels, wait until last on these), and shake the pan. Add all the vegetables except the tomato, and toss or stir evenly. Add the wine and simmer a moment; now add the cream and pasta and toss together.

5. Lift the mixture into heated bowls or onto plates, and garnish evenly with the tomato concasse. Serve.

GRILLED SWEETBREADS IN CORN CAKES
with Kumquat Jelly

Sweetbreads as an entrée are discussed on page 172. In this preparation we have sweetbreads as an appetizer. This is another situation where you can reduce the amount of work required in preparing certain foods by using a bit of foresight. You might plan on blanching an extra pound of sweetbreads when you serve a dinner of sweetbreads on Friday night; then you can cash in with a light meal or appetizer of sweetbreads on Sunday.

It is not crucial to grill the sweetbreads—they can be sautéed; but do grill if you can, since the grill's smoke goes well with the sweetness of the jelly.

Serves 6 to 8

SWEETBREAD PREPARATION

1 pound sweetbreads, blanched and
   trimmed (see page 173)
3 tablespoons extra virgin olive oil
Salt and pepper
3 tablespoons butter
1 leek, white part only, chopped medium
3 tablespoons herbes de Provence vinegar

6 pearl onions, blanched and peeled
1 tablespoon chopped chives
1 tablespoon chopped tarragon
1½ cups heavy cream
1 tablespoon Dijon mustard
1 teaspoon cayenne

CORN CAKES

2 cups fresh corn kernels
⅓ cup milk
⅓ cup flour
⅓ cup cornmeal
¼ cup clarified butter
2 large eggs

1 egg yolk
1 tablespoon basil leaves
1 tablespoon oregano leaves
Salt and pepper
Clarified butter for frying cakes

JELLY

2 tablespoons sherry vinegar
6 kumquats, pitted and chopped medium

12 ounces orange marmalade
1 tablespoon cayenne pepper

1. Fire a grill to medium high.

2. Oil and season the sweetbreads with the olive oil, salt, and pepper, and keep them cool.

3. Heat a small saucepan over medium heat. Add the butter. Add the leek and cook until just softened. Add the vinegar and pearl onions and reduce a moment.

4. Add the chives, tarragon, and cream and reduce by half. Now add the Dijon and cayenne. Stir. Taste and adjust as necessary. Chill.

5. Grill the sweetbreads until medium-rare and chill.

6. Make the corncakes: Process the corn kernels with a few tablespoons of the milk in a food processor until not quite smooth.

7. Put corn mixture in a bowl and add the remaining milk, the flour, cornmeal, and ¼ cup clarified butter. Whisk. Add the eggs, egg yolk, herbs, salt, and pepper. Set aside.

(recipe continues)

8. Cut up the sweetbreads fairly fine and mix with the reserved leek and mustard cream. (Be sure they are in proportion to each other. In other words, add just enough of the cream mixture to bind and flavor the sweetbreads.) Chill.

9. Prepare the jelly: Heat the vinegar in a medium-sized saucepan over medium heat a moment. Add the kumquats. Add the marmalade and cayenne. Mix well and keep warm.

10. Prior to serving, remove the sweetbread mixture from the refrigerator and allow to warm.

11. Heat a skillet over medium-high heat. Add enough clarified butter to just coat the bottom of the pan. Fry the corn cakes (use about 2 ounces of batter per cake) until golden brown on each side and put on a plate.

12. Spoon a little of the sweetbread mixture on the top right-hand area and bottom right-hand area of the cake. Fold the cake over, covering the two dollops of sweetbread mixture. Cut the cake in half to form 2 quarter-cakes.

13. Repeat until all the corn cakes are prepared, filled, and cut.

14. Spoon the kumquat jelly in the middle of each small serving plate, surround with 4 quarters of the filled corn cake, and serve.

PAN-FRIED GULF CRAB CAKES
with Mustard Béarnaise

Crab meat for cakes is traditionally from the blue crab, which can be found in many parts of the world, especially in Chesapeake Bay and the Gulf of Mexico. There are different grades of fresh meat available from mid-spring to very late fall, depending on the weather. For crab cakes, I usually use "flake" meat.

Serves 4 to 8

2 pounds fresh flaked blue crab meat	1/3 cup minced red pepper
4 egg yolks	1/3 cup minced yellow pepper
1/4 cup heavy cream	1/3 cup minced green pepper
1/4 cup chopped fresh herbs such as basil, Italian parsley, or thyme leaves	1/4 cup clarified butter
	4 cups fresh bread crumbs
1 cup minced celery	
1 cup minced onion	

Juice of 1 lemon
    2 tablespoons Pickapeppa sauce
    2 teaspoons Tabasco
    1 tablespoon dry mustard
    1 cup chopped, roasted pecans
Salt and pepper

Flour
    2 eggs
  ½ cup milk
    1 recipe Sauce Béarnaise (page 238)
       made with white wine, with creole or
       Dijon mustard folded in to taste
Peanut oil to fry the crab cakes
Lime wedges, for garnish

1. Carefully clean the crab meat of any shell or cartilage.

2. Beat the egg yolks, cream, and herbs together. Set aside.

3. In a large bowl, combine crab, celery, onion, and peppers and mix together. Add clarified butter, about 3 cups of the bread crumbs, lemon juice, Pickapeppa, Tabasco, dry mustard, and pecans. Mix thoroughly. Pour in herbed egg yolk and cream and mix. Taste for seasoning and add salt and pepper if necessary. Chill.

4. When you are ready to cook, carefully form about ¼ cup of the crab meat mixture into a cake. Lightly flour it, then dip it into an egg wash made by beating together 2 eggs and ½ cup milk. Then coat with fresh bread crumbs and put on a tray. Repeat until you have as many crab cakes as you need. Preheat the oven to 400 degrees.

5. Prepare the mustard béarnaise and keep warm.

6. Pan-fry the crab cakes in peanut oil in a hot skillet for 1 minute on each side and then put them in the oven for about 2 minutes.

7. Put the cakes on warm plates and spoon some of the béarnaise over them. Garnish with lime wedges.

STUFFED BAKED MUSSELS
with Shellfish Béarnaise and Aioli

Mussels are rapidly gaining new converts in this country. In this recipe, the sauce is so heady and rich that half a dozen mussels should satisfy the most demanding appetite as a first course. The aioli, traditionally somewhat thick, can be thinned a bit so you can drizzle it over the mussels by whisking in a little water or stock.

Serves 4

COURT BOUILLON AND MUSSELS

4   tablespoons (½ stick) butter
1   onion, peeled and roughly chopped
1   leek, cleaned and roughly chopped
1   stalk celery, cleaned and roughly chopped
6   cloves garlic, peeled and left whole

1   bay leaf
3   sprigs thyme, stems on
6   whole black peppercorns
2   cups white wine
24 mussels, soaked, scraped, and debearded

SAUCES

1   recipe Sauce Béarnaise (page 238), using white wine or Champagne and white wine vinegar or Champagne vinegar instead of red wine and red wine vinegar

½   cup reduced mussel stock
1   recipe Aioli (page 233)

STUFFING

¼   cup extra virgin olive oil
3   cloves garlic, minced
1   red onion, peeled and finely diced
1   bulb fennel, core removed, finely diced

1   tomato, concassée
Sea salt and cracked black pepper to taste
1   cup freshly made bread crumbs

Lemon wedges and chopped herbs, for garnish

1. Heat to high heat a pan large enough to hold the mussels evenly. Add the butter and the chopped onion, leek, and celery and stir briskly for 1 to 2 minutes. Add the garlic and cook another minute or two. Add the bay leaf, thyme and black peppercorns. Add the wine and cook another minute or two.

2. Add the mussels and cook them, covered, just until they open their shells.

3. Remove the mussels and allow to cool on a plate. Carefully reduce the liquid in the pan until there is only half a cup remaining. Then strain.

4. Make the béarnaise sauce and whisk in the half cup of remaining mussel liquor. Keep warm.

5. Prepare the stuffing: Heat a sauté pan, add the extra virgin olive oil, and bring to medium heat. Add the garlic and cook briefly. Add the diced red onion, fennel, and tomato and cook until softened. Season to taste with sea salt and cracked black pepper. Stir in the bread crumbs and remove from heat.

6. Heat oven to 450 degrees. Remove the mussels from their shells. Twist off half of each shell and discard. Return the mussels to remaining half shells and place on a baking sheet. Add the stuffing mixture to each shell.

7. Put the stuffed mussels in the oven for 4 or 5 minutes. Remove the pan from the oven and spoon on some of the shellfish-infused béarnaise sauce. Return the pan to the oven for a few moments.

8. Remove mussels from oven and arrange on plates. Put the aioli in a ketchup-style squeeze bottle and drizzle it over the mussels. Serve with lemon wedges and freshly chopped herbs showered over each dish.

Scallop Chartreuse
with Sun-Dried Tomato Pesto
and A Rosé Butter Sauce

This dish was inspired by my very good friend and a great chef, Charlie Trotter of Chicago.

Serves 4 to 6

PESTO

- ½ cup Pesto (page 224)
- 1 tablespoon finely chopped sun-dried tomatoes (I suggest the very sweet San Remo as one particularly nice brand.)

SCALLOP MOUSSE

- ½ pound sea scallops
- 1 whole egg
- ¾ cup heavy cream
- 3½ tablespoons very soft but not melted butter
- 1 egg white

Salt and pepper to taste

CHARTREUSE LINING

- ½ tablespoon butter
- 2 large bunches leeks, white part only, cleaned and cooked in lightly salted simmering water until just soft, refreshed in icy water, and drained

SAUCE

- 2 tablespoons shallots, finely chopped
- 1 teaspoon cracked black pepper
- 3 tablespoons red wine vinegar
- ½ cup rosé (I recommend rosé from the Bandol region of France)
- ¼ cup heavy cream
- ½ pound (2 sticks) butter, cut into small pieces and kept cold

Salt and pepper to taste

Basil leaves, for garnish

1. Prepare the pesto and add the finely chopped sun-dried tomato to it.

2. Prepare the mousse: Process the scallops in a food processor. With the machine running, add the whole egg and then the cream. Now, working quickly, add the soft butter. Turn off the machine, scrape the mixture into a bowl, and keep cold.

3. Beat the egg white to soft peaks and fold into the mousse. Add the pesto and fold that in, also. Season with salt and pepper if needed. Refrigerate.

4. Heat oven to 375 degrees. Choose a pan just large enough to hold 4 to 6 half-cup ramekins or soufflé molds. Put a kitchen towel in the pan, fill pan almost half full of water, and put it in the oven.

5. Lightly butter ramekins. Arrange the leek strips, cutting them as necessary to line the buttered ramekins. They should barely overlap each other, with their ends hanging over the sides. Try to avoid any leeks that seem tough or stringy. The inside pieces are a bit more difficult to work with, but they are more tender.

6. Spoon the chilled mousse into the leeks until the containers are full. Fold the leek ends over the mousse to make neat, compact packages.

7. Put the ramekins of mousse in the water bath, being sure there is not so much water in the pan that it washes over the sides of the ramekins. Bake about 15 to 20 minutes, or until a thin skewer inserted into the mousse comes out very warm to the touch, and the mousse is just firm.

8. Meanwhile, prepare the sauce: Reduce the shallots and cracked black pepper in the red wine vinegar and rosé. When the mixture is reduced by three-fourths, add the cream. Reduce it by half. Lower the heat and beat in the butter, piece by piece. Taste and adjust to your liking. Strain through a fine-mesh strainer. Keep warm.

9. If you have not done so already, remove the scallop mousse from the oven. Cool for a few moments. Invert onto a cutting board.

10. Spoon some of the rosé butter sauce onto serving plates. Place one mousse in the middle of each plate. Garnish with perfect basil leaves.

Note: Any extra mousse can be used by simply buttering soup cups lightly, filling them with the mousse, and cooking them in a bain-marie, uncovered, until they are set. They can be served warm or cold.

GAME BIRD RAVIOLI, CITRUS PASTA,
Sauce Adobado

This is an intense, visually striking first course dish. You can use odds and ends and leftovers with terrific results in fillings for ravioli and tortellini. If you roast squab, quail, or pheasant, and end up with some extra cooked meat, just shred the meat from the skin and bones and you have the beginnings of another dish.

Serves 4

1   recipe Basic All-purpose Flour Pasta dough (page 206)

1½   tablespoons zest of orange and lime, combined and incorporated into the dough with the eggs

SAUCE ADOBADO

6   ancho chiles
¼   cup (4 tablespoons) duck fat or butter
1   small onion, finely diced
½   tablespoon finely minced garlic
1   tablespoon ground cumin
¼   cup Spanish sherry wine vinegar

2   cups chicken stock
2   tablespoons freshly squeezed orange juice
2   tablespoons lime juice
2   tablespoons brown sugar
2 to 4 tablespoons tomato purée

RAVIOLI FILLING

1   teaspoon virgin olive oil
1   shallot, peeled and finely chopped
2   tablespoons red wine vinegar
½   cup chicken stock (or other rich poultry stock)

1   tablespoon soft butter

⅓   cup heavy cream
1   cup cooked game-type poultry (such as quail, squab, or duck) meat, finely chopped
Salt and pepper to taste

1. Prepare the pasta dough and refrigerate.

2. Make the sauce: Toast the ancho chiles and soak them in water about half an hour to soften. Remove the stems and seeds. Purée the anchos and set aside.

3. Heat the duck fat or butter in a heavy saucepan on medium-high heat. Add the onion

and allow it to caramelize (get deep brown). Add the garlic and cumin and stir. Add the vinegar, stock, and ancho purée. Simmer.

4. Mix the orange juice, lime juice, brown sugar, and tomato purée together. Whisk this into the simmering sauce and cook 15 minutes on low heat until saucelike in texture. Reserve.

5. To make the stuffing, heat a saucepan on medium heat. Add the olive oil and chopped shallot and sauté until shallot is soft. Add the vinegar and reduce to a glaze. Add the stock and reduce till syrupy. Add the cream and cook 3 to 4 minutes, then strain the liquid into a bowl.

6. Mix the cooked poultry meat with this liquid. Season to taste and set aside.

7. Roll out the ravioli dough and fill with the game bird mixture as described on page 208, making the ravioli 1½ inches square. You should have about 2 dozen.

8. Reheat the sauce.

9. Heat a pot of water to boiling. Cook the ravioli until tender but not mushy. Drain and toss with 1 tablespoon soft butter.

10. Ladle some warm sauce onto four plates. Top with ravioli and serve.

ARTICHOKE AND GORGONZOLA TORTA
with Red Beet Purée

This is a very simple recipe, but the variations are endless, since the tarts are perfect bases for many ideas. After assembling them, top them with whatever suits your appetite. Instead of artichokes and Gorgonzola, you could use: caviar, roasted peppers, tapenade, smoked fish, even fruit. You will need individual tart molds for individual tarts, but if you prefer you can use a larger mold and slice the finished tart like a pie. (The filling recipe makes approximately one quart.)

Makes six 3½-inch individual molds
or one 10-inch tart

RED BEET PURÉE

   2   *medium-large beets, unpeeled*
  ¼ *cup red wine vinegar (more or less to taste)*

2 tablespoons or less clarified butter or olive oil	½ pound cream cheese, at room temperature
1 cup or less lightly toasted processed bread crumbs	1¼ cups sour cream
	3 whole eggs
½ pound Gorgonzola cheese, at room temperature	6 cooked artichoke bottoms
	Extra virgin olive oil

1. First, make the purée: Cook the unpeeled beets, completely covered, in simmering water until you can pierce them easily with a thin, small knife (approximately 40 minutes).

2. Remove beets from the water and allow to cool. Peel them and process them to a fine purée. With the processor running, add enough vinegar to give purée some bite.

3. Remove purée from machine and reserve until needed.

4. Preheat oven to 350 degrees.

5. Prepare molds: Brush each with olive oil or clarified butter and then add enough toasted bread crumbs to just cover the inside. (Use much less than you would for cheesecake.) Press crumbs evenly with the back of a spoon. Set aside.

6. Combine the Gorgonzola cheese and cream cheese and beat until thoroughly mixed. Beat in ¾ cup sour cream. Add the eggs, one at a time, beating thoroughly after each.

7. Pour cheese mixture into molds and bake for 20 to 25 minutes, or 12–16 minutes for smaller molds, until mixture is set.

8. While tarts are baking, slice artichoke bottoms very thin, then dice them thin, and drizzle the dice with a bit of olive oil.

9. Remove tarts from oven. Allow to cool for 10 minutes. Lightly spread remaining ½ cup sour cream over the tops and add the diced artichoke bottoms.

10. Either serve immediately or hold and serve warm or cold, with a little of the purée spooned onto each plate as a dipping sauce.

CRISP POTATO CAKES
with Sour Cream and Caviar

I like to use what are called "chef" potatoes (large, round white ones) for these cakes. They are not too wet, which helps avoid an unpleasant gummy texture. It is a good idea to cook the potatoes more than a few hours in advance (or the night before) to allow them to cool completely. This, too, will help to keep them light and crisp.

12 to 16 cakes, depending on the size you make them

4 or 5 unpeeled chef potatoes, scrubbed
  4 tablespoons (½ stick) butter
  1 large onion, peeled and chopped medium
  1 small bunch scallions, diced
  3 tablespoons chopped Roast Garlic cloves (page 200)
  3 tablespoons chopped fresh basil leaves
  1 teaspoon chopped cilantro
  1 teaspoon chopped fresh thyme leaves

  2 egg yolks
Salt and cayenne pepper, to taste
Peanut oil
  14 tablespoons sour cream (about 1 tablespoon per cake)
  14 teaspoons caviar (black American sturgeon, salmon roe, whitefish roe, or any combination thereof, to make about 1 teaspoon per cake)

1. Put the potatoes in a pot, cover them with cold water, and bring to a high simmer. Cook until almost but not quite done. Drain well and chill.

2. Heat a large, heavy skillet and add the butter. Allow to get foamy. Sauté the onion, scallions, and garlic, stirring, for 3 to 5 minutes. Drain the excess liquid from the vegetables. Add the fresh herbs and cool slightly.

3. Put vegetable and herb mixture in a large bowl. Mix in the egg yolks, salt, and cayenne.

4. Peel the potatoes and shred on the large holes of a box grater.

5. Combine the potatoes with the egg, vegetable, and herb mixture. Taste for seasoning. Preheat oven to 375 degrees.

6. Form potato mixture into small cakes or patties approximately 2 inches square. Reserve on a baking sheet until ready to cook.

7. Heat a skillet over moderately high heat. Add peanut oil and swirl. (You could also use your roasted garlic oil, if you have been making roast garlic and have some left.) Add the cakes to the pan. Do not crowd them. When they are brown on both sides, put them in the preheated oven for about 8 minutes to heat through.

8. Remove cakes to plates, top with sour cream and caviar, and serve.

Lasagnetta
with Gulf Shrimp and California Escargots in a Lemon-Mustard Cream

I began serving lasagnettas like this one in the Cafe at Louie's Backyard one night as part of a whole new menu I was introducing. The same comment kept coming back to the kitchen in one form or another; "Best damn thing I ever ate!" said one petite young lady. The technique is quite simple: two layers of pasta, one on the bottom and one on the top, with the warm cream shrimp and escargot mixture between.

I think you'll be delighted with the lemon-mustard if you make it. You could substitute another prepared mustard, however, such as Dijon.

The California escargots, also known as Petit Gris, are farmed by a company named Enfant Riant, located in Petaluma, California.

Serves 4

Salt
1 quart heavy cream
½ cup Lemon Mustard (page 205)
3 tablespoons butter
1 teaspoon peeled and finely chopped shallots
12 large shrimp, peeled, deveined and sliced in half laterally
1½ cups small farm or other "wild" mushrooms such as chanterelles or shiitakes, cleaned and thinly sliced

1 tablespoon roughly chopped thyme leaves
24 tiny escargots, rinsed and patted dry
2 tablespoons Pernod
Black pepper to taste
½ recipe Basic All-purpose Flour Pasta (page 206) with herbs, rolled out, cut into 2-inch squares, and kept covered

1. Bring a pot of water to boil for the pasta. Add salt.

2. Heat the cream and reduce until just thick enough to coat the back of a spoon. Whisk in the mustard and set aside.

3. Gently heat a sauté pan and add the butter. Just as the butter begins to foam, add the shallots and then the shrimp. Toss or stir a moment and add the mushrooms and thyme. Turn up the heat and add the escargots.

4. When the shrimp is *just* cooked, add the Pernod and deglaze. Add just enough of the lemon-mustard cream to absorb the shrimp and escargot moisture. Season to taste.

5. Drop the pasta squares into the boiling water and cook until al dente. Drain and lay one square of pasta on each plate. Spoon the shrimp mixture evenly onto each and top with another square of pasta. Serve.

Manila Clams in Rioja
with Spanish Sausage

Manila clams are native to the West Coast; they are also known as Japanese littlenecks. They are extremely small and very tender. I am calling for a white Spanish wine from the Rioja region—Marqués de Caceres makes a very nice one that I've seen readily available. Many wines from Rioja are dry, crisp, simple, and perfect for everyday drinking.

Serves 4 to 6

4 tablespoons (½ stick) butter	32 Manila clams, scrubbed (or use other small, fresh clams)
1 large carrot, peeled and finely julienned into 2-inch lengths	1½ cups white Rioja wine (or substitute other dry, light white wine)
1 large leek, white part only, cleaned, finely julienned into 2-inch lengths	1 small bunch fresh cilantro, leaves only, roughly chopped
1 large stalk celery, cleaned and finely julienned into 2-inch lengths	3 ounces chorizo sausage, cooked, cooled, and diced small

1. Heat a sauté pan large enough to hold the clams. Add 2 tablespoons of the butter and coat the bottom of the pan. Add the carrot, leek, and celery and stir a moment.

2 Add the clams and wine. Cover the pan and allow the clams to steam open. Shake the pan a bit. As the clams open, remove them to 4 warm bowls and keep warm.

3. Reduce the wine and clam liquor over high heat until ½ cup remains. Add the cilantro and sausage and swirl in the remaining 2 tablespoons of butter. Pour the mixture over the clams and serve.

BRUSCHETTA
with Roquefort and Tapenade

This is another example of rustic comfort food that, despite its foreign name, will feel immediately familiar. Just think of it as a grilled cheese sandwich with a European education, or even knife and fork fondue.

Bruschetta hails from Italy's Umbria region; it is toasted or grilled bread brushed with good olive oil and often sliced garlic cloves. Other things may accompany it, but bread is the heart of bruschetta.

Serves 4 to 6

Tapenade (page 225)
- ¼ pound (1 stick) butter
- 6 garlic cloves, peeled and sliced
- 1 carrot, peeled and diced small
- 1 Spanish onion, peeled and diced small
- 2 stalks celery, cleaned and diced small
- 2 leeks, white part only
- 2 bay leaves
- 16 basil leaves, roughly chopped
- 2 quarts Chicken Stock (page 240)
- 1 tablespoon cracked black pepper
- 1 quart heavy cream
- ½ pound Roquefort, crumbled
- 1 loaf baguette-shaped bread
- ¼ cup extra virgin olive oil (or more, if necessary to generously coat the bread)

1. Prepare tapenade and set aside in the refrigerator.

2. Heat a large saucepan to medium heat and add the butter. As soon as the butter foams a bit, add the garlic and stir 20 seconds or so. Now add the carrot, onion, celery, leeks, and bay leaves. Stir often for about 10 minutes. Add the basil leaves. Reduce the heat if vegetables begin to show any color.

3. When the vegetables are glossy and softened somewhat, add the stock and cracked black pepper. Allow to simmer until the stock has a rich, concentrated flavor and only about 1 cup remains. Add the heavy cream to the stock and reduce it by about one-third.

4. Put the cream and vegetable mixture into a processor or blender and purée; with the machine running, drop in the cheese, piece by piece, until it is entirely incorporated. Season to taste.

5. Pour the cheese-cream mixture into a stainless steel or glass container and keep warm.

6. Preheat the oven to 450 degrees. Slice the baguette in half laterally and brush it with the olive oil. Spoon just enough tapenade onto the bread to cover it lightly. (Reserve the rest for another use.)

7. Place the bread, cut side up, in the oven and toast about 5 minutes. Remove to a cutting board and cut into 1-inch sections.

8. Ladle 2 or 3 ounces of the cheese-cream mixture onto warm plates and arrange the bread, tapenade side up, clockwise fashion over the cheese. Serve hot.

CARNITAS IN RED CHILI CAKES
with Black Beans, Sour Cream, and Salsa

Carnitas—literally "little meats"—also refers in Mexican cookery to meat that is cooked in a braising liquid until the liquid reduces to the point where only the fat remains and the meat lightly fries in the resulting fat drippings. A meat that has a relatively high fat content is better for a method like this, so pork is the usual choice. The meat should weigh about three pounds, but the addition to the pot of pork bones will enhance the flavor.

This is a case where planning ahead will pay off. Much of the work can be done a day or more in advance.

Serves 8 to 12

3 pounds pork (butt, country ribs, or loin ends)	1 head garlic, cut in half laterally
½ cup virgin olive oil	12 to 16 black peppercorns, bruised
2 carrots, peeled and roughly chopped	2 bay leaves
2 Spanish onions, peeled and roughly chopped	1 small bunch thyme
4 stalks celery, cleaned and roughly chopped	Water
	Salsa (page 223)
	2 cups sour cream

BEANS (see Note)

- ¼ cup olive oil
- 1 smoked pork hock
- ½ pound smoked slab bacon, rind removed, diced small
- 2 jalapeño peppers, diced small to medium
- 1 small Spanish onion, diced small to medium
- 2 stalks celery, diced small to medium
- ½ green pepper, skin and seeds removed, diced small to medium
- 2 cloves garlic, minced
- 1 quart black turtle beans, soaked in water overnight (remove any stones prior to soaking)
- ¼ cup ground cumin powder
- 1 bay leaf

Salt and pepper to taste

- 2 quarts Smoked Stock (page 241), or substitute Chicken Stock (page 240) and double the amount of smoked pork hocks
- ½ cup Spanish sherry wine vinegar

RED CHILI CAKES

- 6 whole eggs
- ¼ teaspoon salt
- ¼ cup chili powder or chili molido, sifted
- 2 to 2½ cups milk
- 2 cups or slightly less flour
- ½ cup clarified butter

1. Cut the meat into 1- by 2-inch strips. Leave all the fat *on* the meat.

2. Put a large pan on top of the stove on medium heat. Add the olive oil and then the chopped carrots, onions, and celery and the halved garlic head, and stir 5 to 8 minutes. Now add the peppercorns and bay leaves. Add the pork and thyme and stir once. Top this mixture with just enough water to cover the meat.

3. Bring the liquid to a high simmer and skim off any residue that comes to the top. Reduce heat and allow the liquid to cook down, stirring from time to time. When the liquid is gone or almost gone (in approximately 2½ hours), remove the meat to a bowl and allow to cool. (Any braising liquid that remains can be strained off, reduced, and reserved for flavoring the meat.) Discard the vegetables.

4. Now, if you haven't any black bean soup on hand, prepare the beans: Clean out the pot you used for the pork and heat it again. Add the olive oil, pork hock, and slab bacon. Allow the bacon to cook until just barely medium, then add the diced jalapeños, Spanish onion, celery, green pepper, and the minced garlic. Stir until vegetables are just glazed. Add the black beans, cumin, bay leaf, and salt and pepper. Stir. Add the stock and stir again. Allow the beans to cook until they are just soft. Stir in the vinegar and adjust seasoning as desired. (The beans may be prepared ahead and reheated for serving later.)

5. Shred the cooked pork into small, bite-sized pieces, season to taste, and put in a bowl.

6. Prepare the red chili cakes as you would regular crêpes (see page 266), and set aside covered with a dry towel.

7. Rub 8 to 12 small soufflé-type dishes with a tiny bit of butter on the bottom and the sides. Lay one chili cake (crêpe) in each of the molds and press them gently against the bottom and sides. Add a few tablespoons of meat to each of the molds. Lay another crêpe on top of the meat and add another layer of meat on top of that. You will notice that the edges of the crêpe extend over the sides of the mold, so you should fold the edges of the cake over the meat. Top each mold with aluminum foil. Set aside. (These can be prepared a full day ahead of time and refrigerated.)

8. Prepare the salsa.

9. When ready to serve, preheat the oven to 450 degrees. Put the molds on a baking sheet and put them in the oven for 10 to 15 minutes (longer if they have been refrigerated).

10. Heat enough of the black bean mixture to cover the base of each plate. With the aid of a spatula, carefully invert the molds over a cutting board and then slide the carnitas onto the beans. Garnish with sour cream and salsa. Serve.

Note: This is another case where you can utilize earlier hard work. If you have made Black Bean Soup (page 27) and had leftovers, you could certainly use them for this recipe.

SALADS

Probably in no other menu category have we experienced in these past few years more evidence of change, experimentation, and new raw products than in salads. It is only the beginning, I'm sure. A number of factors have contributed to this new range—the public's desire to eat more lightly and healthfully, the vigilant efforts and skills of farmers, and the imaginative work of chefs, whether professional or dedicated amateurs, have all conspired to make this welcome trend possible.

In the past, Americans have shortchanged themselves with iceberg lettuce pasted with syrupy-sweet bottled concoctions, mostly either red or green. Now the trend is to enjoy Mother Nature within the cycle of her seasons. It doesn't have to be complicated: You don't need a written recipe for the simple perfection of tender greens drizzled with good olive oil, vinegar, and freshly ground black pepper. Yet, if we wish to make a salad the focus of our meal, we can complicate it as we see fit.

Cold salads, warm salads, salads with fish or meat, cheese, or fruit, or combinations thereof, are part of the broad panoply of choices available to us. The ethnic mix in this country is widening our global interest and awareness of nature's bounty. Asia and South and Central America, in particular, are expanding and redefining our list of raw ingredients today.

In the rush to seem inventive we tend to overembrace the newest or even weirdest foodstuffs, yet the inquisitive palate is a vital tool. It may seem that we are up to our necks in radicchio and miniature vegetables. Their place at center stage will pass, and there will be new darlings from the garden. It is the process of natural selection. Radicchio is not new, nor are most of the other things we are sampling in our markets and restaurant tables today—cherimoya, mustard greens, and lobster mushrooms have existed for a long time. Only our awareness and appreciation for them is new, and they are welcome in my kitchen. Still, there is nothing on God's green earth more luscious than a tomato, just plucked off the vine and still full of the summer's heat, rinsed and cut into fat slices with a razor-sharp knife, and eaten with a pinch of salt and pepper, a splash of vinegar—leaning over the kitchen sink.

HOT FRIED CHICKEN SALAD
with Honey-Mustard Dressing

Hands down, this has been the most consistently requested salad I've ever put on a menu. Perhaps it satisfies some primal urge, I don't know, but this recipe is a study in contrasts: hot and cold, spicy and sweet, raw and cooked, crunchy and smooth—and maybe that is the key. The salad needs to be served immediately after you make it or those contrasts are lost. It can serve as a light entrée by itself.

The dressing can be made a day or two days ahead. The chicken is best marinated overnight in the refrigerator. The lettuces can be prepared a few hours ahead and left in paper toweling in a bowl in the refrigerator. At our restaurant we deep-fry the chicken in peanut oil but you can pan-fry this in a deep skillet, taking normal safety precautions.

Serves 6 to 8

SALAD DRESSING

3	egg yolks
1½	tablespoons honey
3	ounces (6 tablespoons) creole mustard
½	cup or slightly less balsamic vinegar

1½	cups safflower oil
½	cup extra virgin olive oil
2	tablespoons roasted sesame oil

MARINADE AND CHICKEN

6	whole eggs
2	cups heavy cream
2	jalapeño peppers, stems and seeds removed, sliced thin
1½	tablespoons crushed red pepper flakes
1½	tablespoons cayenne pepper

Salt and ground black pepper to taste

1½	tablespoons hot paprika
4	boneless, skinless chicken breasts, cut into small, finger-size pieces

Peanut oil for deep-frying chicken, enough to completely cover

1	head of romaine, outer leaves removed, remainder washed and torn
1	head of red leaf lettuce, outer leaves removed, remainder washed and torn
1	red onion, thinly sliced into rings

4½	cups all-purpose flour
2	tablespoons salt
6	tablespoons black pepper
9	tablespoons crushed red pepper flakes
3	tablespoons cayenne

1. Make the salad dressing: Beat the egg yolks with the honey, mustard, and balsamic vinegar. Gradually add the oils, whisking vigorously, until an emulsion forms. Refrigerate dressing in a covered container.

2. Prepare the marinade: Beat the eggs until thick and lemon colored. Slowly beat in the remaining ingredients. The marinade should be creamy, with a sweet/tart taste. Add the chicken strips to the marinade and refrigerate at least 12 hours or overnight.

3. An hour or two before serving prepare lettuces and chill. Prepare onion rings and set aside, covered. Mix the flour with the salt, pepper, pepper flakes, and cayenne in a large, shallow bowl.

4. When ready to serve, heat the oil to approximately 350 degrees. Remove the chilled chicken meat, allowing excess marinade to drip off. (You can simply strain the marinade off into the sink since you'll be cooking all the chicken at once.) Roll the chicken "fingers" in the seasoned flour.

5. Fry the chicken, turning it from time to time, until it is light brown.

6. Toss the lettuces in a bowl with just enough salad dressing to coat the leaves lightly. Mound the leaves in large chilled bowls.

7. Remove the hot chicken to toweling and cut up into bite-sized pieces. Arrange them over the greens and top with rings of red onion. Serve immediately.

MEDITERRANEAN BREAD SALAD

This dish demonstrates that the Mediterranean region exerts as much influence on Key West's cuisine as does the Caribbean. This salad can be a nice luncheon by itself. It is important to use excellent bread, tomatoes, and oil—for me, the magic and power of the dish are in the flavors of its simple ingredients.

Serves 4

4 ½-inch-thick slices of Italian bread
Virgin olive oil to sauté the bread
8 thin slices of buffalo milk mozzarella
4 slices tomato, drizzled with olive oil and seasoned with sea salt and freshly cracked black pepper

6 handfuls of mixed lettuces such as romaine, arugula, radicchio, curly chicory, Belgian endive, and watercress
½ cup extra virgin olive oil
1 cup virgin olive oil
½ cup Italian red wine vinegar
Cracked black pepper to taste

1. Heat oven to 400 degrees. Warm the olive oil for the bread in an ovenproof skillet and sauté the slices of bread until golden on both sides.

2. Lay 2 slices of the mozzarella on each slice of bread and top each with a slice of tomato. Place the pan in the oven and warm the cheese and tomatoes through.

3. Meanwhile, mix the greens together and add the oils. Toss. Add the vinegar and pepper and continue to toss gently.

4. Remove the pan from the oven and put the slices of bread in deep, room-temperature bowls, one slice per bowl. Now, generously mound the lettuces over the bread, cheese, and tomato combination and serve. The lettuces will completely cover the bread, tomato, and cheese. It is meant to be that way—a pleasant surprise.

CAESAR SALAD STEAK "TARTARE"

Every now and then when the blue jeans get a little snug, my wife says something like, "Let's just eat Caesar salad for a couple of nights." Faced with the spectre of food denial, my mind races for an intelligent way to placate her and also satisfy my need for more flavors. This salad is probably not cuisine minceur, but it's loaded with protein, garlic, greens, and Parmesan, and these are the things that make me happy.

Serves 4

TARTARE

1 pound trimmed filet mignon
4 egg yolks, stirred
Freshly ground black pepper
2 tablespoons capers, drained and rinsed well
¼ cup finely chopped red onion

¼ cup chopped fresh parsley
1 tablespoon Tabasco
1 tablespoon Worcestershire
12 to 16 anchovy fillets, soaked thoroughly and patted dry

DRESSING

3 egg yolks
1½ cups extra virgin olive oil
½ cup canola oil
3 tablespoons red wine vinegar
1 tablespoon
    minced garlic

2 ounces anchovy fillets, rinsed and
    finely chopped
2 tablespoons fresh lemon juice
½ tablespoon cracked black pepper
½ tablespoon Dijon mustard
½ cup freshly grated Parmesan

2 ½-pound loaves of sourdough bread, or
    1 loaf of French bread
½ cup olive oil
Sea salt and cracked black pepper, to taste

2 heads romaine, interior leaves only,
    washed and spun dry
1 small red onion, cut into rings and
    chilled
Cracked black pepper
Parmesan cheese

1. Prepare the tartare: Either finely chop or process the meat. Remove meat to bowl.

2. Briefly process the remaining ingredients and add them to the beef. Mix well and refrigerate.

3. Prepare the dressing: Beat the egg yolks by hand with a whisk or in an electric mixer until pale.

4. When the yolks are mixed, add the oils in a slow, steady stream. You will probably need to add a small portion of the vinegar during this time so that the emulsion doesn't get too thick to accept the oil.

5. Add the remaining vinegar. Now add everything but the cheese as you whisk. Add the cheese and adjust for taste. You should have about 2½ cups. Chill.

6. Cut two shapes of croutons—16 medium-to-large flat pieces and 24 to 36 small cubes.

7. Heat a skillet and add half the oil. Sauté the cubes until crisp. Add salt and pepper and drain on paper toweling; keep warm.

8. Clean and reheat the skillet. Add remaining oil and sauté the flat croutons. Drain on paper toweling and keep warm.

9. When you are ready to serve, put the cubed croutons, the romaine, and the onion in a bowl and toss with just enough dressing to coat. Mound the salad in large bowls. Spread the flat croutons with the tartare and surround the rim of the bowl. Season with cracked pepper all over and offer more fresh Parmesan tableside, to grate over the dish.

GRILLED PARMESAN POLENTA CROSTINI
with Eggplant and a Spinach Salad

How something so seemingly boring can, in reality, be so irresistible captivates me. Such is the case with polenta. The cross between its creaminess and its crunchiness gives it a very interesting texture. It is the perfect base for many sauces. I also like it in this salad that features both cold and warm temperatures.

Serves 6

POLENTA

2½ cups milk	1¾ cups yellow cornmeal
2½ cups water	¾ cup freshly grated Parmesan
4 teaspoons salt	3 tablespoons butter, cut into pieces
3 tablespoons cracked black pepper	

EGGPLANT MIXTURE

2 medium-sized eggplant, peeled, and top and bottom removed
1½ cups extra virgin olive oil
1 roasted red bell pepper

1 roasted poblano (or jalapeño) chile
2 tablespoons Spanish sherry wine vinegar
Salt and pepper to taste

SPINACH SALAD

¼ cup red wine vinegar
Salt and cracked black pepper
1 cup extra virgin olive oil

2 avocados, peeled, seeded and cut into small chunks
6 double handfuls of tender young spinach, cleaned

1. Heat oven to 425 degrees.

2. Prepare the polenta: Heat 2 cups of the milk, all the water, and salt and pepper in a saucepan and bring to a boil.

3. Whisk the remaining ½ cup milk in a bowl and add the cornmeal. Add this to the boiling mixture. Whisk quickly until thick. Add the Parmesan.

4. Add 2 tablespoons of butter to the corn mixture, stir until butter melts, and pour into a buttered baking sheet with a rim (approximately 12 by 14 inches). Dot the top with

the remaining 1 tablespoon butter. Cover the mixture with foil and cool 15 minutes.

5. Now bake until stiff, approximately 30 minutes. Remove and allow to cool. Lower the oven temperature to 400 degrees.

6. Slice the eggplant into "planks" ½ inch thick. Brush them *liberally* with extra virgin olive oil (use the entire 1 cup) and season. Spread them out on a baking pan and bake 8 to 10 minutes on each side. They will lose their whiteness and look glossy and oily. Remove them from the oven.

7. Cut up the eggplant into a rough-textured mixture and put in a bowl. Cut up the bell pepper and chile and add to the eggplant. Add the ½ cup of extra virgin olive oil, the wine vinegar, and salt and pepper, and toss all together.

8. Cut the cooled polenta into circles, squares, or any other attractive shapes and heat up a grill to moderate heat. Brush the polenta circles with oil and slowly grill them.

9. Make the salad vinaigrette: Mix together the red wine vinegar, salt, and pepper. Add the extra virgin olive oil and whisk.

10. Heat a small pan and warm enough of the eggplant mixture to top the grilled polenta. Remove the polenta from the grill and generously spoon on the eggplant mixture.

11. Toss the avocado chunks and spinach leaves with enough of the vinaigrette to coat them lightly. Arrange dressed salad on 6 plates, and serve with the warm eggplant crostini.

GOLDEN LENTIL SALAD
with Poached Artichoke Hearts

The artichoke was not well known to Americans until the 1900s, and it didn't really become mainstream until the 1960s when the crops in California found increasing audiences across the country. I distinctly remember the first time I ate one—not only was the vegetable oddly shaped, but there were two separate procedures for eating the thing, to boot! But I ate it, and loved it. I still do.

For this recipe you begin by discarding all of the outer leaves. If you wish to poach the loose leaves for a snack, by all means do so. You can cook the artichokes a full day ahead of serving them.

Serves 4

ARTICHOKES

4 large artichokes, all leaves removed and choke scraped off, evenly pared, leaving a thin portion of the inner stem

Juice of 3 lemons

¼ cup olive oil

1 onion, peeled and roughly chopped

1 carrot, peeled and roughly chopped

2 stalks celery, cleaned and roughly chopped

1 head garlic, cut in half crosswise

2 bay leaves

LENTILS

2 cups lentils (preferably small French ones)

1 teaspoon sea salt

12 basil leaves

12 Italian parsley leaves

10 cloves garlic

1 carrot, peeled and finely diced

1 Spanish onion, peeled and finely diced

1 stalk celery, cleaned and finely diced

2 yellow bell peppers, stems and seeds removed, cut into medium-large dice

1 cup extra virgin olive oil

1 cup safflower oil or other salad oil

¾ cup tarragon vinegar

¾ cup tomato concasse

Fresh tarragon leaves, for garnish

Freshly grated Parmesan cheese

Cracked black pepper

1. Clean and pare the artichokes, add all the lemon juice, and toss in a bowl. (The lemon juice discourages discoloration while contributing flavor.)

2. Heat a saucepan just large enough to hold the artichokes. Add the olive oil and then add the onion, carrot, celery, and garlic. Cook a few minutes. Add the bay leaves and place the artichoke hearts on the bed of vegetables. Add enough water to cover them.

3. Cover the pot and steam gently until the artichokes are just tender, 15 to 20 minutes. Remove from heat and chill artichoke hearts. Discard broth and vegetables.

4. Wash the lentils in cold water and rinse. Put them in a saucepan and just cover with water. Add the salt.

5. Make a bouquet garni by tying the basil, parsley, and garlic cloves in cheesecloth and add them to the lentils. Bring lentils to a boil and then reduce them to a simmer.

6. After 10 minutes add the diced carrot, onion, and celery and cook 5 minutes. Now add the diced yellow peppers and cook about 10 more minutes. There should be almost

no water left in the pan; if there is some, drain it off. Pour the lentils onto a large platter to cool.

7. Prepare a vinaigrette by combining the olive and safflower oils and the tarragon vinegar. Place the cooled lentils in a bowl and stir in enough of the vinaigrette to coat them lightly.

8. Spoon lentils evenly on 4 plates. Place an artichoke heart in the center of each plate. Surround the artichokes with the tomato concasse and spoon some of the remaining vinaigrette over the artichokes. Garnish with fresh tarragon leaves.

9. Serve with freshly grated Parmesan cheese and cracked black pepper.

CRABMEAT, MANGO, AND AVOCADO
with Olive Oil and Lime Vinaigrette

Serves 6

VINAIGRETTE

¼ cup lime juice
¾ cup extra virgin olive oil
Cracked black pepper to taste

1 large mango, peeled and cubed into medium chunks, chilled
1 avocado, peeled, seeded, and cubed into medium chunks, chilled

4 small handfuls of mixed fresh lettuces, washed, spun dry, and kept cold
1 pound lump crabmeat, picked over and cleaned, then chilled

1. Mix the vinaigrette ingredients and chill until ready to assemble the salad.

2. Combine the mango and avocado in one bowl. Ladle on enough of the vinaigrette to coat and delicately mix them together; be careful not to mash the avocado.

3. Ladle enough of the remaining vinaigrette over the lettuces to coat them lightly. Toss.

4. Arrange the lettuces casually on plates. Mound the avocado and mango combination over the lettuces. Shred the crabmeat by tearing it with your fingers and strew it over the avocado and mango. Serve cold.

BRAIDED SASHIMI OF RED SNAPPER AND YELLOWFIN TUNA
with Tart Herbal Dressing and Mixed Lettuces

The sushi craze has had a far-reaching impact on the way we think about fish: We no longer treat it with the same disrespect we have shown over the last twenty years. Naturally, it is imperative that the fish you use be of the most pristine quality. I have braided, or woven, the fish for the sake of artful presentation, but if you wish, you can prepare this dish more simply by chopping the two fish in the fashion of a tartare.

Makes 4 salad-size portions

- ¼ pound boneless, skinless red snapper, trimmed and evenly cut
- ¼ pound boneless, skinless yellowfin tuna, trimmed and evenly cut
- ½ to ¾ cup Port Wine Vinaigrette (page 230)
- 4 small handfuls mixed lettuces, cleaned, spun dry, and kept cool
- 1 cup Aigrelette Sauce (page 231)

1. Cut the fish into ribbons 3 inches long by slightly less than ½ inch wide. Keep as cold as possible.

2. Lay 3 or 4 strips of the snapper vertically on your cutting board. Now braid 3 or 4 strips of tuna through them horizontally.

3. Keep the fish covered and cold while you make the vinaigrette, prepare the lettuces, and make the sauce.

4. When ready to serve, dress the greens with just enough vinaigrette to coat them lightly and place a portion on each plate. Put a small dollop of the Aigrelette Sauce next to the lettuces. Lay the sashimi on each plate and serve.

WARM WHITE BEAN SALAD
with Cracklings, Duck Livers, and Greens, Sherry Vinaigrette

More and more people in this country have begun to share the Europeans' appreciation for salads that are served warm. Some salads should be served quite cool while others can be warm throughout—my hot fried chicken salad is an example of a dish that should be both hot and cool, and certainly needs to be served as soon as it is assembled.

When I make this white bean salad I always sneak in a little mango chutney as a mystery ingredient. Its tangy fruit works well with the sharpness of vinegar, the richness of liver, and the faint bitterness of greens. Note that the beans must be soaked overnight.

Serves 4

BEANS

2   cups white beans, rinsed and soaked overnight
½   cup duck fat or olive oil
6   whole cloves garlic, peeled
1   stalk celery, cleaned and finely chopped

1   onion, peeled and finely diced
1   carrot, peeled and finely diced
1   bay leaf
1   tablespoon cumin
1   quart chicken stock

VINAIGRETTE

½   cup Spanish sherry wine vinegar
1½   to 2 cups extra virgin olive oil
1   tablespoon cracked black pepper

2   tablespoons rendered duck fat or olive oil
1   pound duck livers, lobes separated
3   tablespoons Mango Chutney (page 203), optional
1   head radicchio, cleaned, patted dry, and torn up

1   head Belgian endive, cleaned, patted dry, and torn up
¼   head Napa cabbage, cleaned, patted dry, and torn up
Salt and pepper
¼   cup prepared cracklings (see page 10)

1. Drain the beans and prepare them: Heat a large, heavy saucepan on medium heat and add the duck fat or olive oil. Add the garlic cloves and cook about 1 minute. Now, add the celery, onion, carrot, and bay leaf. Stir and cook until vegetables are glazed.

(recipe continues)

2. Add the beans and cumin to the glazed vegetables and stir. Add the stock and lower the heat. Cook gently until the beans are just soft (approximately 1½ hours; it may be necessary to add more stock if it evaporates during cooking). Reserve beans in their liquid.

3. Make vinaigrette by mixing all of the ingredients together. Set aside.

4. Heat a large skillet on medium-high heat. Add 2 tablespoons of duck fat or olive oil and heat it well. Sear the duck livers well on each side and then remove them to a warm plate.

5. Add the chutney to the pan. Then add the radicchio, endive, and cabbage and season with salt and pepper.

6. Add the reserved beans and liquid, the cracklings, and the vinaigrette and gently but quickly toss them all together.

7. Arrange the warm salads on 4 plates and place the livers in and around the melange of greens, cracklings, and beans. Serve.

GRILLED VEGETABLE SALAD
with Pesto Vinaigrette

If you are planning to serve an entrée from the grill, you may wish to combine it with this salad. In some ways it seems like so much work to clean the grill, load up, start the fire, wait half an hour for it to be perfect and then cook a piece of fish or meat on it for 5 minutes. Why not get double duty out of your effort and pull two courses from one source? Just grill your vegetables before the fire reaches its peak, and make the salad. In that way, you can cook the entrée while you enjoy the first course.

This salad, accompanied by large, grilled slices of sourdough bread brushed with olive oil and spread with a soft cheese, makes a nice luncheon.

Serves 4

VINAIGRETTE

½ cup red wine vinegar	1 cup safflower oil
½ cup balsamic vinegar	¼ cup Pesto (page 224)
2 cups extra virgin olive oil	1 teaspoon freshly cracked black pepper

1 medium-sized eggplant, ends removed, cut into "planks" ½ inch thick
Salt and pepper
2 medium-sized zucchini, ends removed, cut into planks ½ inch thick
2 medium-sized yellow squash, ends removed, cut into planks ½ inch thick
4 tomatoes, cored and cut into thick slices crosswise

½ head radicchio, washed and shaken dry
1 head romaine, inner leaves only, washed and shaken dry
1 head Belgian endive, washed and shaken dry
1 head curly chicory, washed and shaken dry

1. Prepare a fire in the grill.

2. Whisk together all the ingredients for the vinaigrette.

3. Salt the eggplant liberally and allow it to drain in a colander.

4. Lay the other cut vegetables in a shallow baking dish and pour on just enough of the vinaigrette to coat them. Turn them occasionally while the fire gets hot.

5. Rinse the eggplant planks and pat them dry. Add them to the other vegetables in the vinaigrette.

6. Combine all the greens in a large mixing bowl and keep cool.

7. Using tongs, place the vegetables on the grill and cook until slightly soft, turning once and removing them to a plate when they are ready.

8. Add a pinch of salt and pepper to the vegetables and arrange them on plates, cutting them as necessary for presentation.

9. Toss the lettuces lightly in some of the remaining vinaigrette. Arrange the lettuces in the center of the grilled vegetables.

10. Pour a bit more of the vinaigrette over the grilled vegetables. Serve.

BELL PEPPER, ENDIVE, JICAMA, AND AVOCADO SALAD
with a Salsa Vinaigrette

Serves 6 to 8

1 green pepper, stems, ribs and seeds removed
1 red pepper, stems, ribs, and seeds removed
1 yellow pepper, stems, ribs, and seeds removed

3 heads Belgian endive, cores removed
1 small jicama, peeled
1 avocado, peeled and pitted
Juice of ½ lemon

SALSA VINAIGRETTE

3 tablespoons Spanish wine vinegar
¾ cup extra virgin olive oil
1 tomato, concassée in medium dice
½ red onion, finely diced

1 jalapeño, finely diced
2 tablespoons coarsely chopped cilantro leaves

1. Finely julienne the bell peppers, endive, and jicama and mix. Keep cold.

2. Cube the avocado flesh in medium-sized dice and squeeze lemon on it.

3. Prepare the vinaigrette: Whisk the vinegar and oil together and stir in the remaining ingredients.

4. In a large bowl, mix enough of the salsa with everything but the avocado to moisten well. Divide this mixture on plates and garnish with diced avocado.

SMOKED DUCK SALAD SZECHUAN
with Somen Noodles and Oriental Vegetables

People have often asked me for this recipe. Although Szechuan cooking can be fiery, in this dish the chiles' power is very subtle. The intense meaty flavor of the duck breast goes a long way, so you'll only need a small portion of the meat. Do note that the duck must marinate overnight in the refrigerator.

If you have never cooked somen noodles, please let me offer a warning. They cook much faster than the directions on the package indicate. Once you've tried them, I'm sure you'll fall in love with their beautiful shape, taste, and presence in the dish.

Serves 4 to 6

MARINADE AND DUCK

1 cup dark molasses	1 teaspoon finely chopped fresh gingerroot
½ cup apple cider vinegar	1 pinch grated fresh nutmeg
¼ cup freshly squeezed lemon juice	1 teaspoon fresh thyme leaves
½ cup Dijon mustard	10 to 12 ounces Moulard duck breast (one
½ cup tomato sauce	half of a full breast), to yield 5 or 6 ounces of
1 clove garlic, minced	meat when trimmed of skin and fat
½ teaspoon cayenne	

1 recipe Tamari-Sesame Dressing (page 230)	1½ cups finely julienned mixed vegetables such as purple cabbage, Napa cabbage,
1½ cups cooked somen noodles (available in oriental grocery stores)	carrot, cucumber, daikon, snow peas, bell peppers
1 tablespoon sesame oil	Enoki mushrooms or edible flowers such as nasturtiums, for garnish

1. Combine all the ingredients for the marinade and cover the duck breast with it. Refrigerate overnight.

2. The next day, make the dressing by mixing the garlic, basil, and pepper with the vinegar and tamari and whisking in the oils. Keep dressing cool.

3. Remove the duck breast from the marinade and smoke it until just cooked through. (If you don't have a smoker available, you can grill the breast.) Chill the meat.

(recipe continues)

4. Cook the somen noodles until just al dente and rinse under cold water. Drain thoroughly and toss with the sesame oil. Chill.

5. Prepare the vegetables.

6. Remove the skin from the duck and discard it. Slice the breast on a severe angle into thin, flat pieces. (They should be *quite* thin.) You will probably have more than you need. Save any leftovers for another use.

7. Arrange the chilled noodles in a tight nest in the center of a large serving platter.

8. Toss the vegetables in a bowl and dress with enough vinaigrette to coat them lightly. Surround the noodles with the vegetables.

9. Dip the duck slices into the vinaigrette and arrange them around the noodles.

10. A small stand of enoki mushrooms, or a few nasturtiums, may be placed in the nest of pasta as a fitting garnish.

STEAMED ASPARAGUS SPEARS
with Black Pepper Pesto Vinaigrette

The sweet, vernal flavor of asparagus is so perfect that the simplest accompaniments are the most welcome ones.

Serves 4 to 6

BLACK PEPPER PESTO

1 large clove garlic	½ cup washed Italian parsley leaves
½ cup toasted pine nuts	1½ teaspoons coarsely ground black pepper
½ cup washed parsley leaves	¾ cup virgin olive oil

VINAIGRETTE

1 cup extra virgin olive oil
¼ cup red wine vinegar
¼ cup black pepper pesto

24 tiny asparagus spears, blanched or
   steamed until just cooked, then cooled
   and dried

1. Put all of the pesto ingredients except the olive oil in a food processor and pulse a few times. Now, with the machine running, slowly pour in the oil. The pesto should be slightly coarse. Adjust seasoning to taste.

2. Mix all of the vinaigrette ingredients together and chill, covered.

3. Arrange 6 spears of asparagus on each of 4 chilled plates.

4. Whisk the pesto-infused vinaigrette and spoon a small amount on the center portion of the spears.

ACHIOTE-MARINATED SKEWERED QUAIL
with Torn Greens and Papaya-Chile Vinaigrette

Achiote is a seed from certain trees indigenous to South and Central America and the West Indies. It is also known as annatto seed. *The seeds impart a pungent flavor but not a spicy one and they cause a dramatic color transformation that will lend a brilliant orangey red cast to the quail.*

Serves 4

1 cup virgin olive oil	Salt and pepper to taste
¼ cup achiote (or annatto) seeds	4 handfuls fresh greens, washed, dried,
8 tiny semiboneless quail	and torn into small pieces

VINAIGRETTE

1 poblano chile, seeds and skin removed, diced small	1 cup extra virgin olive oil
1 small ripe papaya, seeds and skin removed, diced small	¼ cup Champagne vinegar

1. Heat the 1 cup virgin olive oil in a small saucepan until quite warm. Stir in the achiote seeds and remove from the heat. Allow to cool.

2. Put the raw quail in a medium-large bowl and season with salt and pepper. When the olive oil is cool, pour it through a fine strainer and put the seeds in a cheesecloth. Tie the cloth securely shut and add it to the oil. Now pour the oil over the quail and add the seed bag to the bowl. Allow quail to marinate between 1 and 3 hours, refrigerated.

(recipe continues)

3. Fire up the grill or broiler to high heat.

4. Make the vinaigrette: Mix together half of the poblano and half the papaya with the extra virgin olive oil and Champagne vinegar. Set aside.

5. Soak 16 small, wooden skewers in water (this prevents them from burning up). Now thread two skewers crosswise in an X through each quail and lay birds in a flat pan. Discard the marinade.

6. Grill the quails, turning them from time to time. They should be crisp and juicy. Remove them to a warm platter when they are done.

7. Put the prepared greens in a bowl and toss with enough vinaigrette to barely coat them. Mound the greens on 4 plates. Arrange the quail attractively in front of the greens. Drizzle any collected drippings the quail may have rendered onto the plates. Garnish the plates with the remaining diced papaya and poblano chile. Serve.

Avocado and Tomato Salad
with Smoked Trout-Buttermilk Dressing

Maine's coastal area has a relatively new neighbor—Duck Trap Farms. One of their fine products is the smoked trout in this salad. The cold smoked delicacy's slight salinity is countered by the spicy heat of a poblano chile in the dressing.

Serves 4

1½ cups sour cream	¼ cup white wine vinegar
½ cup buttermilk	2 avocados
½ cup heavy cream	2 tomatoes, concassée
¼ bunch basil leaves, chopped	1 orange, segments only (all pith and
½ poblano chile, diced fine	seeds removed)
1 pound smoked trout, all skin and bone discarded, flaked	8 sprigs cilantro

1. Combine the sour cream, buttermilk, heavy cream, chopped basil, diced poblano, flaked trout, and wine vinegar and chill, covered.

2. Cut the avocados in half lengthwise and remove the peel neatly. Discard the seed. Place

the four avocado halves flat side down, thinly slice each half into even sections, 6 to 9 per half, and fan slices out slightly on four cool plates.

3. Ladle enough of the trout mixture over avocado slices to almost cover them. Randomly scatter the diced tomato and the orange segments over each of the plates, both on and off the avocado. Garnish each plate with 2 sprigs of cilantro. Serve.

A VINTNER'S SALAD:
Grilled Goat Cheese in Grape Leaves,
Bitter Greens, and Cabernet Sauvignon Vinegar

Nothing could have prepared me for the majestic, sweeping beauty of the Californian treasures known as the Napa and Sonoma Valleys. My long-awaited pilgrimage to this viticultural heaven occurred in May of 1985 and I eagerly look forward to a return soon.

The components of a salad like this are natural alliances that made immediate sense to me as I enjoyed the extremely generous hospitality of our hosts, Bruce and Barbara Neyers, of Joseph Phelps Wineries.

Serves 4

Eight 2-ounce disks of goat cheese
- 2 *tablespoons extra virgin olive oil*
- 2 *tablespoons finely chopped thyme leaves*
- 16 *grape leaves, fresh picked or packed in brine (if using brine-packed leaves, rinse them thoroughly before blanching)*

- 4 *large handfuls fresh greens, such as radicchio, Belgian endive, watercress, arugula, or chicory, cleaned, torn into small pieces, and spun dry*

VINAIGRETTE

    1 *cup extra virgin olive oil*
    ¼ *cup Cabernet Sauvignon vinegar*
Cracked black pepper to taste

1. Lay the goat cheese on a platter and spoon a bit of the extra virgin olive oil on each disk. Scatter the thyme leaves over the cheese.

2. Bring a pot of water to a boil and blanch the grape leaves. Strain the leaves and refresh under cold water. Dry. Trim off the stems and discard.

3. Place each disk of cheese on 2 overlapped grape leaves and fold leaves around the cheese to make neat packages. Reserve.

4. Heat up a grill.

5. Toss the greens in a bowl. Mix together the vinaigrette ingredients and reserve.

6. Grill the leaf-wrapped cheeses.

7. Add just enough vinaigrette to the greens to coat them and arrange the greens on 4 plates. When the cheese packages are warm, divide them among the plates, unfolding the grape leaves (they are not eaten in this recipe). Serve with crusty French bread, and spread the warm cheese on it.

HEARTS OF ROMAINE AND TINY GREEN BEANS
with Blue Cheese and Tuscan Vinegar

Beautiful colors and a combination of crisp and smooth textures highlight this delicate but full-flavored salad.

Serves 4

¼ cup Tuscan red wine vinegar or other good red wine vinegar
1 cup virgin olive oil
¾ pound haricots verts, cleaned and blanched al dente in lightly salted boiling water, toweled dry, and kept cold

4 heads romaine, interior leaves or hearts only (reserve outer leaves for another use), washed, spun dry, and kept cold on dry toweling, covered, in the refrigerator
2 to 3 ounces crumbled blue cheese (Maytag or Nauvoo Bleu are good domestic choices; otherwise a Bleu de Bresse, Gorgonzola, or Stilton)
Cracked black pepper to taste

1. Whisk the red wine vinegar and olive oil together in a bowl.

2. Lightly toss the prepared beans in just enough vinaigrette to dress them. Arrange them in the center of 4 cool plates.

3. Toss the romaine hearts into the same bowl and dress with a bit more vinaigrette. Arrange them on either side of the beans. Crumble the blue cheese over the beans and serve, offering the pepper mill and good bread.

FISH AND
SEAFOOD ENTRÉES

A round 1820, Key West began as a station for "wreckers." John Simonton recognized that the island of Cayo Hueso (Bone Key), with its protective reef, was a place of promise. People could trade prosperously in the bounty from cargo ships that faltered in the treacherous waters immediately outside what would later be called Key West. Although there was no fresh water available on the island, rainwater could be caught and stored successfully. In the city of Havana, Simonton purchased Cayo Hueso on January 19, 1822, from Juan Pablo Salas for two thousand dollars.

Prosper they did. At the end of the nineteenth century, Key West was the richest community per capita in the United States. The wealth poured in from the sea, and the people who settled the island developed businesses that related to the ocean. By the 1930s the free-wheeling town had become notorious, and it began to attract literary folk (Hemingway, Dos Passos, and Robert Frost were part of the famous first wave). Today, fishing and writing remain major interests to Key Westers, and their visitors.

The Overseas Highway that spans the 100-odd miles down to Key West could probably be considered the world's longest fishing pier. The range of waters and types of fish available to the anglers on the edge of US 1 is staggering. Each year more people come to the Keys to participate in the sport of fishing. They vary in ability and interest but they all have one thing in common: an appetite for seafood.

It is a real inspiration to cook with fish of the superb quality available here. On any given day I can obtain the freshest shrimp ("Key West gold"), snapper, yellowtail, grouper, tuna, dolphin, or swordfish. Over the years, I have developed relationships with a small coterie of dedicated professionals who know how to take care of their catch and bring me their best. This chapter is dedicated to the men and women who live their lives fishing the waters around Cayo Hueso, and who bring the fruits of their labors to my kitchen.

CONCH LASAGNE

I created this dish while working in Jupiter, Florida. My friend Proal Perry was coming from Key West to visit me. I was homesick for Key West so conch came to mind. It has a flavor not unlike clams or abalone, but the texture poses a bit of a challenge. Unless you grind it—which I didn't want to do for this recipe—you've got to pound it paper-thin or it will be as tough as hide. Once you've pounded it, whether for this dish or another local favorite, cracked conch, its texture is delicate and fine.

I make this dish with a flavored homemade semolina pasta but it can be done with a quality dried pasta, and since the recipe is somewhat complicated, that's not a bad idea. If you've made lasagne before, this variation will be easy for you to understand. It's basically alternate layers of pasta, fresh tomato sauce, and a seafood mornay—all flavored with Parmesan, ricotta, herbs, and garlic. This is a good party dish because it can be made a day ahead of time and cooked while you mingle with your guests.

Serves 10 to 12

FRESH TOMATO SAUCE

- 2 tablespoons olive oil
- 6 ounces slab bacon, rind removed, cut into small cubes
- ¼ pound (1 stick) butter
- 2 leeks, white part only, split, cleaned, and diced
- 1 Spanish onion, diced
- ¼ pound mushrooms
- 4 stalks celery, diced

- 2 bell peppers, stems, seeds, and ribs removed, diced
- 4 garlic cloves, sliced
- 1 bay leaf
- 8 tomatoes, concassée
- 12 basil leaves, roughly chopped
Cracked black pepper to taste
- ½ cup balsamic vinegar
- 2 tablespoons tomato paste

About 2 pounds lasagne noodles, homemade or a good commercial variety
- 1 pound conch meat, cleaned and pounded very thin

Salad Oil
- 1 quart ricotta (see page 211 if you want to make your own)

SEAFOOD MORNAY

1½ cups clarified butter	½ cup flour, sifted
3 garlic cloves, sliced	2 cups Fish Stock (page 244), heated
1 jalapeño, stemmed, seeded, and sliced	½ tablespoon cayenne
1 Spanish onion, diced	2½ cups cream
2 stalks celery, diced	½ cup Parmesan
1 green pepper, stemmed, seeded, and diced	Salt and pepper to taste

1. Prepare the tomato sauce: In a large, heavy-bottomed pot, heat olive oil and cook the bacon about medium-rare.

2. Add the butter, leeks, onion, mushrooms, celery, bell pepper, and garlic and cook over medium heat until the vegetables are slightly softened. Add the bay leaf. Let the vegetables begin to caramelize a little and then add the tomatoes and basil and stir gently. Season with pepper.

3. Turn heat to low and allow to cook about 10 minutes; then add the balsamic vinegar and tomato paste. Cook 10 more minutes and remove from heat and cool completely.

4. Meanwhile, cook the pasta al dente, drain, and cool. Lightly oil cooked lasagne noodles and set aside on damp cloth toweling.

5. Pound the conch, cut it on the bias into small bite-sized pieces, and scatter it over the bottom of a large bowl.

6. Make the mornay sauce: Heat the clarified butter in a heavy-bottomed pot. Add the garlic, jalapeño, onion, celery, and green pepper and stir. Sauté briefly over medium heat.

7. Before the vegetables start to brown, begin to whisk in the flour in stages, over low heat. This way the flour taste can cook out more readily. Continue to whisk until all the flour is incorporated.

8. Still whisking, add the fish stock in batches. It will fluctuate between thick and loose at first; that's normal.

9. Now add the cayenne and cream. Cook slowly for 20 to 30 minutes, whisking often. The sauce should have the consistency of a thin batter. Strain the sauce through a fine-mesh strainer into the bowl with the conch and add the grated Parmesan. Season and cool.

10. Assemble the dish: Spread the bottom of a baking casserole with a little of the tomato sauce. Now build alternate layers of pasta, seafood mornay, pasta, and tomato sauce, adding generous dollops of ricotta as you go. (You may also add more garlic if you desire.) Finish with a layer of tomato sauce and plenty of ricotta.

(recipe continues)

FISH AND SEAFOOD ENTRÉES

11. Cover with aluminum foil and bake at 350 degrees for 45 minutes, or until warm throughout. Remove the foil, turn the oven off, and allow lasagna to rest about 20 minutes so that it sets before serving.

Note: You may store the assembled lasagne overnight in the refrigerator before baking. However, be sure to cover it with plastic wrap, *not* aluminum foil, for storage. Foil can react with the tomato sauce and shed gray flakes on the lasagne, a depressing discovery after all the work you've put in.

A dry white Italian wine, such as Pinot Grigio, Italian Chardonnay, or perhaps a Gavi dei Gavi, would be a suitable accompaniment to this dish. For more roundness, a dry Chenin Blanc would be a suitable alternative.

GROUPER WITH ASIAN VEGETABLES

This is a dish for its time. It is quite simple to prepare, it's spicy and loaded with vegetables, it's good for you, and I think it's delicious!
Freshness is the key to the vegetables, so vary them according to market availability— just be sure they're Asian-style, in keeping with the dish.

Serves 4

MARINADE

½ cup virgin olive oil	2 bay leaves
1 cup safflower or other salad oil	6 black peppercorns
½ cup soy sauce	1 small bunch fresh cilantro, roughly
Juice of 1 orange, 1 lemon, and 1 lime	chopped
	2 large cloves garlic, cut in half

GINGER-GARLIC VINAIGRETTE

1 cup red wine vinegar	Freshly cracked black pepper
½ cup soy sauce (preferably low-sodium soy)	Four 7- to 8-ounce pieces of fresh filleted grouper, cut on a severe bias
½ cup dark-roasted sesame oil	About 8 cups assorted fresh vegetables such as
½ cup chopped cilantro	cucumbers, purple cabbage, daikon, red and
½ cup chili oil	yellow peppers, bok choy, bean sprouts, Napa
3 tablespoons chopped peeled ginger	cabbage, enoki mushrooms, and fresh water
3 tablespoons minced garlic	chestnuts (2 cups mixed vegetables per serving)
1½ tablespoons sugar	Lime wedges for garnish

1. Mix all of the marinade ingredients together in a stainless steel bowl at least 1 hour in advance to allow flavors to blend.

2. Combine all vinaigrette ingredients and keep at room temperature.

3. Cut the assorted vegetables in small slices or strips on the bias, as is common with oriental preparations. Keep cool in a bowl. Be sure you have chosen vegetables with a good variety of colors and textures.

4. Prepare a hot, well oiled grill.

5. Marinate grouper 2 to 4 minutes (no longer or the fish will taste overly salty from the soy sauce). Remove from marinade and grill until just done. Remove to a platter.

6. Put vegetables in a large, slightly warm bowl and add just enough of the room-temperature vinaigrette to coat the vegetables lightly—you can reserve any leftover vinaigrette for another use. Mix well and then mound the vegetables over the fish. Garnish with lime and serve.

The ginger vinaigrette dressing on the vegetables might argue for a cold, bitter beer, but a semisweet wine such as a California Riesling would be a good choice.

BRAISED STRIPED BASS IN CHARDONNAY
with a Chiffonade of Lettuces

The braising of meat generally involves an initial browning of the exterior but this is not usually the case with seafood. It is helpful to baste your fish periodically during cooking to prevent it from drying out. This is a dish of brilliant colors and subtle, rich flavors.

Serves 4

- 6 tablespoons (¾ stick) butter
- 4 shallots, peeled and finely chopped
- Four 7- to 8-ounce fillets striped bass, scaled but skin left on, boned and cut into 12 "scallops" (three pieces per person)
- ⅓ cup Champagne wine vinegar or Chardonnay wine vinegar
- 1 cup Chardonnay
- 3 cups cream, reduced by almost half
- 4 handfuls mixed lettuces such as radicchio, Belgian endive, red oak leaf, or baby Bibb, cut into thin ribbons (chiffonade), and kept cold
- Salt and pepper

1. Preheat the oven to 350 degrees. Lightly butter the bottom of a heavy-bottomed skillet and scatter in the chopped shallots.

2. Put the fish in the pan, skin side up, being careful not to overcrowd. Add the wine vinegar and Chardonnay but do not completely cover the fish. You want to go only halfway up.

3. Now place a piece of oiled parchment paper on top of the fish, put the skillet on a stove burner, and bring to a simmer. Baste the fish once and then put it in the oven. The thickness of your fish will determine cooking time, but I recommend you test it and baste it every 2 or 3 minutes.

4. When the fish is almost done, discard the parchment paper and, using a spatula, remove the fish to a platter and keep warm. Put the skillet on the burner and reduce the cooking liquid over high heat. When it is almost a glaze, add the cream and cook until almost thick enough to coat the back of a spoon.

5. Put the lettuces in the pan, season, and stir for 30 seconds. Spoon the sauce and lettuces onto serving plates and arrange the fish on top. Serve.

Note: If you substitute another fish, such as snapper, I would advise you to braise the fish and then, while you are waiting for your sauce to reduce, peel off the cooked skin and discard it. It is not as interesting, texturally, as bass skin, but leaving it on during braising helps to keep the fish moist.

A moderately priced California Chardonnay or a young, crisp White Burgundy, like St.-Véran, would be the best choices here.

PAN-COOKED GROUPER
Over Ancho Butter Sauce
with Avocado and Tomato Béarnaise

Most Americans, except perhaps in the far West and Southwest, have had very little exposure to the many interesting uses for chiles. Chiles come in various forms and are called different names by different people. Perhaps this shifting nomenclature has kept many people from trying them, but a more probable cause is fear. "Just how hot are those devils," you shudder when faced with the presence of the gnarled, twisting finger of a fresh cayenne pepper.

With the influence of Mexican and Spanish cooking cutting deeply into the mainstream of American dining, this attitude is changing quickly. Beyond that, many Asian and other oriental cultures also employ the use of chiles, and Americans have fallen in love with foods from that part of the world.

There are many who argue that the presence of chiles is too violent and upsets the delicate subtleties of European-styled cuisine. While it is true that in the past many classically trained chefs went only as far as dried cayenne pepper added sparingly to some sauces, many chefs are now eagerly incorporating chiles, both fresh and dried, into their repertoire.

Serves 6

BUTTER SAUCE

1 tablespoon olive oil	6 tablespoons Spanish vinegar
3 tablespoons peeled and sliced shallots	½ cup heavy cream
3 garlic cloves, sliced	1 pound butter, cut into small pieces and kept very cold in a bowl
24 coriander seeds, toasted	Salt and pepper to taste
1 bay leaf	
6 toasted ancho chiles, stems and seeds removed, soaked in water	

1 recipe Sauce Béarnaise (page 238), made with white wine	¼ cup clarified butter
½ cup diced ripe avocado, at room temperature	6 grouper fillets, skinned and boned, cut into 7- or 8-ounce pieces
½ cup tomato concasse, at room temperature	Salt and pepper
	¼ cup all-purpose flour

1. Make the butter sauce: In a medium-size saucepan, warm up the olive oil. Add the sliced shallots and garlic and stir. Add the coriander seeds and bay leaf and stir, keeping the flame low. Remove the anchos from the water and pat dry. Add half of them to the pan and stir. Cut the other half into thin strips (they are called *rajas*), and reserve for garnish.

2. Now add the Spanish vinegar to the sauce and reduce until glazy. When this is done, add the heavy cream and reduce until thick and bubbling. Keeping the heat low, whisk in the butter pieces one piece at a time until all butter is incorporated. Adjust seasoning. Strain sauce through a fine-mesh strainer and reserve in a warm place.

3. Prepare béarnaise and fold in diced avocado and tomato. Keep warm.

4. Preheat oven to 450 degrees. Put the clarified butter in a large, heavy skillet or sauté pan and bring to high heat.

5. Season the fish with salt and pepper and then lay it skin side down. Dust it with the flour. Now spank any excess flour off the fish and lay it carefully in the hot pan.

6. Shake the pan a bit and sauté fish about 2 minutes on medium to medium-high heat.

7. Turn fish with a spatula. Drain off any excess fat and put fish in the oven until just done (approximately 5 minutes). It will feel slightly springy to the touch.

8. Ladle ¼ cup of butter sauce onto each warm plate and then place a portion of fish on top. Add a generous dollop of the avocado-tomato béarnaise and garnish with the reserved strips of ancho. Serve.

Note: For a lighter dish you can omit one of the sauces.

A dry, assertive white wine with good acidity, such as a White Hermitage or a Spanish Chardonnay, would stand up to the complexity of flavors in this dish.

Soy- and Sesame-Grilled Grouper
with a Tropical Fruit Salsa

This is a summertime dish. It is light, spicy, and a cooling foil to hot evenings.

Serves 4

SALSA

1 papaya, seeds and skin removed, cut into small dice

1 mango, seed and skin removed, cut into small dice

¼ pineapple, core, outside skin, and eyes removed, cut into small dice

½ tomato, concassée

2 jalapeños or serrano chilies, stems, seeds and ribs discarded and cut into small dice

⅓ cup Spanish wine vinegar

½ red onion, peeled and diced small

2 tablespoons olive oil

¼ cup roughly chopped cilantro or mint leaves

MARINADE

⅞ cup peanut oil

¼ cup roasted sesame oil

⅓ cup soy sauce

1 orange, cut in half

10 whole black peppercorns, slightly bruised

2 bay leaves

Four 8-ounce grouper fillets, cut on an extreme bias

1. Prepare the salsa: Gently combine all of the ingredients and keep at room temperature.
2. Prepare the marinade: Combine all of the ingredients and keep at room temperature.
3. Prepare a hot grill and oil it. Slip the fish into the marinade for about 3 minutes.
4. Grill the fish until just cooked through.
5. Place the fish on warm plates and top with the desired amount of salsa. (The salsa will keep in the refrigerator for about a day.)

A Tavel Rosé or a California Blush with low residual sugar would be a refreshing complement.

Florida Stone Crabs and Lobster
with Acorn Squash, Garlic, and Ginger Butter Sauce

Florida lobsters and stone crabs are both fresh in the market in late fall. I associate fall with pumpkins and squash, and their sweet flavors and autumn colors marry well with the sweetness of the shellfish.

Serves 4

Two 1½-pound Florida lobsters, in their shells
- 8 medium-large Florida stone crabs, cooked in their shells
- 2 acorn squash

Salt and cracked black pepper
- 4 tablespoons (½ stick) butter
- 8 large whole garlic cloves, peeled
- 3 shallots, peeled and minced

STOCK

- 1 tablespoon butter
- 2 tablespoons olive oil
- 1 carrot, peeled and finely diced
- 1 onion, peeled and finely diced
- 2 stalks celery, cleaned and finely diced
- 2 tomatoes, concassée

- 2 bay leaves
- 24 whole peppercorns
- 2 cups white wine
- 10 to 12 fresh basil leaves
- 4 sprigs thyme

SAUCE

- ¼ cup peeled and sliced shallots
- 1 bay leaf
- 12 whole black peppercorns, bruised
- 3 tablespoons peeled and roughly chopped fresh gingerroot

- 6 tablespoons white wine vinegar
- ½ cup white wine
- ½ cup heavy cream
- 1 pound butter, cut into bits and kept chilled

1. Remove the lobster meat from the shells by making a circular incision into the area where the head meets the body. Split the tail and pull out the meat; cut each tail in half lengthwise and then crosswise. Discard the intestinal vein, remove the tomalley, and set aside the lobster meat in a bowl. (Reserve tomalley for another use.) Save the shells. Crack the stone crabs open; try to keep the claw pieces in one whole section, on a plate by themselves. Crack open the joints and remove the meat to a bowl. Reserve the shells.

(recipe continues)

2. Make the stock: In a heavy pot, melt the butter in the olive oil. Add the diced carrot, onion, and celery, and toss to coat with the butter and oil. Sauté.

3. When the vegetables are almost tender, add the tomatoes and cook 5 minutes, stirring. Add the lobster and crab shells and the bay leaves, peppercorns, and white wine and reduce to a glaze.

4. Add just enough cold water to cover the shells and bring to a boil. Skim. Add the herbs, reduce to a simmer, and cook until reduced to 1 quart. Strain, then reduce the liquid in a clean saucepan to ½ cup. This is your shellfish glaze.

5. Preheat oven to 375 degrees. Cut the squash in half and scrape out the seeds and fibers. Season squash with salt and pepper and rub with 2 tablespoons of the butter.

6. Lay the garlic cloves on a baking sheet and invert the squash halves over the garlic. Bake the squash from 50 to 60 minutes, or longer if necessary. It should be just soft when you take it out. Allow it to cool a few moments, then peel and cut squash into medium-sized cubes. Reserve the squash and the garlic. Leave the oven on.

7. Make the sauce: In a medium-sized saucepan, reduce the sliced shallots, bay leaf, peppercorns, and ginger in the wine vinegar and wine until liquid has nearly evaporated. Add the shellfish glaze and reduce it by three-fourths. Add the cream and cook until fairly thick. Now beat in the butter piece by piece. Season to taste. Strain through a fine-mesh strainer and keep warm.

8. In a heavy skillet, heat the remaining 2 tablespoons butter on moderate heat until foamy. Season. Add the minced shallots and shake the pan. Now add the lobster meat and cook, turning pieces once. Then put the pan in the preheated oven. When the lobster meat is cooked (about 8 minutes) remove to a plate and keep warm.

9. While the lobster meat is baking, heat two medium-sized sauté pans on top of the stove and put 1 tablespoon of butter in each pan. Put the loose crab meat from the joint and claws in one and the squash pieces in the other and heat through.

10. Ladle the warm butter sauce onto warm plates and distribute the crab and lobster over the sauce, divided evenly among the 4 plates. Arrange the squash between the crab and lobster sections. Arrange the garlic in a similar fashion. (The plate should look something like a clock.) Reheat assembled plates in the oven for a few seconds if food has cooled.

Note: You may skip the glaze procedure for an easier and somewhat less intense dish.

A big, buttery California Chardonnay or its Australian counterpart would be ideal here.

ROASTED SWORDFISH
with Herbs, Smoked Bacon, and Red Wine Butter

This method is not usually associated with modern fish cookery in this country. It is more ancient in style and examples of it are found in cuisine bourgeoise. *The bacon is cooked briefly and then pushed into the swordfish meat to enrich the flavor and keep the meat moist during roasting. The herbs, red wine butter, and garlic all commingle with the juices of the fish to provide a rich, satisfying seafood entrée that has stewlike complexities that pan-frying or quick grilling will not afford. A compote of glazed pearl onions is an ideal accompaniment.*

Serves 4 to 6

3 pounds evenly cut swordfish
½ pound smoked slab bacon, cut into matchstick-size pieces
¼ cup extra virgin olive oil

1½ cups chopped, mixed fresh herbs (thyme, basil, chervil, tarragon)
Peanut oil
Sea salt and cracked black pepper
5 garlic cloves, finely minced

SAUCE

4 shallots, peeled and chopped
1 tablespoon extra virgin olive oil
¾ cup red wine vinegar
1 teaspoon cracked black pepper
1 bay leaf

1 cup red wine
½ cup heavy cream
1 pound butter, cut into small pieces and kept cold

1. Have the fishmonger cut an even-sized section of boneless, skinless swordfish. Naturally, it must be spanking fresh. Divide it in half.

2. Cook the smoked bacon in its own fat until medium-rare. Remove the bacon from the fat. (The fat may be reserved for another use.)

3. With a larding needle or knife, insert the bacon pieces into the swordfish, spacing evenly over the two sections of fish. (This is the same procedure often used with game meats, such as venison.) Now, rub olive oil over the swordfish and rub about ⅓ of the herbs on the fish.

4. Bring a large, heavy skillet to a moderately hot temperature, add the peanut oil to the pan, and sear the fish well on all sides. Remove the fish from the heat and allow it to rest.

5. Heat the oven to 400 degrees. Season the fish with a little sea salt and freshly cracked black pepper. Then top the entire length of the fish with the remaining herbs and the minced fresh garlic. Put the fish in a small roasting pan and place it in the oven. Roast for 20 to 25 minutes.

6. While the fish is roasting, make the sauce: In a medium-sized saucepan, gently stew the chopped shallots in the olive oil. Add the red wine vinegar, black pepper, and bay leaf and reduce to 3 tablespoons. Add the red wine and reduce to ¼ cup. Add the heavy cream and reduce the entire mixture till it thickens.

7. Beat in the butter, bit by bit, until it is all incorporated, and then strain the sauce through a fine-mesh strainer and keep warm.

8. Remove swordfish from the oven and allow to rest in a warm place for 5 to 10 minutes.

9. Slice the swordfish into portions. If the fish is too rare in the center for your taste, just lay it out in the pan and warm it in the oven for a few more minutes.

10. Ladle a few ounces of the warm butter sauce onto each plate and top with the fish. Serve.

A slightly chilled Beaujolais-style Zinfandel would make a nice counterpoint. If you prefer a white wine, a full-bodied Fumé Blanc would be appropriate.

PAN-COOKED SCALLOPS
with Red Pepper Purée
and Blue Corn Cakes

Not only does this taste great, it just happens to be red (the peppers), white (the scallops), and blue (the cakes), so I've served it on the Fourth of July. Edible patriotic symbolism, you might say.

Serves 4

Blue Corn Cakes (page 195)
6 red peppers, roasted and peeled
½ cup red wine vinegar
½ teaspoon cayenne
Freshly cracked black pepper to taste

4 to 6 tablespoons clarified butter
2 pounds jumbo sea scallops, cleaned and ready to cook
1 tablespoon butter, cut into pieces and kept cold

1. Prepare batter for blue corn cakes and set aside.

2. Purée the peppers in a food processor and remove to a bowl. Keep warm. Add vinegar, cayenne, and cracked black pepper to purée.

3. In a large skillet, working in batches, cook the corn cakes in clarified butter. Keep them warm by placing between dry napkins. (It's important to have everything at hand, so you can complete the dish quickly. As is often the case with good food, it must be finished quickly so as not to lose the fleeting qualities of taste.)

4. Now, sautée the scallops in clarified butter. (You can use the same pan you used for the pancakes, just be sure to wipe it out first.) The scallops will only take a minute; sauté them until they just turn opaque, then remove them to a warm bowl. Wipe out the pan and add the purée to it. Beat in the cold pieces of butter, adjust seasoning, and divide purée among 4 warm plates.

5. Arrange the scallops over the purée and add the corn cakes in an attractive manner. Any collected juices from the scallops can be brushed lightly over them just before you serve.

A straightforward Mâcon Blanc Villages or White Rully would suit this somewhat rustic preparation.

Herb-Crusted, Char-Grilled Swordfish
with Lemon Butter

This is a light, healthy entrée that could possibly be included in a spa-type cuisine menu, if you go in for that sort of thing. Personally, I could never manage self-imposed deprivation when it comes to flavors (I can live with light portions), so many of the spa adaptations leave me bored, untempted, and usually on my way to another section of the menu. But, good food is good food and if it happens to be healthy or "good for you," well hell, that's a happy coincidence.

The swordfish can be accompanied with crisply blanched and sautéed green beans.

Serves 4

Sea salt to taste
⅓ cup freshly squeezed lemon juice
Cracked black pepper to taste
½ pound butter, softened
1½ cups chopped fresh herbs (any combination of such herbs as parsley, thyme, basil, tarragon, chervil, or mint)

⅓ cup virgin olive oil, to bind the herbs to the fish
Four 7- to 8-ounce swordfish steaks, skin and any black meat removed (tuna, grouper, or salmon can be substituted for the swordfish)

1. Preheat a grill or broiler to maximum heat.

2. Mix the salt, lemon juice, and pepper into the softened butter.

3. Mix the herbs and oil together and then press on as much as will stick to the fish. (This should be done at least 30 minutes before cooking and *can* be done hours before.)

4. With a heavy cloth, oil the grid of the grill and then lay the swordfish steaks on it. Cook to medium-rare and remove to warm plates. Top each steak with 3 ounces (6 tablespoons) or less of the lemon butter. Reserve any leftover butter for other uses.

The lemon butter in this dish would suggest a dry white wine with good acidity, such as a Premier cru Chablis or Sancerre. A California Sauvignon Blanc would also work well.

GRILLED GINGER-STUDDED SEA SCALLOPS
with Chinese Parsley and Sesame Seed Sauce

There are a few options to consider here. First, the ginger that is "studded" into the scallops could be pickled ginger (see page 202). Second, you can pan-cook the scallops if grilling is a problem. Third, you could substitute for the Chinese parsley and sesame seed sauce anything from a chile-infused hollandaise to a rich garlic cream, or even a simple dab of wasabi and stir-fried vegetables. Here is the recipe, but the choices are all yours.

Serves 4

2 pounds jumbo sea scallops
½ cup peeled fresh gingerroot, cut into short, thin matchstick-size pieces
3 tablespoons extra virgin olive oil
Sea salt and cracked black pepper to taste
3 large jalapeños, stemmed and seeded
4 garlic cloves, peeled

3 cups cilantro (Chinese parsley) leaves, washed
1 cup white sesame seeds, toasted
1 cup black sesame seeds, toasted
¾ cup rice wine vinegar
¾ cup dark roasted sesame oil
1 cup virgin olive oil

1. Using a small knife or skewer, puncture each scallop in 4 or 5 places and fill the holes with ginger strips. Toss the scallops in a bowl, pour the olive oil over them, and mix gently. Crack some fresh pepper over the scallops and allow to rest ½ hour or more.

2. While scallops are resting, make the sauce: Put the jalapeños, garlic, and cilantro leaves into a food processor and pulse 8 to 10 times. Add the sesame seeds and vinegar and pulse again. Scrape down the sides and, with the machine running, add the sesame oil and olive oil.

3. When all the oil is incorporated, season to taste and set aside until needed, covered and refrigerated.

4. Fire a grill to a hot temperature and grill the scallops to your liking. (I encourage you to try them medium rare.)

5. Gently warm the sauce over low heat, ladle it onto 4 warm plates, and top with the scallops. Serve.

A somewhat dry white wine would complement the sweetness of the scallops and offset the heat and astringency of the other ingredients. An Alsace Pinot Blanc or Early Harvest Riesling would be suitable.

GRILLED TUNA
with Ginger, Scallion, Citrus, and Black Bean Relish

I like to briefly marinate many fish that I intend to grill. The marinade gently seasons the fish and helps to make it tender. Also, a citrus marination is a natural counterpoint to the grill's smoky-wood flavors. The following marinade is the one I use most often, and I also think that it complements the somewhat oriental feel of this preparation.

Note that you must soak the black beans overnight.

Serves 4

MARINADE

3 cups light oil, such as safflower or peanut
1 cup soy sauce
1 orange, cut in half and squeezed lightly
1 lemon, cut in half and squeezed lightly
1 lime, cut in half and squeezed lightly
2 bay leaves

1 whole black peppercorn
1 fresh fennel bulb or 1 tablespoon fennel seeds
6 cloves unpeeled garlic, slightly crushed
3 basil leaves
1 sprig fresh thyme

BLACK BEANS

1 red onion, finely diced
3 stalks celery, finely diced
1 large carrot, finely diced
A 2-inch piece gingerroot, finely diced
Olive oil to sauté the vegetables

1 quart black beans, soaked overnight in water and then drained before cooking
1 bay leaf
1 gallon fish stock or water
Sea salt and cracked pepper to taste

RELISH

½ cup rice wine vinegar
1 cup orange juice
½ cup stock reserved after bean preparation

2 oranges, peeled and cut into clean sections, reserve juices
4 scallions, cleaned and cut crosswise into ¼-inch slices

*Four 7- to 8-ounce tuna steaks (yellowfin or
big-eye are excellent varieties for the grill)
   ½ cup roughly chopped cilantro leaves*

1. Make the marinade: Whisk together the oil and soy sauce in a large bowl. Add the remaining marinade ingredients and stir thoroughly. Set aside.

2. Prepare the beans: In a very large pot, sauté the onion, celery, carrot, and ginger over moderate heat in the olive oil until just tender. Add the drained beans. Add the bay leaf and stock or water and cook until beans are just soft. Season.

3. Strain off excess stock for another use and reserve ½ cup.

4. Prepare the relish: Combine the vinegar, orange juice, and reserved stock in a saucepan and reduce to ½ cup.

5. Cut the orange sections into halves and combine them with the scallions, black beans, and reduced stock. Season to taste (more vinegar may be added).

6. Prepare a very hot grill and season it with oil. While the grill is heating, marinate the tuna 2 or 3 minutes; grill it to medium-rare.

7. Put the tuna steaks on warm serving plates and top the fish with the relish. Sprinkle with freshly chopped cilantro leaves and serve.

*A White Graves or non-herbaceous Sauvignon Blanc would pull all the flavors in this dish together.
   If you prefer red wine with tuna (as I do) a Côtes-du-Rhône or Gigondas would work nicely.*

PANÉED GROUPER WITH ALABAMA OYSTERS
and Conch Butter Sauce

After making tomato butter sauce by following the world-renowned chef Fredy Girardet's recipe, I began to make other butter sauces with a tomato base. Gazpacho, creole, and ratatouille butter sauces all yielded very interesting results. But recently it occurred to me to try it with conch, our most famous local shellfish, and everyone really got a kick out of it. I would suggest trying this when you have conch chowder left over. (By the way, panéed is a Southern way of saying pan-cooked in a little more oil than you would use for sautéing.)

Serves 4

Salt and pepper to taste
20 freshly shucked oysters, liquor strained and reserved
Flour for dusting the oysters and grouper

2 whole eggs, beaten
1 to 2 cups fresh bread crumbs, finely processed but not dry

SAUCE

2 cups Bahamian Conch Chowder (page 22)
Reserved oyster liquor
¼ cup Spanish wine vinegar

Cracked black pepper to taste
½ cup heavy cream
1 pound butter, cut into small pieces and chilled

Four 7- to 8-ounce boneless, skinless fillets of grouper, cut on the bias
Clarified butter or peanut oil, to sauté the fish

1. Preheat oven to 425 degrees. Season and roll the shucked oysters in flour, then in the eggs, and then in the fresh bread crumbs. Set them on a piece of parchment paper and chill.

2. Prepare the sauce: Process the chowder for a full minute and then heat it in a heavy, medium-sized saucepan. Add the reserved oyster liquor and allow the mixture to reduce and thicken. Stir it often; it will splatter if not attended to. When it is reduced to ¾ cup, add the vinegar and some cracked black pepper. Reduce by half. Now add the heavy cream and reduce until fairly thick.

3. Beat in the butter, piece by piece, stirring until it is all incorporated. Adjust seasoning as needed. Strain through a fine-mesh strainer and keep warm.

4. Season the fish with salt and pepper and flour lightly.

5. Heat a skillet large enough to hold the fish without crowding. When it is hot, add enough clarified butter or oil to fill the bottom of the pan. Carefully lay the fish in the pan skin side down and shake the pan a little. Allow the fish to cook till lightly golden on each side.

6. Discard any excess oil, put the pan into the oven, and bake until the fish is just cooked through. Remove the fish to a warm platter for a moment. Wipe out the pan and add enough additional oil to the skillet to fry the oysters. When the oil is hot, add the oysters one by one and fry briefly.

7. Ladle the butter sauce onto 4 warm plates. Top with the grouper and surround each fish portion with 5 oysters per serving.

Traditionally, Muscadet is paired with oysters. But with the richness of the butter sauce in this recipe, I would recommend something a bit more full-bodied, such as a Mâcon Villages or Italian Chardonnay.

SAUTÉED SHRIMP
with Anchos, Tequila, and Red Onion Salsa

I began making this dish around 1982 when I was deeply intrigued by American regional cuisine. I was obviously thinking of the Southwest when I hit upon this combination. It is not traditional to use beurre blanc sauces in the cookery of this area of the country, to be sure, but the sauce makes a soothing bridge between the heat of the salsa and the bite of the tequila.

Serves 4

BUTTER SAUCE

4 ancho chiles, toasted and soaked	1½ cups dry white wine
3 tablespoons butter	1 cup heavy cream
¼ teaspoon chopped shallots	1 pound butter, cut into small pieces, and kept cold
1 cup chopped mushrooms	2 tablespoons freshly squeezed lime juice
2 sprigs parsley	Salt
1 bay leaf	Freshly ground black pepper, to taste
1 cup Fish Stock (page 244)	

SALSA

1 medium red onion, diced medium	1 jalapeño, finely diced
1 bunch fresh cilantro leaves, roughly chopped to make ⅓ cup	1 freshly squeezed lime
1 large ripe tomato, skinned, seeded, and diced	1 pinch coarse salt
	2 tablespoons extra virgin olive oil

¼ pound (1 stick) butter	1 tablespoon chopped garlic
2 tablespoons chopped shallots	½ cup Cuervo gold tequila
24 large fresh shrimp, shelled and deveined	

1. Prepare the butter sauce: Toast the anchos by holding them by the stems, with metal tongs, over an open flame. Then drop them into a bowl of water to soften. Remove stems and seeds and cut into strips. Put aside.

2. In a heavy 2-quart saucepan, melt the butter and add shallots, mushrooms, parsley, and bay leaf. Cook until glazy. Add the stock (for additional flavor, add the shells from the

shrimp). Add the wine and ¾ of the ancho strips and reduce again until glazy.

3. At this point, add the cream and stir often. When reduced by ½ to ¾, add the butter piece by piece, whisking constantly. When all butter is incorporated, add lime juice and salt and pepper to taste. Strain sauce through a fine-mesh strainer and reserve, keeping warm but not hot.

4. Combine all of the salsa ingredients and keep cool in a small bowl.

5. Heat a large skillet to medium-high temperature. Add the butter and swirl pan. As the butter begins to foam, add the shallots and shrimp, stirring and tossing. Add the garlic and cook the shrimp, being careful not to burn garlic or overcook shrimp, for no more than 8 minutes.

6. Remove shrimp to a bowl. Drain off and discard cooking butter, then add tequila and deglaze pan. When liquor is almost a glaze, add salsa and stir.

7. Spoon the reserved warm butter sauce onto 4 plates. Arrange shrimp in a circle over sauce. Spoon tequila-infused salsa into center of plates and garnish with reserved ancho chile strips.

A full-bodied Sauvignon Blanc would complement the earthiness of the anchos; or you can try a Dry Riesling as a foil to the heat and the perfume of the tequila.

Sautéed Florida Lobster
with Citrus, Wild Mushrooms, and Roasted Peppers in a Sauternes Butter Sauce

When Louie's Backyard was awarded four stars by the Miami Herald, *this dish was one of the most popular items on the menu. (If Florida lobster is unavailable, you can use shrimp, or Maine lobster.)*

Serves 4

SAUCE

1 tablespoon olive oil
3 shallots, peeled and chopped
6 whole black peppercorns
1 bay leaf
4 basil leaves

½ bottle Sauternes (about 1⅔ cups)
½ cup heavy cream
1 pound butter, cut into small pieces and kept cold

6 tablespoons (¾ stick) butter
Four 1¼-pound fresh lobsters, heads removed, cut in half lengthwise, shells and veins removed, seasoned with sea salt and cracked black pepper
1 tablespoon finely chopped shallots
1½ cups large slices of wild mushrooms such as shiitake, oysters, or trumpets

¼ cup Sauternes (Alexis Lichine is a moderately priced good choice)
Sea salt and pepper to taste
1 cup roasted red bell peppers, cut into fat strips
⅔ cup orange sections
⅓ cup lime sections

1. Make the sauce: Heat the olive oil in a large, deep saucepan until very warm. Add the shallots, black peppercorns, bay leaf and basil and stir until shallots are softened. Add the Sauternes and reduce to ⅓ cup. Add the cream and reduce to ½ cup.

2. Lower the heat and whisk in the butter, bit by bit, until it is all incorporated. Strain through a fine-mesh strainer and set aside.

3. Over medium heat place a sauté pan large enough to accommodate all of the lobster meat comfortably. Add the butter and let it melt.

4. Lay the lobsters in the pan and add the shallots. Lightly brown the lobster and shallots for about 2 minutes. Add the mushrooms and toss lightly. Add the Sauternes.

5. When the lobster is just firm, remove it to a cutting board. Reduce the liquid in the pan until it has almost evaporated, and hold it in a warm place for a moment. Then add the reserved butter sauce to the pan and mix with the mushrooms. Correct the seasoning.

6. Slice the lobster meat into angled sections.

7. Ladle the butter and mushroom sauce onto 4 warm plates. Arrange the lobster meat over the sauce. Arrange the roasted peppers and citrus sections over and around the lobster. Serve.

This wonderfully rich dish calls for extravagance, so I recommend either a full-bodied White Burgundy, such as a Meursault from a good producer, or a big California Chardonnay.

Pan-Cooked Whole Yellowtail
with Key Lime Butter and Basil

In the old days Key West vendors would hawk yellowtail on the streets in the early hours of the morning. The aroma of yellowtail being fried for breakfast was not far behind, for then it was considered a fish for the first meal of the day. Yellowtail is a very delicate, fine, white-fleshed fish. It should be absolutely fresh, for it deteriorates more quickly than most fish. For this recipe, you can substitute snapper if yellowtail does not reach your market. Regular limes lack the tart pungency of our Key limes, but you can use them if you must. The basil should be as beautiful as possible for the proper aesthetic effect.

Serves 4

4 yellowtail, 1¼ to 1½ pounds each, whole weight, cleaned, scaled, and dorsal fins cut out	1 teaspoon each sea salt and freshly cracked black pepper
½ cup all-purpose flour	Clarified butter to sauté the fish

SAUCE

2	tablespoons olive oil	½	cup freshly squeezed Key lime juice
¼	cup diced shallots	½	cup heavy cream
1	bay leaf	1	pound butter, cut into small pieces and kept cold
1	teaspoon cracked black peppercorns		
36	basil leaves (reserve leaves for garnish, put stems in the sauce reduction)		

1. Preheat oven to 425 degrees. Make a series of three shallow incisions on both sides of each fish to allow the heat to reach into the interior.

2. Lightly dredge the fish in flour, tapping the fish gently to get rid of any excess. Season with salt and pepper.

3. Heat a sauté pan large enough to accommodate the fish without crowding (use two pans if necessary). Get the pan very hot and add enough clarified butter to cover the bottom generously.

4. Now, one by one, grasp each fish by the tail and put them in the pan. Shake the pan a bit and when the fish are lightly browned, turn them gently with a spatula to brown the other side.

5. Drain off and discard any excess oil and place the pan(s) in the oven.

6. Make the sauce: Heat the olive oil in a saucepan on moderate heat. Add the shallots and stir about 30 seconds. Add the bay leaf and black peppercorns. Cook 30 seconds. Add basil stems and cook for 10 seconds.

7. Add the Key lime juice and reduce almost to a glaze. Add the heavy cream and reduce by almost half. Lower the temperature a little and whisk in the butter, piece by piece, until it is all incorporated.

8. Strain the butter sauce through a fine-mesh strainer and keep warm. (If you think it will take you longer than 10 minutes to make the sauce, you can make it before preparing the fish. Just keep it warm over hot but not simmering water in a double boiler.)

9. Bring a small pot of water to a boil on top of the stove. Blanch the basil leaves by placing them in a strainer and lowering them into the water for 5 seconds.

10. The fish should take about 10 minutes in the oven. When it is cooked, ladle ¼ cup of sauce on each plate. Place the fish on the plates, garnish with the basil leaves, and serve.

A wine with a hint of sweetness—such as a Vouvray or a California Chenin Blanc—would complement the Key-lime butter and basil, and the delicate texture of the fish.

PAN-SEARED SPICED SHRIMP
with Gumbo Sauce

The word gumbo *comes from the African word* ngumbo, *which we translate as okra. So, while making a sauce and calling it gumbo may be a contradiction in form, it would not be a contradiction in terms.*

One day, with some leftover gumbo (the soup) on my hands, I decided to check it out as a sauce by simply reducing it. It worked marvelously! The intensity of spice was dramatic, as was the deep, shiny black color it became. Treat the gumbo as a dipping sauce.

For this recipe I recommend leaving the shrimp in the shells. It protects the meat from drying out and it gives your guests the informality and fun appropriate to a down-home dish like this. Wash these down with plenty of cold beer.

Makes 6 appetizer portions

24 large fresh shrimp (16 to 20s) in the shell	1 quart Hot Sausage and Shellfish Gumbo (page 25)
½ cup olive oil	Peanut oil
4 teaspoons salt	Lemon slices, for garnish
2 teaspoons freshly cracked black pepper	6 slices Pickled Okra (page 202, or store-bought)
2 teaspoons cumin	
4 teaspoons cayenne	
4 teaspoons brown sugar	

1. Dry the shrimp thoroughly. Split the shells down the back with a sharp knife and remove the veins, but leave the shells on.

2. Lightly toss the shrimp in a bowl with the olive oil. Add the salt, spices, and brown sugar and mix. Work some of the spice mixture onto the exposed shrimp meat inside the shells. Refrigerate a minimum of 4 hours.

3. Reduce gumbo to 2 cups or so. It should be as thick as maple syrup. Strain it of all solids. Keep warm.

(recipe continues)

4. Get a skillet smoking hot and pour in a thin layer of peanut oil. Add the shrimp and toss or stir until they are cooked. You will need to expose the cut part of the shell to get the heat into the meat.

5. Spoon gumbo sauce onto plates and pile on some shrimp. Garnish with lemon slices and pickled okra.

The intensity of this dish would probably overpower most wines, so a cold beer or white-wine Sangria might be best here to put out the fire. If you prefer a wine, however, I would suggest something aggressive like a Tokay d'Alsace.

POBLANO CHILES RELLEÑOS
with Lobster, Avocado, and Pepitas Over Citrus Butter

There is an Italian in me. Every time I step to a grill with a bowl of very lightly oiled peppers or chiles, he steps out and happily does this hot, slow, but soul-satisfying chore. To be sure, roasting peppers can be done while you do three or four other things, for they do not require constant attention. Yet he stands there and watches the variegated flesh turn to charcoal, blister, and wrinkle. Satisfied once the peppers are tucked under a towel in a bowl, the Italian goes back inside and leaves me the second half of the task—peeling them!

Serves 6

¼ pound (1 stick) butter	2 cups cream
¼ cup chopped shallots	¼ cup toasted pepitas (or pine nuts)
2¼ pounds shelled lobster tails, cut in half lengthwise	¼ cup roughly chopped cilantro leaves
Salt and pepper to taste	1 large avocado, skinned and diced medium
¼ cup Spanish vinegar	6 poblano chiles, roasted and peeled, stems left on

BUTTER SAUCE

½ cup freshly squeezed orange juice
3 tablespoons Champagne vinegar or white wine vinegar
3 tablespoons chopped shallots, in medium-fine dice

1 bay leaf
Freshly cracked black pepper
½ cup heavy cream
1 pound butter, cut into small pieces and chilled

1. In a sauté pan, heat butter until slightly foamy. Add the shallots and then the lobster. Turn the meat from time to time until it is cooked through. Season lightly, add the vinegar, and reduce for 30 seconds. Add the cream, stir, and then, using a slotted spoon, remove the lobster to a plate.

2. Reduce the cream until thick and strain it into a bowl.

3. Put the nuts into a food processor and pulse twice. Now add the lobster and pulse twice. Add the cilantro and pulse. Now, with the machine running, quickly add the strained cream. Turn machine off, scrape this mixture into a bowl, and chill. (It is important not to overprocess the mixture. If need be, scrape the processed lobster mixture into a bowl and then stir in the cream, entirely omitting processing the cream.)

4. When the mix is cold, add the diced avocado and gently mix. Season to taste. (The poblano is somewhat spicy, so remember, when you are seasoning the lobster stuffing mixture, to allow for the heat that the chile will bring to the final dish.)

5. Carefully slit open the peppers and cut out the area under the stem that holds the majority of the seeds. Try to keep the chile from ripping. Stuff the poblanos with the lobster mixture and chill.

6. Prepare the sauce: In a small, heavy saucepan reduce orange juice, vinegar, shallots, bay leaf, and black pepper until almost evaporated. Add the cream and reduce to ½ to ¾ cup and then gradually whisk in the pieces of butter until incorporated. Strain sauce through a fine-mesh strainer into a pot or bowl and keep in a warm place.

7. Put the stuffed poblanos on a lightly oiled baking sheet and heat them through in a preheated 350-degree oven. This should take 10 minutes or less.

8. Spoon the warm sauce onto warm plates and top with the poblanos. Serve.

This is a full-flavored dish, with complex combinations of hot, sweet, tart, and rich. A fairly full-bodied white with some tart acidity, such as a Gavi dei Gavi or Alsace Gewürtztraminer would be appropriate.

GRILLED NORWEGIAN SALMON
with a Sour Cream Béarnaise and Salmon Caviar

One cannot deny the appeal of salmon. It is required eating at the table of a true gourmand, even in a place as seemingly remote as Key West. With the increasingly sophisticated levels of fish-farming developing around the world, coupled with express air shipping, one has only to live relatively close to a major airport to enjoy many fresh products from distant places.

Tiny steamed new potatoes make an ideal starch accompaniment for this dish.

Serves 4

Four 7- to 8-ounce portions of salmon
Sea salt and cracked black pepper
½ cup virgin olive oil
1 bay leaf

½ recipe Sauce Béarnaise (page 238) using red wine and red wine vinegar
1 cup sour cream or crème fraîche, at room temperature
2 teaspoons salmon caviar, chilled

1. Fire up a hot grill.

2. Season the salmon with sea salt and pepper and put it in a flat-bottomed dish with the olive oil and bay leaf.

3. Prepare the béarnaise. Taste and adjust seasonings and keep warm in a double boiler, stirring from time to time.

4. Lift the salmon out of the oil and grill it to medium-rare.

5. Put the salmon on warm plates and spoon the béarnaise over the center of the fish. Now place a dollop of sour cream on top of the béarnaise. Garnish with the salmon caviar. Serve.

I like a lusty red wine with grilled salmon, such as a St. Joseph from the northern Rhône. If you prefer a white wine, perhaps try one from the same area, such as a Condrieu or Crozes-Hermitage.

PAN-COOKED SOFT-SHELL CRABS
with Papaya and Lime

Back when I lived in the snow-swept farmlands of northern Illinois, there was one sure signal that summer was soon to return to the heartland: My favorite Midwestern fish purveyors, Roy and Bonnie, would call me and excitedly tell me that the soft-shell crab season had opened in Chesapeake Bay.

To tell you the truth, I would eat a fresh pan-fried soft-shell crab with nothing but a tiny squeeze of lemon any time at all. They are sweet, rich, crunchy, and as intense as any of God's creatures.

Serves 4

½ cup flour
Pinch of salt
2 tablespoons cayenne pepper
12 small soft-shell crabs, cleaned

Basic White Butter Sauce (page 237)
1 cup clarified butter or peanut oil
12 papaya wedges, seeds and skin discarded
6 lime sections

1. Preheat oven to 400 degrees.

2. Combine the flour, salt, and cayenne pepper and lightly dredge the crabs in the flour mixture.

3. Prepare the butter sauce and keep warm.

4. Heat a sauté pan large enough to hold the crabs (or work in batches). Add the butter or oil and heat until very hot. Lay the crabs in the pan, top side down, and pan-fry them for about 2 or 3 minutes. Turn them over to pan-fry the other side, and finish cooking them in the oven for about 3 more minutes.

5. Remove the crabs from the pan and arrange them on plates on a ladleful of the butter sauce. Garnish the plates with the papaya and lime sections. Serve.

One of the several California Chardonnays teeming with tropical fruit flavors would be wonderful with this dish.

CATFISH
with Peanuts, Green Onions, and Bacon Pan Butter

It used to be that catfish was served primarily in the South, but more and more northerners now enjoy these fish. Much of this change is, of course, due to the burgeoning industry of wet-farming the fish. Many farmers are finding good profits in this light, white-fleshed, tasty critter.

Serves 4

Four 8-ounce boneless catfish fillets, skin removed
Salt and pepper to taste
2 eggs, beaten
1½ cups buttermilk
2 cups yellow cornmeal
1 cup all-purpose flour
2 tablespoons olive or peanut oil
6 or 7 ounces slab bacon, cut into rectangles ¼ inch by 1 inch

½ pound (2 sticks) butter, cut into small pieces and kept cold
2 tablespoons lemon juice
8 green onions, roots and upper green ends removed, cut into rings
½ pound raw, unsalted peanuts, lightly roasted, skins removed
Lemon wedges, for garnish

1. Lightly season the catfish fillets with salt and pepper.

2. Whisk together the eggs and buttermilk in a large bowl and dip the fillets into the egg wash.

3. Mix together the cornmeal and flour, coat the fillets with the mixture, and set aside.

4. Heat a sauté pan on gentle heat and add the olive or peanut oil and the bacon. Stir often until the bacon is partially cooked. Remove the bacon from the pan, reserve it, and strain the oils into a clean bowl or jar.

5. Preheat oven to 400 degrees. Heat a skillet large enough to hold the four fillets without crowding (or use two pans). Add the reserved oil to the pan(s) and allow it to get quite hot, adding more peanut or olive oil as necessary. Lay the fillets in and gently shake the pan.

6. When the fillets are golden on one side, turn them over. Remove any excess fat and put the pan into the oven for about 2 minutes. (If the fillets are thin enough, you can cook them entirely on top of the stove.)

7. Remove the catfish to warm plates with a spatula. Wipe out the pan and reheat it almost to the smoking point.

8. Now, working *quite* rapidly, add the butter and then *immediately* add the lemon juice, green onions, and most of the peanuts, shaking the pan. Swirl the pan evenly over the heat. Gradually, as the butter incorporates, it will become saucelike in texture. Pour the sauce evenly over the fish and sprinkle the remaining peanuts and reserved bacon over all. Serve with lemon wedges.

A smoky Fumé Blanc or a California Riesling would work well.

MEAT ENTRÉES

I recently cooked a vintners' dinner for the people from Chateau Montelena in California. They wished to present a vertical tasting of their Cabernet Sauvignons from 1979 through 1983, so the food had to match a solid flow of Cabernets. I devised a very simple, classic progression, beginning with an "amuse" course—tiny samples of foie gras, a wild mushroom terrine, and grilled scallops with a butter sauce. They enjoyed Champagne with this. There followed a salad of mixed lettuces with a vinaigrette, unaccompanied by wine. Then came the two courses with which we poured their beautifully crafted Cabernets. The first was the lamb entrée (the first in this chapter). I felt the bell pepper tones I chose to include in the sauce would be in harmony with the Cabernet's oak and cedar flavors. In fact, the various vintages had characteristics that distinguished them from each other, but the lamb and its sauce was in sync throughout. The second course was a selection of cheeses with homemade breads. The leisurely pace of such a course allowed our guests to linger over the fine vintages for a long while. The wines evolved in fascinating ways as we slowly swirled, sniffed, and finished the glasses on the table. Overlooking a moonlit expanse of ocean, we were content in the knowledge that that night we had done the "right thing."

ROAST RACK OF LAMB
with Roasted Peppers, Garlic, and Shallots

A rack of lamb consists of enough meat for four full portions. For six people you will need one and a half racks of lamb cut into six equal-sized sections. Each portion will have three to four bones in it.

Serves 6

6 portions of rack of lamb (see above)	3 yellow peppers
½ cup virgin olive oil	3 tablespoons Dijon mustard
2 tablespoons roughly chopped rosemary leaves	½ to 1 cup fresh bread crumbs
1 tablespoon cracked black pepper	12 medium-sized cloves Roast Garlic (page 200)
3 bay leaves	1 cup red wine
6 cloves garlic, split in half	3½ cups rich Lamb Brown Sauce (page 249)
3 red peppers	

SHALLOTS

12 whole, peeled, medium-sized shallots	1 bay leaf
½ bunch fresh thyme	6 whole black peppercorns
6 leaves fresh basil	2 cups virgin olive oil

1. Cut the lamb into portions and rub them all over with olive oil. Sprinkle on the chopped rosemary and put lamb in a large bowl. Add cracked black pepper, 3 bay leaves, and the 6 split cloves of garlic to the bowl and toss the meat around a moment. Refrigerate.

2. Preheat the oven to 300 degrees. While it is heating, prepare the shallots: Put the peeled, whole shallots in a small baking dish and add the thyme, basil, bay leaf, and peppercorns. Top the shallots with olive oil. Cover the dish with aluminum foil and bake approximately 1 hour. Remove the foil and test shallots. They should be soft enough to be pierced easily with a sharp knife. If they are, remove them from the oven. Otherwise, cook a bit longer. When they are finished, remove the shallots from the oil with a slotted spoon to a clean bowl. Reserve the oil for salad dressings or other cooking.

3. Roast the red and yellow peppers, then peel them, remove the seeds, and cut into very wide strips.

4. Heat oven to 475 degrees. Remove the lamb from the marinade and put it on a plate. Reserve marinade.

5. Heat a skillet large enough to hold all 6 lamb racks and add a small amount of the reserved marinade oil. When the oil is very hot, sear the lamb on all sides.

6. When all the racks of lamb are seared, arrange them, meaty side up, in a baking pan and place the pan in the oven. Roast the lamb no more than medium-rare, between 10 and 15 minutes. Remove lamb to a carving board and keep warm. Discard any excess oil. Spoon the Dijon mustard evenly over the meaty side of each rack and then roll the racks in the bread crumbs. Put coated lamb in a clean pan and return it to oven to roast for 1 minute to toast breadcrumbs. Remove the meat to a cutting board and allow to rest in a warm place.

7. Place the roasting pan on a burner, add the baked shallots and roast garlic, and cook a moment on medium high heat. Now add the red wine and reduce by three-fourths. Add the lamb brown sauce and the roasted pepper strips. Turn the heat to low.

8. Remove the lamb from the oven and carve it off the bone into neat slices. Arrange them on a large platter and spoon the warm sauce all around. When you serve, be sure each diner gets an equal portion of garlic, shallots, and bell pepper.

The complexity of flavor and texture in this rack of lamb represents the best qualities of a red-meat dish, therefore the wine should be equal to the occasion. This is the time to break out your best Bordeaux from the Médoc region.

Honey-glazed Quail
with Stuffing of Cracked Black Pepper Brioche and Wild Mushrooms

Tiny semiboneless quail have been more widely available in the last few years. Although this recipe calls for them, it will work with almost any bird. You may also use some other combination for the stuffing, but the contrasting sweetness and heat (here achieved with honey and pepper) should remain in some form. (There are many interesting honeys available. I buy several varieties from the American Spoonfood Company in Petoskey, Michigan.)

Serves 4

SAUCE

2 tablespoons roughly chopped shallots
1 teaspoon olive oil
½ cup red wine vinegar

1 small onion, diced small
1 small carrot, diced small
2 stalks celery, diced small
4 tablespoons (½ stick) butter
½ pound wild mushrooms, sliced
2 tablespoons thyme leaves
1 cup Chicken (or other poultry) Stock (page 240)

2 quarts Chicken (or other poultry) Stock (page 240)
2 tablespoons honey

Salt and cracked black pepper to taste
½ recipe Cracked Black Pepper Brioche (page 209), cut or torn into small pieces (reserve the rest for another use)
8 fresh semiboneless quail, cleaned and patted dry
4 tablespoons (½ stick) butter
Peanut oil to sauté the quail

1. Make the sauce: In a medium-sized saucepan, sweat the shallots in the olive oil until glazed. Add the vinegar and reduce to a glaze.

2. Add the stock, skim as necessary, and reduce to 1½ cups. Add the honey and cook until almost as thick as maple syrup.

3. Strain sauce through a fine-mesh strainer and reserve.

4. Prepare the stuffing: Sauté the diced onion, carrot, and celery in the butter until slightly soft. Add the mushrooms and continue to sauté. Add the thyme leaves. Add the stock and heat through. Season, remove from the heat, and put in a bowl.

5. Mix the brioche with the vegetables and set aside.

6. Preheat oven to 450 degrees. Rub the quail inside and out with salt and pepper. Stuff the quail and rub the breasts with 2 tablespoons of the butter.

7. Heat a heavy skillet large enough to accommodate the birds (or work in batches). Add the peanut oil. Add the quail and lightly brown them on all sides, starting them breast sides down. Discard the excess oil and place quail breast sides up in the oven.

8. After 4 or 5 minutes, discard any accumulated oil and then brush the birds with the reserved honey sauce. Return them to the oven. Repeat glazing the birds until they are shining, crisp, and darkly colored.

9. Remove the quail to warm plates. Whisk into the remaining sauce the remaining 2 tablespoons of somewhat cold butter and stir over low heat until butter is incorporated. (This is optional, but it pulls the sauce together very nicely.) Pour the sauce over the quail and serve.

The slight gaminess of the quail and the richness of the stuffing suggest a medium-bodied red with plenty of flavor, such as a Mercurey from Burgundy or a Burgundy-style Pinot Noir (there are several interesting ones being produced in Oregon).

PAN-COOKED YOUNG CHICKENS
with Cornbread-Chorizo Stuffing
and Port-Ginger Sauce

Young chickens, known in France as poussin, are specially raised, meaty little birds relatively new on the American scene. Like Cornish game hens they are served one to a person for a dinner entrée, and they make a nice presentation served whole. The sweet sugars in the jelly in this recipe help to caramelize the chicken for a juicy, moist interior and a very crisp skin. Chorizo can be obtained from Spanish meat markets, or you can make your own from the recipe in this book.

Serves 4

SAUCE

2	shallots, peeled and thinly sliced
2	jalapeños, seeds and stems removed, thinly sliced
1	tablespoon butter
1½	cups freshly squeezed orange juice
1	small bay leaf
¾	cup Spanish sherry wine vinegar
1½	cups strong Chicken Stock (page 240)

1	cup nonvintage port wine (Sandeman is a good and relatively inexpensive choice)
3	cups currant jelly, or a homemade jelly such as Madeira
¾	teaspoon cayenne
One	3-inch piece peeled fresh gingerroot, cut into small matchstick strips
1½	teaspoons sugar
⅓	cup water

STUFFING

½	pound chorizo or kielbasa sausage, cut into small pieces
	Olive oil
1	Spanish onion, diced small
½	red pepper, diced small
	Salt and pepper
4	poussin, cleaned and ready for stuffing
¼	cup (½ stick) butter

½	yellow pepper, diced small
2	stalks celery, diced small
10	fresh sage leaves, roughly chopped
3	cups homemade Cornbread (page 210)
1	cup Chicken Stock (page 240)
2	tablespoons light oil for sautéing
	Orange zest, for garnish
	Lime zest, for garnish

1. Prepare the sauce: In a deep saucepan, sweat the shallots and jalapēnos in the butter; do not brown. Towel off any excess butter. Add orange juice and bay leaf and reduce by half. Add the sherry vinegar and stock and reduce by two-thirds. Now add the port wine and reduce down to ½ to ¾ cup.

2. Add the jelly and cayenne. Gently bring to a boil. (Keep an eye on this, for if it boils over it can be messy.) Once boiled, strain the sauce through a fine-mesh strainer and set aside.

3. Put the ginger, sugar, and water in a saucepan and reduce until all the liquid has evaporated. Reserve ginger for sauce.

4. Make the stuffing: Prick the chorizo skin several times to prevent it from bursting. Then cook the sausage in a 425-degree oven until done, approximately 10 minutes. Save the fat that is released to cook your vegetables. Reserve sausage and cool.

5. Heat a skillet until quite hot and carefully add the reserved sausage fat and enough olive oil to equal ½ cup total. Add the vegetables and sage leaves and sauté until just cooked.

6. Break up the cornbread in a large bowl and add the cooked vegetables and sage. Cut up the sausage into bite-sized pieces and add. Mix all together. Now add just enough stock to moisten the stuffing.

7. Preheat oven to 425 degrees. Rub salt and pepper inside the cavities and all over the birds. Now, stuff the birds and tie their legs together. Rub the butter over the breast area of each bird. Add the oil to a hot skillet large enough to comfortably hold the birds and carefully sear the birds on all sides. Discard the excess oil, and with the breast sides down, put pan into the oven for about 15 minutes. Then remove the pan from the oven and ladle some sauce over the birds. Add the ginger and return to the oven for 5 or 6 minutes, or long enough to crisp the skins. Baste chickens with the sauce 2 or 3 times.

8. Serve birds garnished with orange and lime zests, with side dishes of extra sauce.

This dish calls for an aggressive young red, such as a Moulin-à-Vent from a good producer, or perhaps a Nebbiolo d'Alba or Red Rioja.

PAN-ROASTED DUCK
with Yams, Rum, and Oranges

This preparation of duck has a Caribbean tone—French Caribbean, to be more specific. At our restaurant, we would probably pan-roast the duck's leg and thigh but grill the breast. This may not be easy to do in most homes, so the recipe gives the method for pan-roasting the whole duck. You'll note that the legs and thighs are put in the oven ahead of the breast; this is so the breast is not overcooked. Save the duck bones to make stock later, but use duck stock you've made previously for this recipe.

Serves 4

- 2 whole ducks, butchered into four separate boneless breasts and thigh and leg portions, thigh bone removed
- 1 or 2 yams

SAUCE

- ½ tablespoon olive oil
- 2 shallots, peeled and sliced thinly
- 1 jalapeño pepper, stemmed, seeded, and sliced
- 1 bay leaf
- ½ cup sherry vinegar

- ½ cup Essensia wine (an Orange Muscat wine available through the Andrew Quady Winery, Madera, California) or a Sauternes
- 1 cup fresh orange juice
- 2 cups Duck Stock (page 242)
- 1½ cups excellent orange marmalade

- 2 tablespoons peanut oil
- Salt and pepper
- ¼ cup Myers's dark rum

- 2 oranges, cut into sections, all skin, pith, and seeds removed, for garnish

1. Cut up the ducks and set aside.

2. Bring a pot of water to boil, lower the heat, and gently simmer the yams until you can pierce them fairly easily with a knife. Drain and set aside.

3. Make the sauce: Heat the olive oil in a medium-sized saucepan. Add the sliced shallots and jalapeño pepper and cook, stirring, for 1 minute. Add the bay leaf. Now add the vinegar, Essensia, and orange juice and reduce by half. Add the duck stock and reduce to half a cup. (This will take about 45 minutes.)

4. Strain the sauce into a clean saucepan and reheat to a simmer. Add the orange marmalade and cook until thickened slightly. Remove from heat and reserve.

5. Preheat the oven to 400 degrees. Peel the yams and cut into fairly thick wedges. Reserve.

6. Heat peanut oil in a heavy sauté pan. Season the ducks with salt and pepper. Put the duck leg and thigh portions, skin side down, in the pan and sauté until the skin begins to get crisp and brown. Turn once and then back again. Discard excess fat as necessary. Cook 4 or 5 minutes in this way over medium heat. Discard fat and remove the legs and thighs to a plate.

7. Score the duck breasts' skin in a cross-hatch fashion with four or five slashes in each direction. Add the breasts to the pan, skin side down, and cook over medium heat for 5 to 6 minutes. Remove the breasts from the pan and put them on a plate. Return the legs and thighs to the pan and put them in the oven for 8 to 10 minutes. Discard excess fat; now add the breasts to the pan, skin side up, and roast until the breasts are medium rare—approximately 5 to 8 minutes.

8. Take the duck pieces out of the oven, and remove them to a platter. Wipe out the pan and add the rum. Carefully deglaze the pan, burn off the alcohol, and add enough of the sauce to baste the ducks.

9. Put the legs and thighs back in the pan and return to oven. Keep breasts warm. Baste the legs for 1 to 2 minutes. Add the yam wedges to the pan, but do not put the pan back in the oven.

10. Arrange the duck legs on 4 warm plates and put the breasts on a cutting board. Slice the breasts on a bias. (They should have a trace of pink in the center.)

11. Heat the sauce over a medium-high flame for a moment, then pour it over the leg portions. Arrange the yam wedges around the legs and then arrange the sliced breast around the yams. Add the orange sections, season liberally with freshly cracked black pepper, and serve.

The sweetness of the yams and rum and the acidic fruitiness of the oranges in this dish suggests a supple, forward California Merlot. If you prefer a white, a Mosel Riesling would work nicely.

ROASTED LEG OF LAMB
with Roast Garlic, Mint, Pine Nuts, and Figs

This dish benefits from advance planning. I like to flavor the meat with the garlic, mint, and fig mixture for a day or two before roasting, for more flavor. The dish requires no sauce; its own juices will provide that. But some new potatoes, blanched and roasted in lamb fat and rosemary, are perfect alongside.

Serves 4 to 6

20 cloves Roast Garlic (page 200) or 10 cloves raw garlic, roughly chopped	1 cup diced dried figs, soaked in enough Madeira to cover
½ cup pine nuts, toasted	6 tablespoons (¾ stick) butter
¾ cup roughly chopped mint leaves	1½ cups chopped carrots
About ¾ to ⅞ cup olive oil or roast garlic oil	1½ cups chopped onions
A 9-pound leg of lamb, bone in	1½ cups chopped celery
Salt and pepper to taste	1 whole head garlic, cut in half crosswise

1. Mix together the chopped garlic, pine nuts, and the mint leaves and combine them with ⅓ to ½ cup olive oil or the oil from roasting the garlic.

2. Butcher the lamb, removing the pelvic and upper leg bone (or have your butcher do it, but save the bone to flavor the roast). Leave the hindshank bone in. The meat will be divided into two parts, one large, one small. Bisect the large part vertically, as evenly as possible. Cut away any silverskin that might toughen the roast.

3. Lightly salt but rather heavily pepper the meat. Rub the mint and garlic mixture generously all over the meat.

4. Drain the Madeira from the figs and reserve it for later. Cut slits all over the lamb and push the diced figs into the meat.

5. Now, with butcher's twine, start tying the lamb and reshaping the meat into its original form. Starting at the hip end, tie the string at intervals around the meat, trying to keep the meat compact and uniform. When it is all tied, refrigerate the lamb.

6. When you are ready to roast the lamb, preheat oven to 400 degrees. In a roasting pan on top of the stove, heat the butter and 6 tablespoons olive oil or roasted garlic oil until just foamy. Place the carrots, onions, celery, halved garlic head, and lamb bones, if any, in the roasting pan. Sauté briefly, then add the lamb, fat side up.

7. Put pan in the oven and roast about 1½ hours, more or less, to your liking. (My taste in lamb varies with the cut and preparation, but while I enjoy my lamb racks rare, I prefer the leg about medium-rare. The more developed musculature of the leg requires more temperature than the delicate meat of the loin.) Remove lamb to a cutting board and allow to rest.

8. Pour the vegetables and collected meat juices through a strainer into a bowl. Reserve juices, discard vegetables. Allow juices to settle.

9. In a small saucepan reduce the Madeira reserved from the figs.

10. Skim the fat off the strained pan juices and discard. Add these juices to the Madeira and reduce to desired consistency.

11. Remove the strings as you slice down the lamb toward the hind shank. If the diced figs fall onto the cutting board as you slice the lamb, spoon them over the lamb after you have arranged the meat on plates. Top with the warm juices and serve.

Note: To obtain more juices you can add some lamb stock to the bones and vegetables as the lamb roasts.

This subtle, less intensely flavored leg of lamb calls for a medium-bodied Bordeaux from Margaux or St-Julien, or a Cabernet Sauvignon from the Napa Valley.

FRICASSEE OF RABBIT
with Corn Cakes, Root Vegetables, and Bell Pepper Cream

It is better to begin this dish one day in advance, so you have time to prepare the rabbit stock. If you prefer, you may serve the fricassee on pasta or polenta.

Serves 4 to 6

Two 2½- to 3-pound rabbits, cut into leg and thigh portions and loin portions (chicken can be substituted, but it will have a less intense flavor)
¼ cup cleaned and chopped basil leaves
¼ cup cleaned and chopped oregano leaves
¼ cup cleaned and chopped Italian parsley leaves
Salt and pepper to taste
¼ cup flour
¾ to 1 cup clarified butter (enough to sauté the rabbit parts and cook the corn cakes)
8 tablespoons (1 stick) butter
1 carrot, cleaned and cut into 2½-inch julienne strips
1 leek, cleaned and cut into 2½-inch julienne strips

1 stalk celery, cleaned and cut into 2½-inch julienne strips
1 parsnip, cleaned and cut into 2½-inch julienne strips
4 cloves peeled garlic
2 bay leaves
½ cup white wine
¼ cup herbes de Provence vinegar or white wine vinegar
2 cups stock
¼ cup cream
4 bell peppers, roasted, stems and ribs removed, cut into strips
1 tablespoon Dijon mustard
Corn Cake batter (page 194)
1 tablespoon chopped shallots
1 tablespoon chopped garlic

THE DAY BEFORE

1. Butcher the hind legs, thighs, and loins off the rabbit and clean. Roughly chop the carcass remains, including the forelegs. With them, prepare rabbit stock, following the Duck Stock recipe (page 242). Chill the finished stock overnight.

ON THE DAY OF SERVING

2. Preheat the oven to 400 degrees. Remove the stock from the refrigerator and skim off

and discard any fat that has collected and hardened on the top. Reduce 1 quart of stock to 2 cups to intensify the flavor. Set aside. Save remaining stock for another purpose.

3. Mix the chopped basil, oregano, and parsley in a small bowl. Rub the rabbit meat with the chopped herbs and salt and pepper and allow to rest ½ hour.

4. Lightly dust the rabbit with flour.

5. Get a large, heavy skillet moderately hot and add ⅓ to ½ cup of the clarified butter. Now lay the rabbit legs and thighs in the pan, being careful not to overcrowd them. When they are lightly brown, towel off any excess butter and put the pan in the oven. Roast about 10 minutes and remove from the oven. Take the thighs and legs out of the pan, add 2 to 3 tablespoons clarified butter, and sauté the tiny loins on top of the stove. This will only take a minute. Remove them to a plate. Remove excess butter.

6. Mix 6 tablespoons (¾ stick) butter in the same pan and add the prepared root vegetables. Scrape the bottom of the pan with a wooden spoon. Add the garlic cloves and bay leaves and stew the vegetables a few minutes. Dab off excess butter again. Add the wine and herbs de Provence or wine vinegar and cook until liquid has almost evaporated.

7. Meanwhile, cut the loin and leg meat into delicate, bite-sized pieces and reserve. You will need to cut the meat off the bone in the leg. Add the bone to your stock reduction, simmer, and strain.

8. Add the 2 cups strained stock to the vegetable mixture and cook down to ½ cup. Add the heavy cream and reduce until it is thick enough to coat the back of a spoon. (When your root vegetables begin to soften, remove them from the reducing liquid and reserve in a cool place until later.)

9. Add the roasted pepper strips and mustard to the reduced cream mixture and purée. Strain the purée into a clean pan.

10. Fry the corn cakes as in Step 5 on page 194, using in all about ¼ cup clarified butter instead of peanut oil. Allow 3 cakes per serving. Remove them to an ovenproof plate and cover with a towel. Keep warm.

11. Wipe out the pan and add the remaining 2 tablespoons unclarified butter. Add the chopped shallots and garlic and stew a moment. Add the reserved root vegetables, the sliced rabbit, and just enough of the roasted pepper and mustard cream to moisten the dish. Allow to simmer until just heated through.

12. Arrange the fricassee over the corn cakes. Serve.

This rich stew begs for a sturdy red like a Gigondas. If you prefer white, I would select one from the same area such as a white Châteauneuf-du-Pape.

SAUTÉED VEAL STEAKS
with Rum, Plantains,
and Creole Mustard Cream

Plantains are discussed in my recipe for pork Havana "nueva." This starchy relative to the common banana is employed here to provide a somewhat sweet contrast to the heat of the grainy creole mustard. If you are unable to find the creole variety, Pommery mustard is an excellent substitute.

Serves 4

2 very dark to black plantains	Salt and pepper to taste
1 cup flour seasoned with 1 tablespoon cinnamon	1½ pounds boneless, skinless veal loin or tenderloin, cut into four 6-ounce steaks (they will be small in circumference, but thick)
8 to 16 tablespoons (1 to 2 sticks) butter	
1 quart heavy cream	
1 tablespoon veal or chicken demiglace (optional)	¼ cup clarified butter or oil from Roast Garlic (page 200)
3 tablespoons creole mustard	¼ cup dark rum

1. Skin the plantains by making a shallow incision through the length of each. Cut off both ends and slip the skin off. Cut the plantains on the bias into long pieces of equal size. Dredge the pieces in seasoned flour and tap off any excess. Reserve remaining flour.

2. Heat a heavy skillet until barely hot and add the unclarified butter. Allow it to foam, and tip the pan to coat the bottom. Now add the plantains and cook until lightly crusted and golden on both sides. Remove them to a plate and allow to cool to room temperature.

3. In a saucepan, quickly reduce the cream to the consistency at which it will *barely* coat the back of a spoon. Strain through a fine-mesh strainer into a bowl. Whisk in the demiglace. Now whisk in the mustard and keep sauce warm.

4. Preheat the oven to 450 degrees. Season the veal and dredge it in the flour left from the plantains. Tap off any excess. Heat a clean, heavy sauté pan that will comfortably hold the meat. Add the clarified butter or garlic oil to the pan.

5. When the butter or oil is just hot, add the veal steaks, rolling them around on their sides to cook evenly and adjusting the heat so that they cook gently. Sear each end of the veal to seal in juices.

6. Discard the excess butter or oil, put the veal into the oven, and roast for approximately 3 to 6 minutes, turning the veal once.

7. Wash, dry, and reheat the skillet in which you cooked the plantains. Add the remaining unclarified butter and gently reheat the plantains.

8. Remove the veal from the oven and put it on a cutting board. Discard any butter or oil in the sauté pan and add the rum. *Carefully* deglaze the pan and cook the rum down to 1 tablespoon. Add the cream sauce to heat it for a moment and to reduce it slightly.

9. Divide the sauce among 4 warm plates. Slice each piece of veal into 3 or 4 medallions, arrange them and the plantains over the creole cream sauce, and serve.

Either red or white would work equally well with this dish. For the white, I would recommend a dry aromatic wine with good acidity to stand up to the mustard—like a Sancerre or similarly styled Sauvignon Blanc. A Chinon or Bourgeuil from the Loire would be a nice red.

CAJUN RIB STEAK, SWEET PEPPERS, and Hot Chiles

We have a very powerful meal before us with this dish. The heat of the chiles is a perfect challenge to the richness of the beef; their spark and the garlic's warmth help lift what might ordinarily be a very heavy dinner. It seems natural that many people who live on an island or in a coastal town like Key West crave the flavor of a steak from time to time, but people from all over the world have asked me for this recipe. Part of this recipe was, of course, inspired by Paul Prudhomme. The sauce was my invention to complement this roast. (The initial roasting of the beef must be done a day ahead, and you can make the sauce as much as two days ahead.)

Serves 12

An 18-pound prime rib of beef, bone in
8 to 12 garlic cloves, cut into thin slivers
¼ cup coarse kosher salt
¼ cup butcher-grind black pepper

6 to 8 ancho chiles, toasted and softened in water
2 or 3 Spanish onions, peeled and thickly sliced

1. The flap that covers the meat of a prime rib can be pulled back to expose the meat. (A butcher can explain it for you.) You need to open this flap, leaving it connected, and proceed in the following manner.

2. Preheat the oven to 500 degrees. Take a thin knife and puncture the meat all over. You will need about 40 holes. Push a sliver of garlic deep into each of these holes.

3. Liberally season the meat with salt and pepper. (It will seem like quite a bit.) Discard the stems and seeds of the anchos, cut the softened chiles into strips, and cover the salt and pepper mixture with them. Arrange the onion slices over the chiles and carefully fold the flap over this combination.

4. Put the beef in a roasting pan and roast for 30 minutes. Carefully remove from the oven and allow to cool. Discard accumulated fat. Refrigerate the meat overnight.

SAUCE

¼ cup olive oil	1 yellow bell pepper (or 1 more red pepper), stemmed, seeded, ribbed, and sliced into strips
1 red bell pepper, stemmed, seeded, ribbed, and sliced into strips	
1 green bell pepper, stemmed, seeded, ribbed, and sliced into strips	3 jalapeño peppers, stemmed, seeded, ribbed, and sliced into strips
	1 cup marsala wine
	1 quart rich Brown Sauce (page 248)

1. Heat the olive oil in a heavy saucepan. Add the peppers and stir. Cook a few minutes. Towel off any excess oil.

2. Deglaze the pan with marsala, being sure it ignites to burn off the alcohol. (Naturally, you should exercise caution when deglazing anything.) Reduce the wine to a glaze and add the brown sauce.

3. Cook the sauce until its consistency will coat the back of a spoon. It should be sweet, rich, and spicy.

4. Strain the sauce into a container and chill until you are ready to serve. Discard vegetables.

TO PREPARE AND SERVE

1. Either heat up a broiler or prepare a grill. It should be *very* hot. While it is heating, spoon off any fat that may have accumulated on top of the sauce, and gently reheat the sauce.

2. Broil or grill the beef to the degree of doneness you prefer.

3. Spoon the sauce over the sliced meat and serve with your choice of starch and vegetable. (I recommend a sweet potato gratin for the starch.)

If there were ever a time for a big Zinfandel, this is it. If you prefer a French wine, however, a rich Cornas from the Rhône would be appropriate.

Sautéed Calf's Liver
with Slab Bacon, Applejack Brandy, and Green Onions

This has been a favorite dish with my customers over the years. In a way, it is liver with bacon and onions, but its presentation and flavor are special and thoroughly different. One thing that is essential is that the liver be very fresh and truly from a young calf. In addition, the liver must be cooked rather quickly and served no more than medium-rare or its delicate qualities are gone.

Serves 4 to 6

½ pound slab bacon, rind removed, cut into sections ¾ inch long and ¼ inch thick

½ cup flour

1½ to 2 pounds calf's liver, cleaned and cut into slices about ¼ inch thick

Salt and pepper to taste

¼ cup olive oil or oil from Roast Garlic (page 200)

4 scallions, half of the green part and all of the root removed, and remainder cut into julienne pieces, lengthwise

3 tablespoons applejack or calvados brandy

1 cup Brown Sauce (page 248)

1 tablespoon butter

1. Cook the bacon until just barely done and reserve it and the bacon fat.

2. Lightly flour the liver and season it with salt and pepper.

3. Heat a skillet and add just enough oil to coat the pan (use some of the bacon fat for flavor). Lay the liver in the pan, sauté 1 or 2 minutes on each side over medium-high heat, and remove to warm plates.

(recipe continues)

4. Discard the excess oil and add the scallions and bacon. Now add the applejack and deglaze. Reduce to a glaze. Add the prepared brown sauce and cook a moment. Add the butter in small pinches and swirl it in the pan.

5. Pour sauce over the liver, arranging the scallions and bacon over the meat. Serve at once.

One of the many California Pinot Noirs bursting with ripe fruit would be a good choice here. An interesting alternative would be an Australian Shiraz.

ROASTED CALF'S LIVER
with Madeira, Country Ham, and Sweet Melon

Roasting an entire liver seems to intimidate people who think nothing of roasting a prime rib. It is not difficult, just not typical. This recipe calls for marinating the melon with Madeira overnight. This delicious step is not only good with liver—it's good all by itself.

Serves 6 to 8

1 whole honeydew or cantaloupe melon
About 1⅔ cups (½ bottle) Madeira wine
A 4- to 5-pound fresh calf's liver, cleaned, rolled, and tied
8 to 10 ounces ham fat (or bacon), sliced, for wrapping liver
4 shallots, peeled and thinly sliced

¼ cup balsamic vinegar
3 cups Veal Stock (page 243)
Cracked black pepper
¼ pound (1 stick) butter, cut into pieces and chilled
¾ pound Smithfield ham, rind removed, sliced very thin and diced medium

1. Cut a round "plug" out of the melon. Scrape and shake out the seeds. Pour the Madeira into the hole and replace the plug. Chill overnight.

2. Preheat oven to 375 degrees. Set liver on a rack in a roasting pan and arrange ham fat or raw bacon under the strings so that the liver will be protected from direct heat and the fat will baste the meat while it roasts.

3. Remove the plug from the melon and pour the Madeira into a container; reserve. Peel and slice the melon. Cut the slices into a medium dice and put into a bowl. Pour a small amount of the Madeira over the melon and set aside in a cool spot.

4. Put the liver in the oven and roast for 35 to 45 minutes, or until internal temperature is about 120 degrees. Remove the liver, cut off the strings, and discard the fat or bacon. (Bacon may be reserved for later use.) Pour any collected juices into a clean bowl. Allow liver to rest in a warm place while making the sauce. (The liver will cook a bit more as it rests.)

5. Put shallots and balsamic vinegar in a medium-sized saucepan over medium heat. Reduce by three-quarters, add the reserved Madeira, and reduce to about ¼ cup. Add the reserved liver juices and veal stock and reduce to 1½ cups. Reduce the heat to a low simmer. Adjust seasoning.

6. Slice the liver into slices at least ¼ inch thick and arrange on plates.

7. Whisk the butter into the sauce, continue whisking until it is all incorporated, and pour sauce over the meat. Scatter the diced ham and melon over the liver. Serve, offering the pepper mill.

Note: There is no salt called for in this recipe. You'll get all you need from the Smithfield ham.

The rich qualities of many California Merlots would be particularly suitable here.

SWEETBREADS
with Barsac, Glazed Pearl Onions, and Fettuccine

Barsac is a French wine originating from an area adjacent to Sauternes. It has many of the characteristic sweet, floral perfume qualities of Sauternes, and while Barsac is generally not as highly regarded as Sauternes, it is certainly admired in its own right.

Sweetbreads are the thymus glands of animals; in this recipe, we use calves' sweetbreads. Sweetbreads have a delicate, creamy blandness, are texturally sensual, and make an excellent vehicle for more intense flavors. To improve upon their natural texture, it is wise to soak the sweetbreads in several changes of icy water to remove blood, and then to blanch them in a light court bouillon or water. After blanching, drain them and weight them slightly to firm them up. Peel off the thin outer membrane and discard any excess fat. Then the sweetbreads are ready to be sliced and sautéed.

Serves 4

COURT BOUILLON

10 farm mushrooms, stems removed and caps wiped, thinly sliced	6 tablespoons (¾ stick) butter
1 shallot, peeled and thinly sliced	1 bottle white wine (750 ml)
1 carrot, peeled and thinly sliced	2 bay leaves
½ onion, peeled and thinly sliced	½ bunch fresh thyme
1 stalk celery, cleaned and thinly sliced	6 fresh basil leaves
	12 black peppercorns
2 pounds veal sweetbreads, soaked in 4 or 5 changes of icy water	1 recipe Basic All-purpose Pasta dough (page 206)

PEARL ONIONS

1 pint pearl onions	Cracked black pepper to taste
1 tablespoon butter	1 teaspoon fresh thyme leaves
2 tablespoons sugar	About 1⅔ cups (½ bottle) Barsac (or substitute Sauternes)
½ cup Champagne vinegar	

SAUCE

1 tablespoon butter
3 shallots, peeled and thinly sliced
6 whole black peppercorns
1 bay leaf

About 1⅔ cups (½ bottle) Barsac
1 cup reserved sweetbread court bouillon
1 quart heavy cream

Flour for dusting sweetbreads
Salt and cracked black pepper to taste

2 tablespoons butter

1. Prepare court bouillon: Heat a large saucepot and sweat the mushrooms, shallot, carrot, onion, and celery in the butter. When they are glazed, add the white wine and cook 10 minutes to reduce the wine. Now add 2 quarts of water and the bay leaves, thyme, basil, and black peppercorns. Cook 20 minutes and then add the sweetbreads. Skim as necessary. Blanch the sweetbreads for 8 to 10 minutes.

2. Lift the sweetbreads from court bouillon and drop gently into icy water for 1 minute. Remove and drain. Chill until cooled completely on a rack in a pan, to allow for drainage. Meanwhile, allow the court bouillon to gently reduce to 1 cup and reserve for sauce. (This takes about 45 minutes to one hour.)

3. Peel off and discard the thin external membrane and any fat from the sweetbreads. Now cut the sweetbreads into ¼-inch slices. Put them on a plate and cover. Refrigerate until ready to serve.

4. Cut pasta dough into fettuccine. Form into nests and dry. Set aside enough to serve 4 and reserve remainder for other use. (Alternatively, you can use excellent quality commercial pasta; if you can obtain freshly made fettuccine, so much the better.)

5. Prepare the pearl onions: Bring a medium-sized pot of water to a boil. Cut off the root ends of the pearl onions but leave the outer skin on. When the water is boiling, add a pinch of salt and the onions. Cook 3 or 4 minutes. Drain and cool under running water. Now pop the onions from their jackets into a bowl. Discard the skins.

6. Heat a medium-sized, heavy saucepan, add the butter and swirl the pan to coat the bottom. Add the pearl onions and cook over moderate heat until they brown a bit. Add the sugar and stir a moment to caramelize. Add the vinegar, turn up the heat a little, and reduce it. Add the cracked black pepper, thyme, and half a bottle of Barsac.

7. Reduce the liquid in the pan. Ideally, you want to adjust the heat and time the process so that the onions are cooked through just as the liquid in the pan is gone. If the onions are tender before the liquid disappears, simply remove them with a slotted spoon to a bowl, reduce the liquid to 3 or 4 tablespoons, and then pour that over the onions. Keep the onions warm.

(recipe continues)

8. Begin making sauce: Heat butter in a medium-large saucepan. Add the shallots and cook 1 minute over low heat. Add the peppercorns, bay leaf, and remaining half bottle of Barsac. Reduce this by three-quarters.

9. Add the 1 cup reserved sweetbread court bouillon and reduce again by three-quarters. Add the heavy cream and cook until sauce is thick enough to coat the back of a spoon. Strain through a fine-mesh strainer and reserve.

10. Bring a large pot of water to a boil for the pasta.

11. Remove the sliced sweetbreads from the refrigerator and dust them lightly with flour, salt, and cracked black pepper to taste.

12. Heat a large, deep skillet to medium-high heat. Add 2 tablespoons butter and swirl to coat the bottom evenly. Sauté the sweetbread slices until golden on each side, 1 or 2 minutes. Remove to a warm platter. Wipe out the pan and add the reserved sauce. Heat to a simmer.

13. Drop the pasta into the boiling water and cook until al dente. (The timing will vary depending on whether the fettuccine is fresh or dried.) When the pasta is finished, drain it well and toss into the sauce. Mix with a pair of tongs to coat the fettuccine.

14. Lift the coated pasta onto plates in mounds. Pour a little extra sauce over each serving. Top the noodles with the sweetbreads and glazed pearl onions. Serve.

A full-bodied white Burgundy such as a Meursault can negotiate both the rich texture and subtle taste of the sweetbreads. If you prefer a red, choose one with a nice feel and delicate flavor, like a Volnay.

BRAISED BREAST OF CHICKEN
with "Salt and Pepper"

The "salt" in this dish comes from the intriguing flavor of preserved lemons. You will need to have these prepared and in your larder for a period of time before making this recipe. The "pepper" is finely julienned poblano peppers. You could use banana peppers, or jalapeños, instead of the poblanos for more heat.

Serves 4

≈≈≈≈≈≈

SAUCE

2 shallots, peeled and finely chopped	½ cup pitted pickled Niçoise or other nonsalty olives
12 whole black peppercorns	
1 bay leaf	½ cup heavy cream
¼ cup red wine vinegar	1 pound butter, cut into small pieces and kept cold
¾ cup red wine	

¼ cup virgin olive oil	⅔ cup red wine
Four 10-ounce boneless chicken breasts, skin on, lightly seasoned with salt and pepper	1 cup chicken stock
1 large Spanish onion, peeled and sliced	8 sections Preserved Lemons (page 201), finely julienned (rind only!)
3 poblano peppers, stems, ribs, and seeds removed, finely julienned	2 cucumbers, skinned, seeded, and pushed through the largest holes of a grater; reserve and keep cool
1 large tomato, concassée	

1. Make the sauce: Put the shallots, black peppercorns, and bay leaf in a saucepan with the red wine vinegar and reduce the vinegar to 1 tablespoon. Add the red wine and half of the olives. Continue to reduce until most of the liquid is gone. Add the cream and reduce by half.

2. Now whisk in the butter, piece by piece, until it is all incorporated. Strain sauce through a fine-mesh strainer into a warm, clean bowl or bain-marie. Stir in the remaining olives. Reserve and keep warm.

3. Heat a large, heavy pan big enough to comfortably hold the chicken breasts. Add the olive oil. When the pan is moderately hot add the breasts, skin side down. Shake to keep breasts from sticking.

4. Add the onion slices and cook 1 minute. Add the julienned poblano peppers and tomato concasse and toss the vegetables, fitting them in and around the chicken. Add the red wine and reduce the heat to medium.

5. When the wine is reduced by half, turn the breasts skin side up and add the chicken stock and half of the preserved lemon. Lower the heat to low and simmer very gently just until the chicken breasts are cooked. Remove to a warm place while the pan juices are reducing.

(recipe continues)

6. Spread the cucumber "noodles" on 4 warm plates. Cover with the olive butter sauce. Top the sauce with the braised chicken breasts and top the chicken with the glazy pan juices and vegetables. Garnish with the rest of the preserved lemon. Serve.

A good young Mâconnais, like a St-Véran, or an earthy California Sauvignon Blanc would further harmonize the "salt and pepper" in this dish.

GRILLED VEAL CHOP
Over a Pungent Tomato Sauce and Garlic Rouille

This dish possesses the full, brazen, undiluted sunshine personality of Provençe. There is nothing subtle about it except the veal, and we attempt to pump extra character into that by grilling the meat with fresh herbs generously rubbed into it.

Serves 4

- ¼ cup chopped fresh basil leaves
- 1 tablespoon chopped fresh thyme leaves
- 1 tablespoon chopped fresh oregano leaves
- 1 tablespoon chopped fresh rosemary leaves

- ½ cup virgin olive oil
- Cracked black pepper and coarse salt
- Four 10- to 12-ounce veal rib chops, bone in
- 1 recipe Rouille (page 234), made with 3 or 4 extra garlic cloves if you like garlic

TOMATO SAUCE

- ½ cup extra virgin olive oil
- 3 tablespoons butter
- 3 cloves garlic, minced
- 3 poblano peppers, stems, seeds, and ribs removed, julienned
- 2 leeks, white part only, cleaned and diced

- 1 onion, peeled and diced
- 1 cup red wine vinegar
- ½ tablespoon crushed red pepper
- 1 bay leaf
- 4 cups tomato concasse
- ½ cup pitted Niçoise olives

1. Combine the chopped herbs with the olive oil. Season the meat and rub liberally with the herb mixture. Set aside in the refrigerator.

2. Make the rouille and keep at room temperature.

3. Make the sauce: Heat the olive oil and butter in a medium-sized saucepan until foamy. Add the garlic and poblano peppers. (If poblanos are unavailable, substitute 3 jalapeños.) Cook, stirring, 30 seconds. Add the diced leeks and onion. Cook about 2 minutes. Then add the vinegar and reduce by three-fourths.

4. Add the crushed red pepper, bay leaf, and tomato concasse. Cook about 15 minutes. Remove from heat and stir in the olives. Keep warm.

5. Grill the veal until done the way you like it.

6. Spoon tomato sauce on warm plates. Top with the veal and then spoon some of the rouille over the meat. Serve.

This lusty preparation calls for a wine of the same magnitude.
Try a powerful Côte-Rôtie or a Barolo from a good producer.

GRILLED FILET OF BEEF
with Gorgonzola Butter and
Marinated Deep-Fried Red Onions

When I was a child, it was my good fortune to eat filet mignon at some of the steak houses Chicago was famous for. I loved the charred, crisp exterior and suave, soft, rich meat. I thought it was almost as good as the huge deep-fried onion rings that routinely crowned the beef. (The onions here need a head start of at least six hours.)

Serves 4

4   small red onions, cut into thin rings
2   cups Hot Chile Oil (page 212)
5   cups milk
1/2 cup butter, softened at room temperature
1   cup red wine
2   shallots, peeled and finely chopped
1   tablespoon cracked black pepper

1   cup Gorgonzola cheese
Four 8-ounce beef steaks cut from the tenderloin, completely cleaned
1   tablespoon virgin olive oil
Salt and pepper, to taste
Vegetable oil for deep-frying
1   cup flour

1. Immerse the onions in the chile oil for at least 4 hours. Drain them and then immerse them in the milk for 2 or more hours.

2. Heat a grill.

3. Put the softened butter in a mixer bowl. In a saucepan, reduce the red wine with the shallots and cracked black pepper until only a little bit remains. Add this reduction to the butter in the mixer bowl and begin to beat slowly. Add the Gorgonzola piece by piece, beating until it is all incorporated. Season to taste. Set aside in a cool but not cold place.

4. Rub the steaks with the olive oil and salt and pepper.

5. Heat the vegetable oil in a deep-fry pot to 365 degrees.

6. Take the onion rings out of the milk and drain them on paper toweling. Then dredge them in the flour.

7. Begin to grill the steaks to desired doneness. Meanwhile, deep-fry the onion rings until crisp, and remove them to clean paper toweling.

8. Put the steaks on warm plates and top with the Gorgonzola butter. Heap the onion rings over the steaks and serve.

This simple but forthright dish calls for a good cru bourgeois *Bordeaux. A young California Cabernet or its Spanish equivalent would be suitable alternatives.*

Hot Sausages and Fettuccine
with Chèvre and Ratatouille

Serves 4

1 quart Ratatouille (page 188)	1 pound fettuccine noodles, homemade or
1½ pounds hot Italian sausage	a good commercial type
Olive oil	½ pound chèvre goat cheese

1. Heat the ratatouille.

2. Cook the sausages in a small amount of olive oil and keep warm.

3. Boil the fettuccine and drain. Toss quickly in a bowl with olive oil and, if you like, some of the oil from the cooking of the sausage.

4. Arrange the fettuccine in large nests on warm plates or in shallow bowls. Spoon ratatouille into the center of the nests and top with the sausage. Crumble the chèvre over all and serve.

As a complement to this straightforward, rustic dish I would choose either a red Italian, like a Chianti or other proprietary wine of Tuscany, or a red Bandol from Provençe.

ROASTED CHICKEN
with Lardoons, Wild Mushrooms, Pearl Onions, and a Red Wine Vinegar Sauce

I don't know why, but a dish like this fills me with soft, pastoral images—it is a rustic, familial, soothing, and tempting kind of meal. These days, we seem to dote on parts: We grill chicken breasts, we barbecue turkey legs. Yet there is no thought given to where these things come from. There is a time when a whole, roasted bird should be brought to the table with a platter of garden-fresh vegetables, a bowl of snowy white mashed potatoes, and carafes of wine. The bird is carved and shared. A large crusty loaf of bread should be passed and everyone should pull a piece off and pass it on. Take some vegetables and pass them, too. It is communion, and it can be a vital process in the nurturing of the palate, the understanding of cuisine, and the appreciation of life.

Serves 6

Three 3-pound whole chickens
Salt and pepper
- 1/4 pound (1 stick) butter
- 1 tablespoon roughly chopped fresh thyme leaves
- 6 ounces slab bacon, cut into 1/4-inch by 1-inch strips (these are lardoons)
- 2 carrots, peeled and diced
- 1 onion, peeled and diced
- 2 stalks celery, cleaned and diced
- 6 whole cloves garlic, peeled
- 1/2 cup olive oil
- 1 cup red wine vinegar
- 2 quarts strong Chicken Stock (page 240)
- 1/2 pound wild mushrooms, sliced
- 1/2 pound pearl onions, blanched, skins and roots removed

1. Preheat oven to 425 degrees. Wash the chickens quickly in cold water and rub dry. Season the cavities of the birds with salt and pepper. Truss the birds and rub them all over with ¼ pound butter. Season the outside of the chickens with salt, pepper, and thyme.

2. Gently cook the bacon in a large roasting pan until *just* done. Remove and reserve.

3. Put the diced carrots, onion, celery, and garlic into the roasting pan and add the olive oil. Stir everything around to coat the vegetables. Place the chickens in the vegetables and roast approximately 30 to 40 minutes, basting the birds with their own juices periodically. Turn them over and roast another 20 minutes, approximately. (The juices should just run clear when the thigh is pierced.)

4. Remove the birds to a warm platter to rest in a warm place while you prepare the sauce. Pour the vegetables and pan drippings through a colander into a bowl. Reserve the drippings and return the vegetables to the roasting pan.

5. Put the roasting pan on a burner and turn heat to high. Scrape the vegetables from the bottom of the pan if any are sticking. (If any vegetables have blackened entirely, discard them.) Spoon off any excess grease. Add the vinegar to the roasting pan and reduce by half. Add the stock and again reduce by half.

6. Strain the contents of the roasting pan through a fine-mesh strainer into a bowl. Allow sauce to settle; discard vegetables.

7. Heat a medium-sized saucepan on medium heat. Add the drippings saved from roasting the birds. Add the mushrooms and cook about 2 minutes. Add the pearl onions and cook about 2 minutes more. Season to taste. Add the sauce and cook to desired consistency.

8. If the birds have thrown off any extra drippings while resting on their platter, add those. Add the lardoons and check the seasoning.

9. Arrange the birds on a carving platter and send the sauce to the table in a separate sauce boat.

Either a robust young red, such as a Crozes-Hermitage, or a friendly Red Rioja
would be enjoyable with this dish.

ROAST LOIN OF LAMB,
Poached Raisins, and Black Muscat Compote

Here we stuff the loin of lamb with a finely chopped mixture of garlic, anchovy, and basil. You can cut the recipe in half and serve it as an appetizer, if you like.

The Black Muscat in the compote is an interesting wine. I use the Andrew Quady Winery's Elysium, produced in Madera, California. It has a portlike flavor but it is less viscous than port. If you substitute port you should use a little less to diminish the concentrated sweetness that would occur through reduction.

You can cut up and stuff the lamb, and also do the initial sauce preparation in Step 6, a day ahead if you like.

Serves 4

1½ pounds boneless lamb loin, cut from the saddle, bones reserved for stock (or use other bones)	1 tablespoon extra virgin olive oil, plus additional for searing
Cracked black pepper to taste	½ cup chopped basil leaves
	1 tablespoon chopped garlic
	1 tablespoon chopped rinsed anchovy fillets

SAUCE

¾ cup golden raisins	3 tablespoons butter, cut into small pieces and kept cold
¾ cup black raisins	
1 cup mirepoix vegetables (carrots, onion, celery, and leeks in equal proportions), finely diced	1 cup Elysium Black Muscat wine
	4 cups lamb stock
	¼ cup Armagnac
	Cracked black pepper

1. Butcher the lamb loins, removing both the loins and tenderloins. Reserve the tenderloins for another dish. You want to have 4 equal lengths of lamb loin. (You may wish to purchase the loins boneless to simplify preparation. That's fine as long as you have another source of bones for the lamb stock.)

2. Prepare lamb stock as described on page 249.

3. Make a fairly deep (like a pocket) but narrow incision in each length of lamb almost from one end to the other. (Do not "butterfly" it.) Season the lamb and rub it with the

olive oil. Then pack the basil, garlic, and anchovies into the incisions in the lamb.

4. Tie the lamb with butcher's string in 3 or 4 places to secure the filling. Set aside in refrigerator, covered, until you are ready to proceed. (This step may be done one day in advance.)

5. Heat a small pot of water to a boil and plump the raisins for 10 seconds. Pour them through a strainer and refresh them immediately with cold water. Put them into a bowl.

6. Begin sauce by cooking the mirepoix in a heavy saucepan in 2 tablespoons of the butter until they begin to caramelize. Add the Black Muscat wine and reduce to ¼ cup, then add the lamb stock and reduce it by half. Strain and reserve. (This may be done one day in advance. Remove any fat that accumulates on top.)

7. When ready to serve, preheat the oven to 425 degrees.

8. Heat a sauté pan large enough to accommodate the lamb. Add just enough olive oil to coat the bottom of the pan. Sear the lamb on all sides, then place the pan in the oven and roast for *5 minutes*. Remove the pan from the oven. Put the lamb on a platter and keep it warm while completing the sauce.

9. Pour off any excess oil, but keep whatever meaty particles may be adhering to the sauté pan. Add the Armagnac and tilt the pan toward the heat to deglaze it. Shake it vigorously, and when the flames have subsided, gently scrape the bottom of the pan with a wooden spoon. Add half of the raisins.

10. Reduce until almost all of the Armagnac is gone and then add the prepared sauce from Step 6 and the remaining raisins. Reduce the sauce by half, until rich and glazy. Season with cracked black pepper to taste. Add the last tablespoon of cold butter, swirling the pan constantly to distribute the butter.

11. Untie the lamb loins and carve them. Fan them across 4 warm plates. Spoon the sauce and raisins around the meat. Serve.

This deeply flavored and intense dish pairs wonderfully with some of the best Bordeaux of St-Julien—wines that are soft, supple, and laden with deep fruit extract. A few notable California Cabernets (such as those from Dunn Vineyards or Silver Oak Wine Cellars, for instance) are approaching this high standard as well.

GRILLED VEAL LOIN AND SMOKED LOBSTER
with Mango Compote

The subtle flavor of veal acts as a bridge between the sweet/hot mango-chile compote and the rich/smoky lobster in this light and visually attractive dish. Another nice feature is that you can smoke the lobster a day in advance.

Serves 4

1 pound boneless loin of veal, trimmed of most fat and all of the silverskin
Four 10-ounce lobster tails, shelled and deveined (weight is for meat only)

½ cup olive oil
2 teaspoons salt
2 tablespoons cracked black pepper
2 tablespoons thyme leaves

SAUCE

3 tablespoons butter
1 poblano chile, diced fine, stem and seeds discarded
1 red onion, diced fine
½ cup cilantro leaves

1 cup white wine
6 tablespoons white wine vinegar
¼ cup Spanish vinegar (see Note)
3 cups chopped ripe mango flesh, in medium-sized, even pieces

1. Put the veal in one bowl and the lobster tails in another. Top each with equal amounts of olive oil, salt, pepper, and thyme leaves. Allow to marinate 4 or 5 hours.

2. Fire up a smoker. (You could omit smoking the lobster and grill both the lobster and the veal for a slightly different version of this dish.) When the smoker is ready, remove the lobster tails from the marinade and slowly smoke them until almost cooked through. Remove and set aside. (This can be done a day in advance.)

3. Make the sauce: Heat a medium-sized sauté pan on medium heat and add the butter. Add the poblano chile and diced red onion and sauté, stirring occasionally, until they just begin to color. Chop the cilantro leaves roughly and stir them into the vegetables.

4. Add the white wine and white wine vinegar and reduce to a glaze. Add the Spanish vinegar and mango pieces and stir. Do not allow to cook. You are just heating the mango slightly. (You don't want to ruin the mango's soft texture by overcooking or overheating.) The sauce is ready to serve.

5. Fire up the grill.

(recipe continues)

6. Remove the veal from the marinade and grill it evenly all over. When it is about three-quarters cooked, place the smoked lobster tails on the grill. Complete grilling the veal and lobster, then remove to a cutting board.

7. Spoon the mango compote evenly on four warm plates. Slice the veal and lobster into even pieces and arrange them alternately over the compote. Serve with nests of pasta tossed in Herb Butter (page 236).

Note: I like to heat a quart of Spanish vinegar and add 8 to 10 chipotle chiles to the vinegar. When chiles are quite warm, I pour the liquid through a funnel back into the original vinegar bottle and store for uses such as this. I would use the chipotle-infused vinegar here instead of Spanish vinegar alone, because chipotles are dried-smoked jalapeños, and their smoky character reiterates the flavor of the smoke in the lobster. (See pages 221–22 for a broader discussion of this idea.)

This rich, luxurious dish demands a very special wine. I would choose the best White Burgundy or full-bodied California Chardonnay your budget will allow.

VEGETABLES

The amazing and oft-quoted Mae West once said, "I never worry about diets. The only carrots that interest me are the number you get in a diamond." While I share Madame West's love of wit, I don't share what seems to be her lack of enthusiasm for vegetables. But I am not including a long chapter on the subject, since the vegetables that accompany many of my dishes are intrinsic to the recipes themselves. A rabbit fricassee, for instance, has a host of root vegetables; Florida stone crab and lobster comes with acorn squash and so on. Here I offer a few of my dishes that stand on their own as vegetable dishes, or as accompaniments to other combinations you may wish to create.

Ratatouille, My Way

I love the combination of flavors in ratatouille. With some slight variations, this basic vegetable sauce can be used on a number of things. It can be placed in a crock, topped with cheese, and baked; it can be served as the sauce for a rustic pizza; it can be slightly puréed and added to cream for a sauce to be enjoyed with a grilled marinated veal chop. Of course, it is also lively by itself as a nice vegetarian dish.

In this method, I combine both old and new cooking styles. We need the rich flavors of long cooking that nouvelle cuisine too often forgets, but we employ a step that allows us to enjoy the modern appreciation for vegetables with more texture than in la cuisine ancienne.

It is best to have all of your vegetables prepped and ready to go: This preparation is simple but time-consuming, and the succession in which you cook the vegetables is vital for consistency and flavor.

Serves 10 to 12

TOMATO SAUCE

½ pound (2 sticks) butter

3 large Spanish onions, peeled and sliced medium-thick

8 raw garlic cloves or 12 Roast Garlic cloves (page 200), if available

3 bay leaves

½ to ¾ cup sugar

15 tomatoes, peeled and seeded, chopped

¾ cup herbes de Provence vinegar or red wine vinegar (see Note)

1 large bunch basil leaves, chopped

1 cup pure tomato juice

Cracked black pepper, to taste

Olive oil

Butter

¼ bulb fennel, core removed and thinly sliced

1 sweet red pepper, stem, ribs, and seeds removed, cut into medium julienne

1 sweet yellow pepper, stem, ribs, and seeds removed, cut into medium julienne

1 sweet green pepper, stem, ribs, and seeds removed, cut into medium julienne

1 poblano pepper, stem, ribs, and seeds removed, cut into medium julienne (optional)

3 medium-large zucchini, cut into medium julienne

2 medium eggplants, cut into medium julienne

Salt and pepper to taste

1. Make the sauce: Heat a large saucepan and add the butter, then the onions. Cook, stirring occasionally—your goal is to brown the onions. This caramelizes them and brings out their sweetness. When they begin to color and stick to the pan slightly, add the garlic, bay leaves, and sugar. Cook a moment, stirring. Add the tomatoes, vinegar, basil, and tomato juice. Stirring often, reduce the liquid by half.

2. Season sauce with freshly cracked black pepper. Lower heat and simmer on a low flame, stirring occasionally, while you go on to the vegetables.

3. Set up a large colander over a large bowl near your stove. Heat a large sauté pan. Add equal parts of olive oil and butter (how much butter and oil depends on how large your pan is—you want enough fat in the pan to cook your vegetables without making them greasy).

4. Cook the vegetables in batches according to their type. Do not mix them in the same pan because they require different periods of cooking time. Sauté the vegetables over high heat, seasoning them slightly with salt and liberally with pepper, only until they are just cooked. As you finish one batch, put the vegetables in the colander; the excess oil and juices will fall into the bowl. You will note that the eggplant will absorb much more butter and oil than the other vegetables. That's okay, they'll taste better. Add the fat as you see that the vegetables require it.

5. When the vegetables are all in the colander, stir them a little to rid them of any trapped excess oil and then add all the vegetables to the tomato sauce. Cook the vegetables and tomato sauce together over moderate heat for 10 to 15 minutes. (Discard the oil and vegetable drippings in the bowl, but then set the colander back up over the empty bowl.)

6. Now pour the vegetable and tomato mixture into the colander and stir it to release the juices.

7. Put the collected juices in a clean, heavy saucepan large enough to accommodate them. Heat this liquid until it becomes thick and intensely flavored. Its thickness will be about midway between a tomato sauce and tomato paste. Be careful not to burn it.

(recipe continues)

8. Put the vegetables into a dish large enough to hold them. Pour the reduced cooking liquid over the vegetables and mix gently. The ratatouille can be served immediately or refrigerated for later service.

Note: The herbs de Provence vinegar is worth looking for. The added herbal fragrance gives a very pleasing cleanness to the sauce.

GRILLED SUMMER VEGETABLE TERRINE
with Ratatouille Sauce

When summer moves across America, gardens are loaded with many varieties of the season's generous bounty. Often, the casual gardener is beset with the question of what to do with all those zucchinis, yellow squash, tomatoes, and eggplants. This recipe uses all of these vegetables in a rich, warming dish that can serve either as an accompaniment to another entrée or as an entrée itself.

The flavor of the grill adds an interesting note to this dish, but I have done it with very nice results by baking the vegetables in an oven, so do whichever suits you. It is served cold here, and partners nicely with slices of goat cheese dressed in a balsamic and extra virgin olive oil vinaigrette.

For a spicier version of this dish, I have puréed creole sauce as a substitute for the ratatouille. A fresh tomato sauce is fine, too.

One 6- by 8-inch terrine or casserole

1 zucchini, washed, peeled, and cut into planks ¼ inch thick	Sea salt to taste
	2 cups Ratatouille (page 188)
½ eggplant, washed, peeled, and cut into planks ¼ inch thick	Wine vinegar to taste
	A little butter to grease the terrine mold
1 yellow squash, washed, peeled, and cut into planks ¼ inch thick	1 cup freshly grated Parmesan
	1 cup fresh bread crumbs
Olive oil	2 tablespoons olive oil
Cracked black pepper to taste	

1. Liberally brush the raw vegetable slices with olive oil on both sides, and season.

2. Put the eggplant planks in a pan with holes or on a rack set over another pan. Weight

the eggplant and leave for 30 minutes. It will exude a bitter liquid; discard that.

3. Fire up the grill or heat the oven to 400 degrees.

4. Rinse the eggplant, pat it dry with paper towels, and reseason it.

5. When the fire is hot grill the vegetables on both sides. They should be relatively soft but not falling apart. Hold them in a large bowl or dish as you finish each batch.

6. When all the vegetables are grilled, allow them to rest, reserving any juices that may collect. (They can be added to your ratatouille sauce for flavor.)

7. Process the ratatouille in a processor until just barely chunky. Check it for flavor. Add salt, pepper, or wine vinegar as desired. The ratatouille should not be too wet; if it seems so, pour off some of the liquid.

8. Preheat oven to 350 degrees. Lightly butter a 6- by 8-inch terrine. Starting with eggplant and working in layers, alternate the sauce with layers of eggplant, zucchini, and yellow squash. Sprinkle grated Parmesan and bread crumbs on each layer before adding the next. Top the last layer with bread crumbs that have been moistened with olive oil and mixed with a bit more Parmesan.

9. Cover the dish with aluminum foil and bake about 40 minutes. Remove the foil. Towel off any excess liquid. Cool completely, overnight if possible.

10. Insert a knife around the outside of the mold and gently invert the terrine. Chill until ready to serve. Slice with an electric or serrated knife.

Braised fennel
with Prosciutto and Parmesan

It is hard to understand why fennel is not more widely consumed in our country. This vegetable, native to Italy, has a sweet, pungent, licorice-like flavor that is delicious—especially when it is as texturally delicate and smokily flavored as in this recipe. I like to serve this with a fairly subtle dish like poached breast of chicken.

Serves 4 to 8

8 *bulbs fennel, cut in half and cores removed (discard tops)*
3 *tablespoons lemon juice*
3 *tablespoons butter*
1 *quart Chicken Stock (page 240)*

½ *teaspoon freshly ground black pepper*
1 *quart heavy cream*
8 *thin slices prosciutto*
½ *cup grated Parmesan*

1. Preheat oven to 350 degrees. Prepare fennel and toss with lemon juice in a bowl. Then arrange the fennel in a well-buttered baking pan or casserole dish.

2. Bring the stock to a boil and pour it over the fennel. Crack pepper over the fennel and cover the pan with a piece of buttered parchment paper. Bake 1 hour or more, turning the bulbs or basting them from time to time.

3. When the fennel is very easily pierced with a knife, remove from the stock with a slotted spoon. Discard any outer leaves, and keep the fennel warm.

4. Strain the stock through a fine strainer. Measure 2 cups for the sauce and reserve the remainder for another use. Reduce the 2 cups stock until glazy. Add the heavy cream and reduce the mixture until it is thick enough to coat the back of a spoon.

5. Meanwhle, either grill, broil, or pan-fry the prosciutto until just cooked. Allow it to cool and then dice it.

6. Put the fennel in individual ovenproof serving dishes or one large attractive dish. Pour the stock and cream mixture evenly over the fennel. Sprinkle the Parmesan and prosciutto over the dish. Return it to the oven and brown briefly. Serve.

A SAVORY FLAN

This is a very adaptable dish. If you think of it as a molded omelet, it will be easier to imagine the different ingredients that you would enjoy with it. The only thing to remember is that if you add a wet ingredient like freshly cooked spinach, be sure to drain it before adding to the eggs or your proportions will be upset. This dish can withstand the serving conditions of a buffet, and it is so much nicer than ordinary scrambled eggs for your guests' bruncheon.

Serves 12

12 whole eggs	1 tablespoon butter
1 quart heavy cream	Salt and pepper to taste

OPTIONAL INGREDIENTS

- 2 cups blanched chopped spinach, well drained
- 2 cups cooked acorn squash
- 2 cups sautéed onions
- 2 cups sautéed mushrooms

- 1 cup chopped roasted garlic or peppers
- 1 cup grated cheese
- 1 cup assorted chopped fresh herbs
- 1 cup diced Westphalian ham

1. Preheat oven to 375 degrees. Put a folded towel in the bottom of a roasting pan larger than the flan pan, fill the pan less than half full of water, and put it in the oven to heat. In a stainless steel bowl, beat together eggs and cream.

2. Select a stainless steel pan about 4 inches deep and approximately 7 inches by 10 inches. Butter it lightly. Add your chosen ingredients to eggs. Salt and pepper to taste and stir gently.

3. Pour egg mixture into the prepared pan and cover with foil. Carefully lower flan pan into bain-marie (water should come halfway up the outside of the flan pan). Bake approximately 40 minutes. Remove foil. Brown for a minute and serve.

SWEET POTATO GRATIN

This is one of my most sought-after recipes. I have used it to accompany rack of lamb, Cajun rib steak, and other hearty meals. It is baked slowly for a long time, and will hold up nicely if you wish to include it in a buffet-style meal. The gratin can be assembled 12 hours before cooking.

Serves 8 to 12

- 1 small handful Roast Garlic (page 200), chopped
- 1 small bunch basil leaves, roughly chopped
- 3 jalapeño or poblano peppers, seeds and stems removed, thinly sliced
- 1 handful toasted pine nuts
- ½ small red onion, thinly sliced

- 6 egg yolks
- 1 quart heavy cream
- 5 sweet potatoes, peeled and very thinly sliced
- 5 Idaho potatoes, peeled and very thinly sliced

Salt and cracked black pepper to taste

1. Preheat oven to 350 degrees. On the bottom of a 6- by 9-inch baking or casserole dish, mix the garlic, basil, chiles, pine nuts, and red onion. (You can alternate this mixture between the potato layers, if you prefer.)

2. Beat the yolks and cream together.

3. Alternate layers of sweet and white potato and some of the egg and cream mix. Season as you go. Push down evenly with the palms and outstretched fingers of your hands to send the cream into the layers.

4. Cover with aluminum foil and bake for about 2½ hours. Remove the foil and brown for a few minutes before serving.

CORN CAKES

These cakes can be the starch accompanying a grilled steak or as the partner to my fricassee of rabbit.

Makes approximately 36 cakes

¾ cup sifted flour	2 cups heavy cream
¾ cup cornmeal	3 tablespoons chopped fresh herbs (basil, oregano, parsley, thyme, chives, or any combination of them)
2 egg yolks	
2 eggs	
2 cups corn kernels, from freshly shucked corn	7 tablespoons melted butter
	Salt and pepper to taste
	Peanut oil, for cooking

1. Place the flour and cornmeal in a bowl.

2. In another bowl beat together the egg yolks and eggs.

3. Process the corn kernels in a processor with half of the cream and add them to the egg mixture. Add the rest of the cream to the egg mixture. Add the chopped herbs.

4. Whisk the egg mixture into the cornmeal and flour. Whisk in the melted butter. Season to taste.

5. Heat a small amount of peanut oil in a skillet and cook each cake until crisp and lightly browned on each side. (Allow about 2 tablespoons [⅛ cup] of batter per cake.)

BLUE CORN CAKES

Makes approximately 24 cakes

¾ cup blue cornmeal	2 eggs, separated
⅓ cup all-purpose flour	3 tablespoons finely chopped chives
1 teaspoon baking powder	1 cup milk
Salt and pepper to taste	2 tablespoons melted butter
½ teaspoon sugar	Clarified butter or peanut oil for frying cakes

1. Blend together the cornmeal, flour, baking powder, salt, pepper, and sugar in a large bowl.

2. Put the egg yolks and chives in another bowl and mix. Add the milk, stirring. Stir this into the cornmeal mixture and add the melted butter.

3. Beat the egg whites until stiff and gently fold them into the cornmeal mixture. Refrigerate until required.

4. When ready to cook, heat clarified butter or peanut oil in a skillet and when it is fairly hot, add 2 tablespoons (⅛ cup) of batter per cake. Fry until crisp on both sides.

SCALLION PANCAKES

These little cakes are best cooked in a moderate amount of oil or clarified butter. Other vegetables can be added or substituted for the scallions and/or ginger; corn and herbs work well. You do have to be aware of the liquid nature of the vegetables you choose so you don't dilute the batter.

Makes 1 quart batter,
enough for 24 to 28 cakes,
depending on their size

4 whole eggs	½ pound (2 sticks) butter
4 egg yolks	1 large bunch scallions, chopped
4 cups milk	A 2-inch piece of fresh gingerroot, peeled and minced
4 teaspoons salt	½ cup peanut oil or clarified butter
1 pinch cracked black pepper	
3 cups all-purpose flour	

1. Combine in a large bowl the eggs, egg yolks, milk, salt, and pepper. Beat well.

2. Sift the flour into another bowl. Make a well in it and whisk in the egg mixture.

3. Heat a large skillet and add the butter. Stir it around allowing it to get foamy and slightly brown. Toss in the chopped scallions and sauté quickly. Add the ginger, stir, and remove from the heat. Mix the ginger, scallions, and butter into the batter.

4. To cook, heat a skillet until fairly hot. Add enough oil or clarified butter to just coat the bottom of the pan. Spoon in about 2 tablespoons (⅛ cup) of batter per cake and fry until golden on both sides.

LITTLE VEGETABLE PANCAKES

These are terrific with sour cream and caviar or as an accompaniment to an entrée.

Makes approximately
1½ quarts batter (48 pancakes)

1 pound cleaned and coarsely chopped vegetables of your choice, especially ones with good body (carrots, broccoli, parsnips)	6 eggs
	3 egg yolks
	2 tablespoons chopped basil or other herbs as desired
5 cups Chicken Stock (page 240), or substitute water with 1 tablespoon salt	¾ cup flour
	Salt and pepper to taste
	Peanut oil for frying

1. Cook the vegetables in the chicken stock until slightly overcooked. Set aside.

2. Strain off stock into a saucepan and reduce until glazy, about ½ cup. (This step is optional.)

3. Put the cooked vegetables (and glaze if you made it) into a food processor and process entirely.

4. In a large bowl beat the eggs and yolks together. Add herbs. Whisk in the flour and the vegetable mixture. The mixture should be somewhat thick. (You will be able to judge this by pan-frying.) Season to taste.

5. Get a skillet hot. Add enough peanut oil to just coat the bottom of the pan and add the batter in 2-tablespoon (⅛-cup) portions. Fry until golden and crisp on both sides.

LARDER

I have vivid recollections of the lushness of summer in the lake country of Illinois—My childhood in the 1950s, replete with sights and smells, food and gardens. I remember Sundays and the church women, with their strong bodies and hearty laughter, bringing their cookies, cakes, and pies to the "congregation" hour in the basement of our Methodist Church after the Reverend Fletcher gave his sermon. After that my family and I would go to Grandpa Ray's house on Ray's Lane, and my mother would talk and listen to him while he loaded up our car with enough corn, tomatoes, peas, beans, carrots, and strawberries for a week from his incredible garden. My sisters always knew they could find me hiding up in his apple trees eating the tart, small, red apples the horse couldn't reach, or on rainy days in his huge handbuilt old barnlike house staring at the collection of stuffed animals he had shot on his property over the past fifty or sixty years. Predators once, trophies now.

I remember little of my mother's cooking, for she went out to support us when I was just ten and our grandmother, "Nana," took over the preparation of meals. But I *can* vividly recall canning and jelly-making times with my mother. I think her almost messianic zeal for it must have been born during the Second World War, when it seemed everyone had a victory garden.

In the next few pages we will discuss some foods for your larder. If you put in a little time and effort on a rainy day, or while waiting for the telephone repairman, you will be vastly rewarded. Whether entertaining friends or merely grabbing a bite for yourself, there is a resource here that can take you from something ordinary like cheese and crackers to something extraordinary like duck sausage with jalapeño pepper jelly in a warm tortilla. With the jelly and the sausage done weeks ahead of time, what could be simpler?

Roast garlic

When garlic is prepared this way, it is subtle, haunting, and lovely to look at tucked into a lamb stew or festooned around a crisply roasted squab. You can roast as much—or as little—as your heart desires. Being a garlic lover, I roast a lot. Many of my recipes call for roast garlic. You don't have to use it; you can use raw garlic, but remember that raw garlic is two to four times stronger in flavor. I also find many uses for the garlic-infused oil that is a by-product of this recipe—I use it to sauté everything from lamb to green beans.

12 to 16 heads fresh garlic	*2 to 3 tablespoons fresh thyme and rosemary*
Good quality olive oil to cover	*1 bay leaf*
	12 black peppercorns

1. Preheat the oven to 300 degrees. Cut off the tips of the garlic heads and peel off the papery outer skin.

2. Arrange the heads, root side down, in a pan just large enough to hold them, fitting them snugly side by side. Pour the oil over the garlic and scatter the herbs into the oil. Add bay leaf and peppercorns.

3. Cover the pan with aluminum foil and bake 30 minutes. Take the foil off, baste the heads and replace the foil. Lower the temperature to 275 degrees and bake 30 minutes more. Remove the pan from the oven and take off the foil.

4. With a pair of tongs, take the heads out of the oil and put in a bowl or pan to cool. Strain off the olive oil and reserve for other uses.

5. Gently squeeze out the cloves of garlic and reserve for intended use. They can be refrigerated for up to a week.

Note: The cooking time can vary so check on the garlic from time to time as it cooks. The consistency should be such that each clove is easily pierced with a thin knife and not falling apart or soft. But if any overcook and get mushy, you can use them for other things, like a roasted garlic butter.

PRESERVED LEMONS

The preserved lemon is a startling taste experience to the uninitiated. There are interesting uses for them in Moroccan dishes (see Paula Wolfert's Mediterranean Cooking*), but I've recently begun to use them myself for more Western styles of food such as my chicken with "salt and pepper."*

6 lemons, scrubbed, patted dry, and each cut lengthwise into 6 wedges	1 cup freshly squeezed lemon juice
1 cup kosher salt	6 tablespoons virgin olive oil

1. Toss the lemons and salt together in a large bowl.

2. Transfer them to a mason jar. Pour the lemon juice over the cut lemons and salt and add the olive oil. Cover tightly with the jar lid.

3. Let the jar stand in a warm place for at least a week, shaking it once every day. The lemons will keep at room temperature over a month.

Note: Before using the lemons, wash them to eliminate the excess salt. Remember, too, that you will be using only the rinds.

Pickled Okra

I often use this to garnish gumbo.

2	pounds okra, in excellent shape, rinsed and patted dry	2	tablespoons dill seeds
12	dried chiles (cayenne, pequin, or the like)	1	quart cider vinegar
6	garlic cloves, halved	1	quart rice wine vinegar
2	tablespoons mustard seeds	1	quart water
		24	whole black peppercorns

1. Boil the canning jars and lids as described in canning manufacturer's directions.

2. Combine the okra, chiles, garlic cloves, and mustard seeds and divide evenly into the hot canning jars.

3. Boil the dill seeds, vinegars, water, and peppercorns in a saucepan and add to the jars.

4. Put the caps on and process according to approved canning procedures.

Pickled Ginger

Pickled ginger has a fresh, cleansing tartness. You can thinly slice the pickled root into "chips" to accompany sushi, or you can mince the ginger, fold it into soft butter, and serve it with grilled chicken or fish. Also, it can be minced and put into a vinaigrette for an oriental-style salad dressing.

½	pound fresh gingerroot, peeled	½	cup water
2	teaspoons salt	¾	cup sugar
1	cup rice wine vinegar		

1. Rub the ginger with salt and allow to drain for 2 hours. Then rinse thoroughly and place in a sterilized jar.

2. Heat vinegar, water, and sugar to a boil and stir until sugar dissolves. Pour this over the ginger, cover, let cool, and refrigerate.

Note: This is not a long-term pickle; use it within a month.

MANGO CHUTNEY

Despite what you may have heard, there is no mystery to the preparation of chutney. This recipe is very easy to make and is so much better than the store-bought variety. Yes, there are a large number of ingredients, but I'll bet you have many of these spices taking up space in your cabinet right now. This chutney tastes best if stored for one month prior to using, but it can be enjoyed sooner.

Makes 4 to 6 quarts

6 mangoes, peeled and cut into strips
1 quart apple cider vinegar
2 cups granulated sugar
2 cups dark brown sugar
2 cups chopped onion
6 cloves garlic, minced
4 teaspoons cracked black pepper
½ teaspoon salt
4 teaspoons cayenne

1 tablespoon cinnamon
1 tablespoon minced fresh gingerroot
½ teaspoon ground cloves
2 teaspoons ground allspice
2 teaspoons ground mustard seeds
1 cup raisins
1 cup currants
3 pounds Granny Smith apples, peeled, cored and chopped

1. Combine all ingredients in a large bowl and store overnight in the refrigerator.

2. The next day, put the mixture in a large heavy pan. Bring it to a boil, reduce heat, and simmer 30 minutes, or until syrupy.

3. Spoon into sterilized jars. Cover and process as per canning instructions. Cool.

APPLE CHUTNEY

Makes 1 gallon

1½ tablespoons ground ginger
¼ teaspoon ground cloves
¼ teaspoon ground allspice
½ tablespoon ground nutmeg
2 bay leaves
3 sweet bell peppers (1 green, 1 red, and 1 yellow, if possible), chopped
Juice of 4 lemons

3 cups raspberry vinegar
1½ cups Pepper Jelly (page 205) or other tart jelly
1½ cups sugar
1½ cups Michigan dried tart cherries, or raisins
18 Granny Smith apples, peeled, cored, and chopped

1. Tie the spices in cheesecloth and place this "bag" in a large bowl. Add the chopped peppers.

2. Briefly heat the lemon juice, vinegar, jelly, sugar, and cherries or raisins. Pour the heated mixture over the spice bag and peppers and allow to steep while you prepare the apples.

3. Add the chopped apples to the bowl and mix briefly with a wooden spoon. Refrigerate the entire mixture overnight.

4. The next day, put the mixture into a heavy saucepan and gently heat and simmer until thick, approximately 30 minutes. Allow to cool.

5. Remove spice bag and process chutney in preserving jars according to canning instructions.

Pepper Jelly

You will find that this sweet and fiery condiment can accompany many things once you begin to experiment with it.

Makes 1 quart

Enough red peppers, stemmed, seeded, and ground or processed to equal 2 cups
Enough jalapeños, stemmed, seeded, and ground or processed to equal ¼ cup or more, to taste

6½ cups sugar
1½ cups apple cider vinegar
A 6-ounce bottle liquid fruit pectin

1. In a heavy saucepan, bring the prepared peppers and jalapeños to a boil with the sugar and cider vinegar. Allow to simmer about 5 minutes and then remove from the heat and stir occasionally for 20 minutes.

2. Now return the mixture to heat and boil it hard for 2 minutes. Remove from the heat and quickly stir in the pectin. Skim as necessary.

3. You can follow a safe canning procedure as recommended by the manufacturer and store in a cool dry place for a standard period of time; or pour the jelly into sterile jars and cool, then refrigerate and use within 3 weeks.

Lemon Mustard

Makes 1 cup

1 tablespoon virgin olive oil
2 shallots, peeled and finely diced

1 bay leaf, crumbled
¾ cup freshly squeezed lemon juice
½ cup Dijon mustard

1. Heat a small saucepan. Add the olive oil and warm it.

2. Add the shallots and allow them to soften. Then add the bay leaf and lemon juice and cook until the liquid is reduced by three-fourths.

3. Strain this liquid into the mustard, and whisk together. Reserve until needed.

BASIC ALL-PURPOSE FLOUR PASTA

The ratio of egg to flour for pasta is the simplest of ratios to remember, one to one. A good pinch of salt and a few drops of olive oil complete the ingredients.

Makes approximately
14 to 16 ounces of pasta,
or enough for 24 ravioli

2 extra-large eggs	1 tablespoon virgin olive oil
1 teaspoon salt	2 cups all-purpose flour

1. Beat the eggs, salt, and olive oil together in a bowl.

2. Mound the flour on a work surface and make a small well in the center. Pour in the egg mixture.

3. Working with a fork, begin pulling the flour into the egg mixture. After a few minutes, complete mixing the dough with your hands until you can form a compact ball of dough. Wrap the ball in plastic wrap and refrigerate for at least ½ hour.

4. Roll out dough as described for Semolina Pasta (page 208).

SEMOLINA PASTA

When I decided it was time to teach myself how to make pasta, I went to my oldest ally in cookbook resource material, the late James Beard. Much in the way Alice Waters recalls going from recipe to recipe in Elizabeth David's books to teach herself cuisine, there was a period of time in my life that James Beard's work offered me similar guidance. His work still aids me, and although I never met the gentleman, he helped change my life.

This recipe, the one used at our restaurant, is basically his, but there are many variations available to the cook. Do remember that too much liquid in an additional ingredient can create difficulties in rolling your dough. Make it stiff. (The fraisage technique described below is a great pectoral workout!) The preceding recipe for all-purpose flour pasta is simpler to make, but semolina flour has a distinctive texture that I find attractive—it is firm and less likely to soften from overcooking.

Makes 1 pound

≈≈≈≈≈≈≈≈

4 cups semolina flour
3 whole eggs
6 egg yolks

1 teaspoon salt
2 tablespoons water (less if you use "wet" additions)

1. Mound the flour in the middle of your work table. Make a well in the center of the mound.

2. In a large bowl beat together eggs, yolks, salt, water, and any additional ingredients (e.g., saffron, herbs, minced chiles, poppy seeds, puréed cooked vegetables, and so on).

3. Pour egg mixture into the well and whisk flour from the interior of the ring of flour into the eggs. When this is no longer practical use your fingers to mix the dough. Use strength and bear down with the heels of your hands.

4. Do your best to form the dough into a ball. Wrap with plastic film and refrigerate at least 45 minutes, or overnight.

5. Now for the fraisage method. Work on a surface lightly dusted with semolina. Pull off a piece of the dough about the size of a walnut. Take another piece the same size and work them together, pressing them along the floured surface with the heels of your hands. Continue to do this until you have worked the whole ball. The pasta is now ready to be rolled and cut.

WORKING, ROLLING, AND CUTTING PASTA

I use a hand-cranked rolling machine. Mine is larger than the average household variety, but the technique is the same. Follow the manufacturer's instructions if there are any, but if not, here are some pointers:

• Pasta dough loves to be worked. I've taken the most seemingly incohesive mass of dough and worked it into smooth, compact, shimmering sheets of pasta by just rolling and rerolling it over and over again. It may need more flour, but eventually it will work.

• Begin by cutting the ball of dough with a knife into 4 manageable sections. While you work with one, cover the others with a clean, dry towel. Rub some flour on your hands and sprinkle some on the machine and the table the machine is clamped to. Now, form the dough into a rectangle with a rolling pin. (I've used a wine bottle in a pinch.) Set the machine for the widest setting and begin rolling the dough. You may need to sprinkle on more flour if the dough seems wet. It is a textural consistency that you are looking for. As you make the pasta thinner by turning the knob to tighter settings, you will soon be able to hold the ribbon of pasta up to the light and see the shadow of your hand through it.

(recipe continues)

• Hang the uncut sheets of pasta over a broomstick balanced on 2 chairs, or something similar. The sheets must not be too long or their own weight will cause them to rip and fall to the floor. Allow them to dry *a little;* it will help the cutting process.

If you are planning to make ravioli or a similar filled pasta, your dough would now be ready for doing so. It is important to remember that you should have your filling already prepared, and that it not be too wet or too texturally rough. It is also wise not to make too much dough ahead of time or you will be racing to fill the pasta before it dries out.

There are a number of possible shapes and methods to consider for ravioli or other filled pastas, but for the sake of simplicity I'll discuss a square one. Cut the pasta into sections ("ribbons") approximately 24 inches long and 4 inches wide, and place on a lightly floured work table. Place small mounds of filling (approximately one teaspoon per mound) across the lower half of the ribbon, leaving about 2 inches between mounds. Beat together in a small bowl one egg and one tablespoon of water; take a small brush and lightly brush this egg wash between the mounds of filling and around the edges of the ribbon. Now fold the top half of the ribbon over the lower half that holds the filling (figure 1 below).

With gentle pressure, seal the pasta, taking care to push out any air pockets that might form. Your pasta will now resemble small pillows. Cut the ravioli with a pasta cutter or a knife along the two outside edges and the bottom length of the ribbon (figure 2). Then cut between the fillings to form the individual ravioli (figure 3).

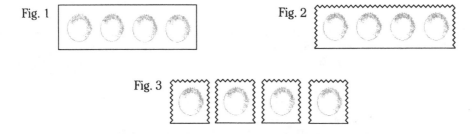

Place the prepared ravioli on a lightly floured pan or plate and cover with plastic wrap. These ravioli can be refrigerated for a few hours before cooking or carefully wrapped and frozen for later use.

• Your machine comes with a few cutting attachments. Choose the shape you want and attach it to the machine. Sprinkle some flour on the cutter and roll it a few times without any dough in it. Take up a sheet of the dough and position yourself almost facing the cutting blades. Hold the pasta with the side of your hand along an outstretched forefinger. Feed the dough into the cutters and turn the rolling crank. When you have fed about half the dough through, drop the uncut portion behind the machine and pick up the cut dough emerging from the machine. Lift it up slightly as you finish cutting. You will have a section of cut noodles. Spread them back over the broom handle to dry slightly and continue working in this manner until you have finished all the dough.

• Lift up a portion of the noodles, wrap them in a loose, circular nest around your first 2 or 3 fingers, and lay them on a flour-dusted baking sheet. They are ready to be cooked.

• I believe in cooking pasta to order. The cook who would precook and chill pasta would precook and chill rice. You've worked so hard to create this wonderful pasta, why diminish your own efforts by precooking (or overcooking) it?

• When you are ready to cook your pasta, bring a large pot of water to boil. When it is boiling rapidly, add a little salt and then stir in the pasta with a wooden spoon. Swirl it once and allow the water to return to a boil. For fresh pasta, begin testing the strands for doneness after 30 seconds. Fresh pasta can cook amazingly fast in comparison with the dried commercial pasta that you may be used to cooking. Drain thoroughly and, if it is not going into some other type of sauce, twirl in a little butter to prevent it from sticking together.

• Any fresh pasta you will not be cooking immediately can be stored in an airtight container for a few days after the nests have dried thoroughly.

CRACKED BLACK PEPPER BRIOCHE

This bread is best made over the course of two days. It is delicious with sweet butter.

Makes 2 loaves

4 *packages yeast*	3¾ *cups flour*
¼ *cup sugar*	5 *eggs, at room temperature*
1¾ *teaspoons salt*	1 *pound butter, at room temperature*
6 *tablespoons lukewarm water*	1½ *tablespoons coarsely ground black pepper, preferably freshly ground*

1. Measure yeast, sugar, and salt into mixer bowl. Add water. Mix briefly, on low speed, using the paddle. Allow to sit for 15 minutes.

2. Add the flour all at once and mix on low speed.

(recipe continues)

3. Add one egg on low speed and mix thoroughly.

4. Switch to medium speed and continue adding eggs, one at a time. Be sure each egg is completely incorporated before adding another. Scrape down sides of bowl as necessary.

5. Add the butter, approximately 1 tablespoon at a time. When all the butter has been incorporated, continue beating 1 minute longer. Add the black pepper and mix thoroughly.

6. Scrape the dough into a bowl, cover with plastic wrap, and allow to rise until doubled in bulk, about 1½ hours. (Do not place the bowl in too warm a spot or the butter will separate from the dough.)

7. When dough has doubled, punch down, cover with plastic wrap, and refrigerate for at least 6 hours, or overnight.

8. The next day, punch the dough down and divide it in half. Butter two standard loaf pans. On a lightly floured surface, shape the dough into two 9- by 4-inch rectangles. Starting at a long side, roll each rectangle tightly and place seam side down in the pans. Allow to rise until doubled, from 1 to 2 hours. Preheat oven to 375 degrees.

9. Bake for 40 to 45 minutes, or until well browned and hollow-sounding when tapped. Remove the brioche from the pans and cool on wire racks. Cool completely before slicing.

Cornbread

This is an adaptation of one of James Beard's recipes.

Makes one 9- by 12-inch loaf

1 cup flour	2 cups milk
3 cups yellow cornmeal	½ cup heavy cream
2 teaspoons salt	½ cup melted butter
2 teaspoons sugar	2 cups corn kernels, cut from freshly
2 tablespoons baking powder	shucked ears
6 eggs, well beaten	

1. Preheat oven to 400 degrees. Butter a 9- by 12-inch baking pan.

2. Sift the dry ingredients into a large bowl and stir.

3. In another bowl, beat the eggs, milk, cream, and corn kernels to mix.

4. Stir the egg mixture into the flour mixture with a *wooden spoon.* Stir in the melted butter.

5. Pour batter into the prepared pan and bake for approximately 30 to 35 minutes.

CRÈME FRAÎCHE

This basic cream is a bit more sour than, say, whipped cream. It can be part of sweet or savory preparations. It can cut some of the intense sweetness from certain desserts, and is great with fresh berries.

> 1 cup heavy cream
> 1 teaspoon buttermilk

1. Stir the buttermilk into the cream. Cover with plastic wrap.

2. Leave at room temperature 12 to 24 hours, depending on your climate. The cream should be fairly thick. Then refrigerate. It will thicken more, to the consistency of sour cream, when refrigerated.

HOMEMADE RICOTTA

The simplicity of making your own ricotta is stunning! You'll feel the wonderful glow of accomplishment that comes when you do something you had always thought was too difficult.

> 1 gallon whole milk
> 1 quart buttermilk

1. Heat the milk and buttermilk in a large saucepan somewhat slowly until it reaches a temperature of 180 degrees F. (An instant-read thermometer is very helpful.)

2. Remove the pan from the heat and set it aside to allow curds to form, approximately half an hour.

3. Set up a strainer over a large bowl and line the strainer with damp cheesecloth. You will need a very broad section of cheesecloth.

(recipe continues)

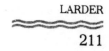

4. Pour the milk and buttermilk mixture through the cheesecloth, and allow it to settle a few minutes.

5. Now, carefully gather up the ends of the cheesecloth and tie them together with a string. Tie that onto the sink's faucet and allow to hang until the liquid drips out. It will take an hour or more. Cut open the bag over a clean bowl and you have fresh ricotta.

Note: You can infuse the ricotta with various flavors as you make it. For instance, saffron, freshly snipped chives, or tarragon can be added to the milk and buttermilk as they are cooking. You could use orange zest, chiles, or garlic, as well.

Hot Chile Oil

- 1 quart virgin olive oil
- 3 ounces dried red chiles, finely chopped or processed

1. Put the oil and chiles in a heavy saucepan and slowly heat to a simmer. Cook 5 minutes and turn off heat. Allow oil to stand until cool.

2. Pour oil into a container. Do not strain off the chopped chiles. Store in the refrigerator until ready to use.

Curry Powder

Makes approximately 1½ cups

- 5 tablespoons hot chile powder
- ½ teaspoon freshly ground black pepper
- ½ teaspoon ground ginger
- ½ teaspoon mustard seeds, toasted briefly in a dry skillet, and then ground
- ½ teaspoon fenugreek
- ½ teaspoon cardamom
- A 2-inch piece cinnamon stick, ground
- 3 tablespoons turmeric
- ¼ cup cumin
- ¼ cup coriander seeds, toasted briefly in a dry skillet, and then ground

Combine all of the above ingredients in a mixing bowl and store in an airtight container in a cool, dry place.

Note: I advise that you buy an electric spice mill or electric coffee mill and grind your own seeds. Keep them in small amounts and use them within 2 months, or start fresh.

Herb-Cured Salmon

This is an extremely adaptable method of preparing salmon. For instance, the fish can be sliced on an extreme bias off the skin; you could fold a few slices of the salmon into freshly cooked crêpes. Or you could grill the salmon briefly and serve it with a compound mustard butter. Then again, pasta tossed with cured salmon and some reduced cream is always nice. The choices are endless.

¼ cup extra virgin olive oil
A 6- to 9-pound salmon, skin on, head removed and flesh taken off the bone (you will have 2 fillets)
1 cup herbs (dill, thyme, basil, or cilantro, or any combination of these)

½ cup salt
½ cup black peppercorns, toasted in a dry skillet
1 cup sugar

1. Drizzle the olive oil all over the flesh of the salmon.

2. Roughly chop the herbs and scatter half of them over the flesh. Now, *pack* the flesh with a mixture of salt, peppercorns, and sugar. Top the fillet with the remaining herbs. Then match the two sides together and stack one side on top of the other.

3. Carefully lift the salmon into a glass or ceramic dish large enough to hold it without bending it. (It is okay to slice the fish crosswise into equal sections prior to curing it.) Now put another pan on top of the fish and try to weight it evenly. (A few cans or a skillet will work; it doesn't need to be very heavy. You want just enough pressure to help push out the liquid.)

4. Refrigerate the fish overnight. Turn it over in the morning and reweight it.

5. In the afternoon of the second day, check your fish. It should be getting firm. If it is not quite firm, put it back in the refrigerator for the second night.

(recipe continues)

6. By the next morning the fish will be ready. Remove it from the refrigerator, carefully wipe off the cure, and discard the residue.

7. Cut a small piece of the fish. If it tastes too salty, rinse the fish with cool water to remove any remaining salt. Pat dry and lay both sides skin side down. Drizzle a bit more olive oil and fresh herbs over the fish and refrigerate until ready to use.

Tasso

As the king of creole cookery, Paul Prudhomme, tells us, tasso is a highly seasoned Cajun ham. You can purchase tasso through his company, which I did until my good friend, professional chef Tom Trieschmann, offered me his method for making our own. It is wonderful and nitrate-free, important for anyone concerned about health. (It is more perishable this way, but it is so good you will use it up before you have to worry about it!) Tasso can be used anytime you would normally want smoky ham in a dish. Try it instead of Canadian bacon for eggs Benedict, or in a salad with black-eyed peas and a mint vinaigrette.

BRINE SOLUTION

3	quarts cold water
1½	cups kosher salt
6	tablespoons sugar

A 5-pound piece boneless pork butt, also known as a Boston butt
3 plus tablespoons kosher salt
3½ tablespoons sugar
¾ cup cracked black pepper

6 plus tablespoons ground white pepper
7 tablespoons cayenne
9 tablespoons medium-finely chopped Roast Garlic cloves (page 200)
7 tablespoons chopped chives

1. Prepare the brine solution and submerge the pork in it, weighting it as needed, for 2 full days in the refrigerator.

2. Remove the pork from the brine and pat dry.

3. Mix together all the remaining ingredients except garlic and chives.

4. Rub garlic all over the pork. Then rub it with the spice mix and chopped chives. Cover pork and refrigerate for 3 full days.

5. Build a fire in a smoker, or use your grill as a smoker (see manufacturer's instructions), and smoke the meat slowly. (We use hickory and fruitwood for hams.) The internal

temperature must reach 150 degrees; if you can't get it that high, put the pork in a 175-degree oven until it reaches the correct temperature.

6. Store the tasso in the refrigerator. It should be used within 10 days.

CHORIZO SAUSAGE

This is a lusty, zesty hot sausage that can be enjoyed with a simple cheese, a loaf of crusty bread, and a bottle of zinfandel, or in any number of more complex preparations. (Chorizo can be frozen if you choose to make it in a large batch like this. If not, cut the recipe in half.)

Makes 10 pounds, cooked weight

10 pounds boneless pork shoulder	3 cups red wine (Spanish, if possible)
5 pounds unsalted skinless fatback	¼ cup finely chopped garlic
½ cup kosher salt	½ cup crushed red pepper
2 tablespoons freshly cracked black pepper	⅓ cup cayenne
1½ cups paprika	10 jalapeños, minced
2 tablespoons cumin powder	3 tablespoons oregano
2 tablespoons freshly ground coriander seed	2 tablespoons chili powder
2 tablespoons sugar	Peanut oil, for cooking the sausage

1. Cube pork and fat and combine with all the remaining ingredients. Cover and refrigerate overnight.

2. Coarsely grind through the meat grinder, twice. Stuff into casings. Refrigerate.

3. When you are ready to cook the sausage, I suggest that you preheat the oven to 325 degrees, cut a section of the sausage, and wind it in a circular shape in a heavy skillet. Add a small amount of peanut oil to the pan and put it on a burner. As it gets warm, pierce the casing with a small, thin knife every ½ inch or so. This will help to keep the sausage from bursting. After it browns on one side, carefully turn it with tongs to brown the other side. Then put the pan in the oven and bake about 10 minutes. The sausage should be firm to the touch and cooked through. If not, return to the oven and continue to cook until done. Remove and reserve for whatever you require.

LAMB SAUSAGE

Makes 4 to 5 pounds,
cooked weight

5 pounds coarsely ground lamb shoulder	1½ tablespoons chopped fresh rosemary
3½ pounds pork shoulder, cut into ½-inch pieces	1 tablespoon chopped fresh mint leaves
7 ounces lamb fat, all the fell (the papery outside) removed	3 ounces lamb glaze (optional)
4 pounds skinless unsalted fatback	2 cups Pinot Noir red wine
1½ tablespoons finely chopped garlic	1½ tablespoons kosher salt
3 tablespoons freshly cracked black pepper	1½ tablespoons chopped shallots
	2½ tablespoons Dijon mustard
	Casings as needed to contain sausage

1. Use the same basic method of sausage-making as for chorizo (page 215).

Note: You *can* prepare these as patties and fry.

DUCK SAUSAGE WITH PRUNES

When you begin something that becomes a major part of your life, whether it be cooking or acting or jogging, you are not always conscious that you are beginning. When was the first time you ever cooked? Or jogged? Who can remember? But occasionally something happens that does allow you to be aware of an intensity of experience, a jump to a higher level where everything is new again. I experienced such a jump when Gordon Sinclair hired me to operate Sinclair's, the restaurant he was opening in Lake Forest, Illinois, back in the summer of 1982. Gordon allowed me the freedom I had always wanted and my staff and I spent the next eighteen months in a state of near volcanic activity. I have included many ideas and recipes from that time in this book. Some have been sharpened or focused in different ways, but I'll always remember that kitchen, those cooks, and Gordon Sinclair. We made this duck sausage at Sinclair's, and served it with grilled breasts of duck and scallion pancakes.

〰〰〰〰

3 pounds duck meat from the legs, all bone, skin, and sinew removed (reserve breasts for another use)

2 or 3 pounds duck livers

2 pounds boneless pork shoulder

¼ pound unsalted fatback

1 tablespoon finely chopped garlic

1½ tablespoons finely ground black pepper

¾ tablespoon coriander seed

1 tablespoon chopped fresh sage

¼ cup duck glaze (optional)

1¼ cups applejack brandy

1½ tablespoons kosher salt

½ tablespoon freshly grated nutmeg

½ teaspoon cloves

1 tablespoon chopped shallots

1½ tablespoons Dijon mustard

½ pound diced prunes

Casings as needed, if you are making link sausage

1. Combine all the ingredients except the prunes in a large bowl. Refrigerate until very cold.

2. Now, coarsely grind the mixture through a meat grinder twice. Add the prunes and chill overnight.

3. The sausage may be formed into patties and fried or stuffed into casings for link sausage.

SAUCES, STOCKS, AND SALAD DRESSINGS

I'd like to try to help you understand a fundamental pattern that, I hope, will open up many possibilities for you. In other words, I want you to be able to grasp the power of creativity that working with food offers you. Many analogies can be made to convey this idea, but I am going to use paint, that is, paint as it relates to the blending of colors.

Food scholars and chefs speak about the "mother sauces," and in a way, it is the offspring of those sauces that I'm referring to here, but in terms of colors. There are really only seven colors in the rainbow. In school they taught us the mnemonic Roy G. Biv to remember red, orange, yellow, green, blue, indigo, and violet. Well, I have no mnemonic device to help you remember the foundational sauces, and in any case there may be several other basic sauces that could be included in this list, even though some of these are not true "mother sauces." But if you can think of them, you probably will have already absorbed my point.

I have chosen the following sauces because of their modern popularity: butter sauce, hollandaise, tomato sauce, vinaigrette, mayonnaise, cream sauce, and brown sauce. Think of each of them as the color *white*. Now if you think of any of these basic sauces as plain white paint and you wish to add, say, tomatoes, and you think of the tomatoes as red paint, you will be blending white and red. Any of the above sauces can be "tinted" with different flavors, or "paints." It is simple enough to learn these basic sauces and then alter them, expand them, and "paint" them into different colors, or flavors!

Now think flavor every time you read the word color. For instance, cream sauce becomes creole mustard cream sauce by the addition of a color (flavor), mustard. Brown sauce becomes Marsala brown sauce by the addition of a color (flavor), Marsala. Vinaigrette can become Mango-chile vinaigrette, mayonnaise can become basil mayonnaise, butter sauce can become a gazpacho butter sauce. Do you see the doors opening? Each sauce, each color, each flavor that you can play with?

A few scenarios to further illustrate my paint analogy can and should be considered. It is important to be able to distinguish between combinations that will work with a particular dish, and those that won't.

Often the shading or tinting of a basic sauce will work because it reiterates the basic premise of a dish. The Sauternes in the butter sauce with my sautéed Florida lobster recipe works because the sweetness of the Sauternes echoes the inherent sweetness of the lobster. It is tone on tone.

More often, however, I will call for a juxtaposition of flavors to offer a dramatic transition within a single dish by choosing a tint that will contrast with the main thematic taste of the entrée. The port mustard cream that I serve as a sauce with ginger ravioli with smoked capon and chutney is illustrative of an attempt to offer a broad spectrum of sensations for the palate. Heat, sweet, tart, smoke, and more collide and embrace as they connect with the tastebuds in that dish. A simple cream sauce could not offer these vibrant and challenging tangents.

But let's discuss some pitfalls to avoid. If you were to use a smoky plum tomato sauce (tomato sauce being the white paint and the smoke being the tint) with say, smoked salmon and smoked salmon butter, you would undoubtedly smoke your guests out of the dining room—a classic case of too much of a good thing.

Or, let's imagine a delicate pair of sweetbreads that have been poached in a carefully made court bouillon commingling herbs, mushrooms, root vegetables, and Champagne. The sweetbreads are cleaned, gently pressed compactly to insure a velvety texture, and readied for a sauce chosen by the chef. Unfortunately, he has elected to tint a harmless and otherwise useful mushroom-scented white butter sauce with a tropical fruit salsa, and, for good measure, a Thai-inspired peanut sauce. It's something akin to the gent who would wear a paisley tie with a striped shirt and checked pants. Third-degree overkill.

Like the laws of color or fashion, there are laws of flavor. Sometimes personal prejudices override the preferential bell curves of broad population, but unless you are cooking solely to suit yourself, I advise that your culinary choices bow to the wisdom of honest good taste. Your improvisation is still dinner to someone, so use balance and harmony. Think of the totality of the dish and of the meal. Everyone makes mistakes, but in cuisine we are sometimes literally required to eat them.

SALSA

This is salsa cruda, an uncooked sauce with a uniquely fresh taste. It provides spice, crunch, and color to a vast variety of foods.

Makes 4 cups

1 small red onion, peeled and finely chopped

1 jalapeño, stemmed, seeded, and finely chopped

1 banana pepper, stemmed, seeded, and finely chopped

½ cup roughly chopped cilantro leaves

1 teaspoon salt

1½ tablespoons virgin olive oil

3 tablespoons Spanish sherry wine vinegar

4 cups tomato concasse

1. Mix together all of the ingredients except the tomatoes.

2. Now, slowly add the tomatoes, being careful not to overmix them. They will become dull-colored and too soft if they are handled too much.

Note: Other versions of salsa can substitute serrano chiles or even the smoked, dried jalapeños known as chipotles for the jalapeño and banana chiles. Also, lime juice can replace the Spanish sherry wine vinegar, and Tabasco or cayenne can add more spice.

SALSA COLORADA

You may find other uses for this salsa, which is thinner in consistency than any other I make, but one of my favorites is on top of white bean soup. The sharp tang of this reddish purée adds a nice punch to the solid, meaty simplicity of the beans.

Makes 1½ cups

2 roasted red peppers, peeled and seeded
2 tomatoes, concassée
2 roasted jalapeños, peeled and seeded
2 large garlic cloves, minced
½ tablespoon salt
¼ cup toasted almonds (whole or blanched sliced)

1 hard-boiled egg yolk
3 tablespoons sherry wine vinegar
1 teaspoon cayenne
3 shallots, peeled and roughly chopped
½ cup olive oil

1. Put everything except the oil in a food processor and pulse evenly until almost puréed. Add the oil with the machine on. Taste and adjust as desired.

2. Refrigerate until ready to use.

PESTO

You can make pesto in a food processor or in a large mortar with a pestle. Either way, the steps are the same. The vinegar is optional, but I like its sweet pungency. It underscores the basil and adds counterpoint to the richness of the oil and nuts.

Makes approximately ¾ cup

2 cups fresh basil leaves
1 or 2 cloves garlic, peeled
¼ cup toasted pine nuts
¼ cup parsley, stems removed
¼ to ½ cup extra virgin olive oil

¼ teaspoon salt
¼ cup freshly grated Parmesan
½ tablespoon red wine vinegar or Spanish sherry vinegar (optional)

1. Pulverize the basil with the garlic and then the nuts. Add the parsley and slowly add the oil.

2. Work in the salt, Parmesan, and vinegar if you like. Taste and adjust to your liking.

Tapenade

Tapenade, though a Mediterranean dish by birth, fits Key West's Caribbean personality just as well—simple, direct, earthy. This recipe is Paula Wolfert's and is available in her excellent book Mediterranean Cooking. *There are other versions of tapenade, some with egg and some with California olives and salsa. Think of it as a somewhat salty, vibrant condiment. Smear it over a crouton, or enjoy it with a goat cheese tart adorned with roasted peppers.*

Makes 1¾ cups

1 cup black Mediterranean-type olives, pitted and roughly chopped
2 ounces anchovy fillets, drained and rinsed
1 teaspoon Dijon mustard

2 tablespoons capers, drained and rinsed
2 tablespoons lemon juice
Cracked black pepper to taste
2 tablespoons Cognac
¼ to ½ cup fruity olive oil

1. Blend everything but the oil in a food processor or chop fine with a knife, and then mix in the oil. Store in a cool place until ready to use.

SAUCE CREOLE

There are many excellent cooks in Louisiana—Alex Patout, Emeril Lagasse, and Dooky Chase to name a few. But these days creole cookery has become synonymous with Paul Prudhomme. His stature is awesome physically, and, more to the point, artistically. I refer to his work whenever I wish to touch the source of this unique regional style of preparing food.

For some fascinating sociological reason, the creole and Cajun styles of cooking remained singularly untainted during a period in history that saw widespread upheaval in almost every other part of our country. This was probably due, in part, to the somewhat daunting geography of the bayous, but on a deeper level, I think the purity of the cuisine can be attributed to the unity and kindred spirit of the refugees.

The people that fused Indian, American, and French cooking all came to that land as virtual outcasts from society. Through the eighteenth, nineteenth, and twentieth centuries, they have created an individual expression of cuisine as compelling as any known to any culture.

Thanks to the recent explosion in popularity of creole and Cajun cooking, we have come to know a great deal about the rich history of these strong-willed people. You should use this knowledge, and not limit your perception of this treasure trove of culinary wonder to drive-up establishments and late night television hucksters. Go to the sources, like Prudhomme, and then experiment with flavors and techniques, enlightened and instructed by the real thing.

Makes approximately 1½ quarts

½ cup duck fat or clarified butter	1 tablespoon sea salt
5 cups finely chopped onions	1 tablespoon white pepper
4 teaspoons sugar	2 teaspoons black pepper
3½ cups finely chopped celery	1 tablespoon Tabasco
3½ cups finely chopped carrots	¼ cup roughly chopped thyme leaves
1 cup finely chopped green pepper	1 tablespoon roughly chopped basil leaves
1 cup finely chopped red pepper	3 cups Fish Stock or Shellfish Stock (pages 244, 245)
1 cup finely chopped yellow pepper	
3 tablespoons butter	6 cups finely chopped tomato concasse
4 teaspoons minced garlic	2 cups tomato sauce
2 bay leaves	

1. Heat the fat or butter in a rondeau until hot. Add 2 cups of the chopped onion and cook over high heat until onion begins to brown and caramelize. Add sugar and allow to darken more, but do not burn.

2. Now add the remaining onion, celery, carrots, bell peppers, and butter. Continue to cook over high heat until peppers are almost tender.

3. Add the garlic, bay leaves, salt, and white and black pepper. Stir well. Add the Tabasco, herbs, and 1 cup of stock, and cook over medium heat about 5 minutes.

4. Add the tomato concasse and tomato sauce. Reduce heat and cook slowly 10 to 15 minutes, stirring occasionally. Now add the remaining stock and cook until sauce has thickened slightly, about 15 minutes. Cool until needed.

BASIC VINAIGRETTE

Makes approximately 1⅓ cups

⅕ to ⅓ cup vinegar
1 cup virgin olive oil
Cracked black pepper to taste

1. Whisk ingredients together until well combined.

JUNIPER-GIN VINAIGRETTE

I developed this recipe to serve with carpaccio of venison. The use of juniper with game meats is historic.

1 cup olive oil
1 cup salad oil
⅔ cup Cabernet Sauvignon vinegar
½ cup gin
10 to 12 juniper berries

3 bay leaves
Pinch of cayenne
Pinch of salt
3 or 4 cloves crushed garlic, in a sachet bag (see Note)

1. Mix all the ingredients together until well combined and serve with carpaccio.

Note: A sachet bag is simply a piece of cheesecloth in which you assemble ingredients whose flavor, but not presence, you want in a dish. You tie the cloth snugly and put it in the mixture, but remove it before serving.

Chardonnay-Hazelnut Vinaigrette

An easy but wonderful dressing—the ingredients are terrific. Try using it very simply with a bowl of different greens, or with cold poached salmon and finely cut vegetables.

2 cups hazelnut oil	1 tablespoon Dijon mustard
1 cup safflower oil	Sea salt and cracked black pepper to taste
1 cup Chardonnay vinegar	

1. Whisk all the ingredients together in a bowl and chill.

Sauce Mignonette

The fascinating writer and sportsman A. J. McClane is a world-class authority on many, if not all, matters relating to the creatures of the sea. I have a dog-eared collection of his work, which has answered many questions for me. In his volume The Encyclopedia of Fish Cookery, *he states that "there are ten species of oysters which enter the world's markets in volume, but only four are found along the shores of North America." You will hear many, many names for oysters, but there are only ten species—it is their* locality *that identifies them. McClane adds an important fact: "Northern oysters are at their best in the fall and winter months, while Gulf bivalves are firm and ripe from December onward."*

Spanking fresh oysters need no sauce, except for the spark of freshly squeezed lemon. But I confess that even if they are fresh, I like the option of doing a dozen with this sauce, anyway.

Makes 1 cup

½ cup Champagne vinegar	2 tablespoons sliced shallots
½ cup dry white wine	Cracked black pepper to taste

1. Mix all the ingredients in a bowl and serve in a small crock with oysters.

Warm Bacon Dressing

This is a simple vinaigrette that you can use on various salads. A spinach salad with the cooked bacon would obviously be a perfect choice. One visually stunning idea: Warm some of the vinaigrette in a sauté pan. Quickly warm some spinach and croutons in the same pan and mound the mixture on plates. Top with a freshly soft-cooked 5-minute egg, peeled and then gently slashed open. The yolk will run onto the greens, adding a rich, creamy texture to the dish.

Makes approximately 2 cups

½ pound slab bacon, rind removed, cut into ¼- by ½-inch dice	½ cup virgin olive oil
	½ cup red wine vinegar
Bacon fat from cooking the bacon	Salt and cracked black pepper to taste
½ cup salad oil, preferably safflower	1 tablespoon Dijon mustard

1. Heat the bacon, salad oil, and olive oil in a large sauté pan until bacon is just cooked.
2. Whisk in the vinegar, salt, cracked black pepper, and Dijon. Hold in a warm place.

Tamari-Sesame Dressing

Makes 1 cup

1 large clove garlic, finely minced
2 tablespoons chopped fresh basil leaves
½ teaspoon salt
¼ teaspoon freshly cracked black pepper
⅓ cup red wine vinegar
⅓ cup tamari, or soy sauce
⅓ cup sesame oil
1 tablespoon plus Hot Chili Oil (page 212)

1. Combine all the ingredients and refrigerate until needed.

Port Wine Vinaigrette

I developed this vinaigrette to accompany a salad composed of mixed lettuces, toasted walnuts, Stilton, and a wild mushroom terrine. The combination of the cheese, nuts, and port is classic. This salad can follow an entrée, as an interesting way to combine a cheese course with an after-dinner salad.

Makes 4 cups

1⅓ cups excellent red wine vinegar
1 cup virgin olive oil
2 cups extra virgin olive oil
1 cup port (nonvintage Sandeman)
Cracked black pepper to taste

1. Mix all together and keep chilled.

AIGRELETTE SAUCE

I scratched down the basis for this recipe years ago. (It seems to me that it came from the world-renowned chef Georges Blanc in Vonnas, but I could be wrong.) We've used this version for many different dishes. It's tangy and redolent of herbs, and I like it with asparagus, poached chicken, and grilled fish. The sauce can be kept for a couple of days in the refrigerator, like a mayonnaise.

Makes 3½ cups

4 egg yolks	¼ cup white wine vinegar
½ cup extra virgin olive oil	¾ cup assorted chopped fresh herbs
½ cup peanut oil	(different herbs relate to different foods,
½ cup olive oil	but basil, tarragon, thyme, cilantro,
2 tablespoons stock or water	and parsley all go with the foods I've
¼ cup dry white wine	mentioned)
¼ cup Dijon mustard	Sea salt (if desired)
¼ cup lemon juice	Black pepper

1. Whisk egg yolks in a stainless steel bowl. Beat in the oils, very slowly at first. When they thicken add the stock and white wine.

2. Now add the Dijon, lemon juice, and vinegar. Lastly, add the herbs, salt, and pepper. Taste and adjust. If sauce is too tart, you can add another egg yolk and a bit of oil.

BASIC HOMEMADE MAYONNAISE

A general note on egg-emulsified dressings: Even though you are commonly instructed to add the oil and then the water or other liquid, you will find that it is usually necessary to add a little of the liquid before all the oil is incorporated; otherwise the eggs and oil can become so thick the mixture "breaks."

Makes 2 cups

4 egg yolks
2 tablespoons lemon juice
Salt and freshly cracked black pepper
½ cup peanut oil, or other light oil

1½ cups virgin olive oil
Warm water to thin, as needed
2 teaspoons Dijon mustard

1. With all ingredients at room temperature, put yolks and lemon in a stainless steel bowl. Season them and whisk them thoroughly.

2. Whisk in the oils drop by drop, adding the water as necessary if mayonnaise becomes too thick. Add the mustard. The more full-flavored your olive oil, the stronger the flavor of the mayonnaise. (If you are using it as a sauce or condiment, I suggest the full-flavored oils, an extra virgin instead of virgin, perhaps—but I recommend a light olive oil for a spreading mayonnaise.)

FENNEL MAYONNAISE

This is an excellent mayonnaise to liven up a cold tuna salad.

3 cups Basic Homemade Mayonnaise
   (above)
½ cup finely chopped fresh fennel bulb,
   core removed
2 teaspoons aniseed

2 tablespoons Pernod
1 tablespoon lemon juice
¼ cup red wine vinegar
1 teaspoon kosher or sea salt
1 teaspoon cracked black pepper

1. Thoroughly combine all ingredients in a bowl and chill until needed.

RED PEPPER MAYONNAISE

The next time you are grilling steaks or burgers, add some lightly oiled peppers to the grill. Let them char fairly completely and then follow the usual procedure for steaming, peeling, and seeding them. Cut the cleaned peppers into large strips. Put them into a bowl or crock, top with olive oil, and chill until you're ready to make this simple mayonnaise. (Of course, you could get the grill going early enough to have this mayo with your burgers.)

> 5 red peppers, roasted, stemmed, seeded, and cut into large strips
>
> 3 jalapeño peppers, roasted, stemmed, seeded, and cut into large strips

> 3 cups Basic Homemade Mayonnaise (page 232)

1. Process the peppers in a food processor until well blended. Add the mayonnaise and purée 30 seconds more. Chill. (For a straight chile mayonnaise, omit the red peppers and increase the jalapeños to 6 or 8.)

AIOLI

Aioli is one of the magnificent, simple sauces that make life a better thing. Robust, sunny, and addictive, it goes well with fish, meat, bread, pasta, and of course, vegetables. This can be made in a food processor, but I prefer the mortar.

Makes 2½ cups

> 4 or 5 large cloves excellent garlic
> 1 pinch kosher or sea salt
> 2 egg yolks

> 2 cups extra virgin olive oil
> Warm water to thin
> 2½ tablespoons fresh lemon juice

1. Put the garlic in a mortar with the salt and pound it to a pulpy smoothness. Add the yolks and work them in.

2. Transfer the mixture to a mixing bowl and beat in the oil, drop by drop. As the emulsion becomes very thick, beat in a little warm water.

3. Add the lemon juice toward the end. Taste and adjust as needed. The result should be like a thick mayonnaise.

Note: A few cloves of finely chopped Roast Garlic (page 200) make a nice addition at the end.

ROUILLE

Traditionally, this spicy Provençal condiment is the "legal" garnish for bouillabaisse, but you don't have to limit this wonderful concoction to the famed soup of Marseilles. The addition of jalapeño is not classical, but exciting nonetheless.

Makes 1 quart

1 jalapeño	¼ cup fish fumet (or water or other stock)
1 red pepper	Pinch each saffron and cayenne
1 ripe tomato	3 egg yolks
5 to 8 garlic cloves	¾ cup extra virgin olive oil
A 1-inch piece baguette-style white bread, crust removed	¾ cup light olive oil

1. Roast the red pepper and the jalapeño, then peel and seed. Roast tomato in the oven, then skin and seed. Finely dice the garlic or crush cloves with a mortar and pestle.

2. Soak the bread in the fumet with the saffron and cayenne until the bread is soft. Squeeze the excess liquid out of the bread.

3. Beat the egg yolks in a mixer until pale and add the bread mixture and garlic. Now slowly add the olive oils, emulsifying them as you would a mayonnaise.

4. Purée the pepper, chile, and tomato and fold into the oil mixture. Taste and adjust seasoning if necessary.

Tonnato

Tonnato means tuna. This is basically a mayonnaise, but "tuna mayo" doesn't exactly roll off the tongue and send pleasure alarms through your nervous system, now does it? So let's not anglicize this dish in either name or preparation. Tonnato is most frequently paired with veal to produce the Italian specialty vitello tonnato, but this sauce can be served on many other foods, like swordfish. Or try it on poached chicken or cold pork roast. This can be stored in the refrigerator for 4 or 5 days.

Makes 1½ quarts

6 egg yolks
3 cups olive oil
1 cup Fish Stock (page 244)
Sea salt and cracked pepper to taste
¾ cup lemon juice

¾ pound cooked tuna meat (if fresh is unavailable, use canned tuna packed in olive oil)
12 anchovy fillets, lightly rinsed
6 tablespoons capers

1. In an electric mixer or food processor, beat the egg yolks. Add the oil very slowly, adding a bit of stock from time to time to prevent the mixture from breaking. Add salt, pepper, and lemon juice.

2. Chop up tuna, anchovies, and capers, and add them to the liquid. Add stock to somewhat runny consistency.

3. Put tonnato in a bowl, cover, and chill overnight, but bring to room temperature before serving.

Southern Slaw Dressing

This is a creamy dressing that I like to use on a mixture of such cabbages as red, green, and Napa. The slaw is a nice bed for steamed shrimp that have been chilled, peeled, and cooked with a Cajun rémoulade sauce.

Makes 3 cups

¾ cup mayonnaise	6 tablespoons creole mustard
¾ cup sour cream	5 tablespoons tomato juice
¾ cup buttermilk	Cayenne to taste
1 teaspoon salt	Paprika to taste
2 teaspoons freshly chopped herbs (basil, mint, thyme, and the like)	Salt and pepper to taste

1. Combine all the ingredients.
2. Toss shredded or julienned cabbages in the dressing and chill for an hour before serving. (This amount will dress almost 2 quarts of julienned vegetables.)

Herb Butter

Sometimes, you can expend more energy thinking about making sauces than you need to. The simplicity of this butter—called a compound butter—offers a nice touch of flavor without complicated preparations. You can make variations on this theme or start with a wholly fresh concept—for instance, mushroom butter, pistachio butter, ginger-mustard butter, or others.

This butter freezes without any loss of flavor. Make a batch and roll it into logs in aluminum foil or parchment paper, mark the date, and keep the logs frozen until you need the butter. It tastes good on pasta, bread, or sautéed with fresh vegetables, but I use it primarily on simply grilled fish and seafood.

5 pounds unsalted butter, slightly softened at room temperature	3 tablespoons fine sea salt or kosher salt
3 tablespoons white pepper	½ cup plus 1 tablespoon peeled, hand-chopped shallots

   3/4 *cup assorted chopped fresh herbs (a*
       mixture of herbs such as basil, thyme,
       parsley, and tarragon would be good,
       but it is important that they pair well

    with the foods you plan to serve the
    butter on)
  1/4 *cup freshly squeezed lemon juice*
   2 *tablespoons Pernod*

1. Put the softened butter in a large bowl. Add all of the remaining ingredients and mix together as thoroughly as possible.

2. Taste and adjust seasoning. Roll into logs as described above and freeze.

Basic white butter sauce
(Beurre Blanc)

White butter sauce is made slightly differently in most restaurants from the way you would prepare it at home because restaurants often require that a sauce be held for the number of hours of service. Classic butter sauce, an emulsion sauce held together only with butter, cannot be held for more than a short time. So cream is added if the sauce needs to be held longer. If you are serving your butter sauce almost immediately after its preparation, you can omit the cream.

Makes 2 cups

   6 *tablespoons white wine*
   3 *tablespoons white wine vinegar*
  1/4 *cup finely chopped shallots*
   1 *bay leaf*
   1 *teaspoon cracked black pepper*

  1/2 *cup heavy cream (optional)*
   1 *pound butter, broken or cut into small*
       bits, kept cold
Salt and pepper to taste
   1 *teaspoon lemon juice*

1. Put the white wine and white wine vinegar into a medium-sized heavy saucepan with the shallots, bay leaf, and cracked pepper and reduce over a medium heat.

2. *Optional* (proceed to Step 3 if not using cream): When the shallot mixture is reduced to 3 tablespoons, add the cream and reduce by half.

3. Whisk the butter in, piece by piece, until it is all incorporated. Strain sauce through a fine-mesh strainer. Add salt (optional), pepper, and lemon to taste.

4. Keep warm in a double boiler.

SAUCE BÉARNAISE

I usually serve béarnaise with red meat. For that reason, I prepare it with red wine and red wine vinegar. For service with fish I would follow the same recipe, but generally use white wine and white wine vinegar.

For 8 servings

½ cup red wine
½ cup red wine vinegar
¼ cup finely chopped shallots
1 teaspoon freshly cracked black pepper
½ cup chopped fresh tarragon leaves

1 tablespoon chopped fresh chervil
6 egg yolks
1 pound softened butter, broken into pieces
¼ teaspoon cayenne pepper
1 tablespoon lemon juice (only if necessary)

1. Put the red wine, red wine vinegar, chopped shallots, freshly cracked black pepper, tarragon, and chervil in a small, heavy saucepan and reduce liquid until almost evaporated. Cool briefly.

2. Put the egg yolks in a stainless steel bowl. Heat a pot of water that will hold the bowl without letting the bowl come into contact with the water, like a double boiler. Keep on moderate heat.

3. Add the reduced wine and shallot mixture to the egg yolks and whisk them very well prior to heating them.

4. Now put the bowl over the simmering water and *whisk,* not stir, the eggs. Allow them to thicken gently and evenly. When you can draw a line with the whisk across the bottom of the bowl and see the bottom for a quick count to 3, they are thick enough.

5. Remove the bowl from the heat and beat in the softened butter. When all the butter is incorporated, whisk in the cayenne pepper and the lemon juice, if it is needed. (Taste and add at your discretion.)

BEER COURT BOUILLON

This is the way we prepare shrimp to serve with creole rémoulade.

6 cups rich Fish Stock (page 244)	4 Spanish onions, peeled and cut up in slices
1 teaspoon whole black peppercorns	2 heads garlic, cut in half laterally
1 teaspoon dry mustard	1 quart beer (we use Dixie, but any light lager will do)
1 teaspoon cayenne pepper	
1 tablespoon thyme leaves	
1 tablespoon shredded basil leaves	1 pound large shrimp

1. Combine all ingredients except shrimp in a large saucepan and bring to a rolling boil. Skim. Lower the heat and simmer for approximately 30 minutes to allow flavors to blend.

2. Add whole unpeeled shrimp and cover. Simmer briefly, checking for doneness often, just until shrimp are tender.

3. Strain shrimp and ice quickly. (Do not leave the shrimp in the ice any longer than necessary. It waters them down and toughens the skin.)

SPICY MOLASSES MARINADE

I like to use this marinade on poultry, especially the large, meaty Moulard duck breasts before smoking them. When they come warm out of the smoke, juicy and medium-rare, it is wonderful to pull off the little tenderloin on the inside of the breast and pop it in your mouth. (This marinade is excellent on pork, also. It is not necessary to smoke anything you marinate like this—grilling is great, too. The marinade works best overnight, in the refrigerator.)

Enough to marinate 4
large chicken breasts

1 cup dark molasses	2 cloves garlic, minced
1/2 cup cider vinegar	1/2 teaspoon cayenne pepper
1/3 cup fresh lemon juice	1/2 teaspoon ground ginger
1/2 cup Dijon mustard	Pinch fresh grated nutmeg
1/2 cup tomato sauce	1 teaspoon minced fresh thyme leaves

1. Mix everything together and store in the refrigerator in a glass or stainless steel container.

CHICKEN STOCK

Makes approximately 3 quarts

BOUQUET GARNI

12 whole black peppercorns	2 bay leaves
6 sprigs thyme	6 sprigs parsley
6 basil leaves	

1 tablespoon virgin olive oil	2 onions, peeled and roughly chopped
3 tablespoons butter	3 stalks celery, cleaned and roughly chopped
3 carrots, peeled and roughly chopped	

½ pound mushrooms, cleaned and roughly
  chopped
1 head garlic, cut in half crosswise
5 pounds chicken carcasses, chopped up

3 cups white wine
1½ gallons water, or enough to cover the
  bones

1. Make the bouquet garni: Tie all ingredients together in a cheesecloth bag.

2. Heat a large stock pot on medium-high heat. Add the olive oil and butter. Melt briefly. Reduce heat to medium. Add the carrots, onions, celery, mushrooms, and garlic.

3. Stir this all together and cook until the vegetables are shiny and glazed, about 10 minutes. Add the chicken bones and the bouquet garni.

4. Add the white wine and reduce by half. Add the cold water, and heat to just boiling. Skim and reduce heat.

5. Simmer until the stock has a pronounced chicken aroma and flavor (approximately 2½ hours on low heat). Strain and chill.

Smoked Stock

In the restaurants I have worked in, we have used various smokers over the years. They have included the inexpensive home varieties that worked well enough to suit any of the recipes included in this book. If you have room for your own smoker, you can include items such as smoked stock in your larder. If a smoker is unavailable or impractical for you, you might be able to locate someone in your community who is smoking meats or seafoods commercially. They might have bones available for you. It can't hurt to ask.

You can create a smoked veal or lobster stock if you wish, but I use a smoked poultry stock most often.

Makes approximately 3 quarts

1 recipe Chicken Stock (above)
1 smoked turkey carcass, or 5 pounds
  smoked chicken bones
1 smoked pork hock

1. Cook the carcass and hock in the stock at a simmer for about 1½ hours. Strain. Chill.

Duck Stock

Makes approximately
3 quarts

BOUQUET GARNI

12	whole black peppercorns	6	sage leaves
6	sprigs thyme	2	bay leaves
6	basil leaves		

5	pounds duck carcasses, chopped up (feet included if obtainable)	3	stalks celery, cleaned and roughly chopped
3	cups red wine	½	pound mushrooms, cleaned and roughly chopped
1	tablespoon virgin olive oil		
3	tablespoons butter	1	head garlic, cut in half crosswise
3	carrots, peeled and roughly chopped	2	tomatoes, cored and cut up
2	onions, peeled and roughly chopped		About 1½ gallons water

1. Preheat oven to 425 degrees. While it is preheating, prepare the bouquet garni by tying all the ingredients in a cheesecloth bag.

2. Scatter the duck bones in a roasting pan and roast until they are deep brown but not black. Remove from the oven, pour in 1 cup of red wine, and scrape any matter clinging to the bottom of the pan using a wooden spoon.

3. Heat a large stock pot on medium-high heat. Add the olive oil and butter. Melt briefly. Reduce heat to medium. Add the carrots, onions, celery, mushrooms, garlic, and tomatoes and cook until the vegetables are shiny and glazed, about 10 minutes. Add the bouquet garni.

4. Add the red wine and reduce by half. Add the duck bones and any liquid left in the roasting pan. Add about 1½ gallons of cold water, bring just to the boiling point, skim, and reduce heat.

5. Simmer until the stock has a pronounced duck aroma and flavor, approximately 2½ hours, on low heat. Strain and chill.

Note: To make duck glaze, degrease the prepared, chilled stock and reduce to approximately 2 cups.

VEAL STOCK

This recipe is for a dark veal stock, which is the basis for brown-sauce-related dishes. For a white veal stock you would not roast the bones, and after the stock came to its first boil, you would strain off the water entirely, wash off the meat and bones, and top with fresh water.

Makes 1½ to 2 gallons

BOUQUET GARNI

24 whole black peppercorns
8 sprigs thyme
12 basil leaves

12 sprigs parsley
3 bay leaves

10 pounds veal knuckle bones, cut in half by a butcher
½ cup peanut oil
6 tablespoons (¾ stick) butter
2 tablespoons virgin olive oil
6 carrots, peeled and roughly chopped
4 onions, peeled and roughly chopped

6 stalks celery, cleaned and roughly chopped
1 pound mushrooms, cleaned and roughly chopped
3 heads garlic, cut in half crosswise
4 or 5 tomatoes, cored and cut up
A 750-ml bottle red wine
About 4 gallons water

1. Preheat oven to 475 degrees. Make the bouquet garni by enclosing all the ingredients in cheesecloth and tying cloth tightly.

2. Scatter the veal bones in a roasting pan and drizzle with the peanut oil. (This helps to brown the bones.) Roast the bones until deep, dark brown. Turn them once during this roasting period. Remove from the oven.

3. Heat a large stock pot (or two, if necessary) and melt the butter and olive oil. Add the carrots, onions, celery, mushrooms, garlic, and tomatoes and cook until the vegetables are shiny and glazed, about 15 minutes. Add the bouquet garni and red wine and reduce by half.

4. Add the bones and cover completely with cold water. Bring just to a boil. Skim and reduce heat.

5. Simmer until the stock has a rich, meaty aroma and flavor. This will take 12 hours, at least. Strain, discard bones and vegetables, and chill.

FISH STOCK

Where there's fish, there are bones. You can make use of them by making stock, which is really quite simple yet the secret success formula for many soups and sauces. Since I live in Key West, I use local fish like grouper and snapper for stock. The basic rule is to use a nonoily variety of fish—your fishmonger can help you choose. It is of utmost importance that the fish frames and heads be fresh. I like to buy whole fish, so I can inspect the eyes for clarity and the gills for a rich, red color and smooth, even shape. (If the gills are dull and shaggy, the fish is past its prime.) Then the fillets can be cut off and the stock made with the head and frame.

Fish stock is unlike other stocks in that it is cooked for a relatively short period of time (longer cooking can cause it to become bitter). Thus, you can buy fish, make the stock, and serve it all relatively quickly. It is important to strain fish stock carefully and to chill it completely. Once it has settled, always ladle off the stock you want; a cloudy, disagreeable sediment forms on the bottom of the pot, and if you stir the stock or pour it, you will break up that sediment and send it into the clean stock above. When you get to the bottom of the pot and see the sediment, stop ladling and discard it.

**Makes approximately
2½ gallons**

BOUQUET GARNI

4 basil leaves	1 tablespoon whole black peppercorns
2 bay leaves	1 teaspoon whole fennel seeds
2 sprigs parsley	1 teaspoon whole coriander seeds
3 sprigs thyme	

¼ cup virgin olive oil	1 cup white wine
1 carrot, peeled and chopped medium	5 pounds fish heads and frames, gills removed and rinsed until no blood remains, roughly chopped
1 leek, white part only, cleaned and chopped medium	
1 onion, peeled and chopped medium	Water
1 head garlic, cut in half crosswise	

1. Make the bouquet garni: Enclose all the ingredients in cheesecloth and tie tightly.
2. Heat the olive oil in a large stock pot until warm. Add the carrots, leek, onion, and

garlic and stir about 5 minutes. Add the fish heads and frames, cover the pot, and let cook for about 5 more minutes. Add the bouquet garni. Add the wine and cook about 2 minutes.

3. Cover the fish bones, herbs, and vegetables with cold water. Leave the pot uncovered. Bring to a low boil and skim the white residue that comes to the top. Reduce the heat and cook 45 minutes. Turn off the heat and allow the stock to settle.

4. Strain stock through cheesecloth and chill. Discard vegetables and bones. Reserve until needed.

Note: If you like, you can freeze shrimp shells for stock and use them with the fish heads for added flavor.

SHELLFISH STOCK

1 cup shellfish shells
1 quart Fish Stock (above)

1. Add fresh shells (lobster, shrimp, crayfish, or crab) to fish stock. Heat to a boil, skim, and lower the heat.

2. Cook for about 30 minutes. Strain and chill until needed.

SAVORY CARAMEL SAUCE

The concept of caramelization can be applied to savory dishes, but to take what is conventionally a dessert sauce and turn it into a savory one requires a radical shift from the original direction. This is accomplished by substituting stock and vinegar for what is usually water.

Makes 3 cups

13 ounces Duck Stock (page 242)	½ cup sugar
¾ cup red wine vinegar (Cabernet Sauvignon, if possible)	2 cups heavy cream
	½ cup duck glaze

1. Combine the stock, vinegar, and sugar in a heavy saucepan and cook to the caramel stage. It is difficult to see the caramelizing color because of the red of the vinegar, but I look for small puffs or wisps of smoke just on the edges of the pan.

2. Carefully whisk in 2 cups heavy cream, then the duck glaze. Cook briefly. Carefully remove any foam that comes to the surface.

3. Strain through a fine-mesh strainer into a bowl and reserve.

THOUGHTS ON SAUCE-MAKING

Apparently the French chef André Guillot introduced into the lexicon of cuisine the term *stratified* to describe a certain sauce-making procedure. While many chefs have used this method, his description helped me to understand the principle more completely than before.

The more I cook the more I seem to utilize this stratification procedure. The results are obtained by a series of rapid reductions whereby the sauce reaches a degree of thickness that we equate with "sauciness" without the application of any traditional thickening agents, or roux.

In the old school of cooking to which I was initially exposed, we were taught to make our brown sauce with a roux. The popular wisdom argued that it was "better" and since we knew of no alternative at the time, we, of course, had to concur. With the advent of nouvelle cuisine we came to discover ways to achieve a rich, intense, glossy brown sauce without roux; it was much finer than its muddy ancestor. I give recipes for brown sauce and lamb brown sauce that are made in this newer style. I still feel there is a place for brown sauces such as these. But I've come to realize that cuisine is limitless in its capacity to teach and to reveal nuance and delight (if we are only willing to accept it) and that perhaps the simplicity of the stratified sauce allows the truest, most natural flavors to pour through.

Stratification depends upon the reduction of a wine or vinegar, followed by the reduction of a protein-rich stock, and then the final addition of cream or butter. In the body analogy earlier in this book, this would be seen as bones plus meat plus flesh; here we see that it is structurally complete. Let us say we are pan-roasting a bird such as quail or squab. Without having a brown sauce in our larder, we can still obtain a wonderful sauce through stratification. The bird is roasted and allowed to rest in a warm place while the sauce is developed. Any excess oil or drippings are discarded from the pan, while any particles remaining in the pan are left alone. Then perhaps we add a fruity vinegar and reduce it substantially, follow with a poultry stock (duck, chicken, quail, or squab), and then at the last moment, whisk in a bit of butter and pour it over the bird. In my opinion, this would be suitable procedure for a delicate dish such as this.

However, consider my recipe for Cajun rib steak. Here I feel a different approach is better. When we roast a prime rib a great deal of fat is rendered. By the time we properly degrease the drippings, we will have spent a great deal of time. By having the brown sauce ready in advance, we can serve the entrée just after it has rested an appropriate length of time. In addition, the rich, vegetable sweetness of the sauce does not overwhelm the robust spiciness of the dish.,

If we draw a comparison to the science of wine, a brown sauce may be likened to a forward and hearty wine such as Zinfandel and the stratified stock reduction may emulate the complexity of a Cabernet Sauvignon. Each has its respective merits and each has a place in modern cooking.

Brown Sauce

Brown sauce is used with all manner of meats, and some poultry. Many cookbooks contain recipes for this foundational sauce; I will include mine because its balance is weighted more generously to the vegetable flavors than many others. You can alter the brown sauce by the addition of such things as mushrooms, wines, mustards, and so on. I suggest making your brown sauce in as large a batch as you can; then freeze it in small containers that are well wrapped and dated.

**Makes approximately
2 quarts**

½ cup peanut oil, for caramelizing the vegetables	A 750 ml bottle red wine
1 pound slab bacon, rind on, cut into ½-inch cubes	3 to 5 unpeeled heads garlic, cut in half crosswise
6 stalks celery, cleaned and diced medium to medium-large	25 whole black peppercorns
8 onions, peeled and diced medium to medium-large	4 bay leaves
	1 bunch oregano, stems on
	1 bunch basil, stems on
	1 bunch thyme, stems on
6 carrots, peeled and diced medium to medium-large	3 tomatoes, cut in half
¾ cup tomato paste	2½ gallons Veal Stock (page 243), previously prepared

1. Heat a heavy, large, flat-bottomed saucepan or stock pot on medium-high heat. Add the peanut oil and bacon and cook until the bacon is almost half done.

2. Add the celery, onions, and carrots and turn heat to high. (In classical French cooking these vegetables used in this manner are known as a mirepoix.) Stir once to coat the mirepoix with fat. It is very important to have enough vegetables to cover the bottom of the pan, and it is best to use a large-bottomed pot so that there is greater surface heat in contact with the cooking vegetables. The idea is to bring the vegetables' inherent sugars to the surface; in this intense heat the vegetables will darken and caramelize, adding sweetness and a dark color to your sauce. If you stir the vegetables too often, especially in the beginning, you will cause them to release too much of their liquid. (This is called "sweating" the vegetables, and you would want to work a sauce this way if you wished it to be very light in color. That is not the case here, however.)

3. Once the vegetables begin to stick, stay close to the pot—it is a short road between sweet and burnt. Add the tomato paste and stir with a wooden spoon, being sure to scrape the bottom to free any vegetables that may be sticking. Now add the wine. (The aroma is wonderfully intense at this point.)

4. Add the garlic, peppercorns, bay leaves, herbs, and tomato. Allow mixture to cook a moment, reducing the wine. Now add the stock. Bring sauce to a boil once, then skim it, reduce heat, and allow it to reduce slowly to a glossy intensity. This will take several hours.

5. When the sauce is reduced and flavorful, turn off the heat and allow it to rest 20 to 30 minutes. Strain it first through a large-holed strainer to remove the larger items, and then through a fine-mesh strainer to remove the small impurities. Cool.

6. Refrigerate the sauce overnight. The next day there will be a layer of hardened fat on top of the sauce. Carefully remove it and discard.

7. If you are going to use the sauce within 2 or 3 days, you can store it in the refrigerator. Otherwise, freeze the sauce in batches.

LAMB BROWN SAUCE

A lamb brown sauce is made much like a regular brown sauce with several small but key differences. First, you begin with a lamb stock, which is made just like veal stock, substituting lamb shanks for veal bones, and white wine for red wine. I also add two extra heads of garlic and one small bunch of fresh rosemary.

The next difference is that although you prepare lamb brown sauce by the (veal) brown sauce recipe, you substitute white wine for the red wine, and add two sprigs of rosemary.

DESSERTS

The first time I tasted Frangelico liqueur, I remembered with an instant and visceral clarity the flavor of the cones that held ice cream in the small drug store in Diamond Lake, Illinois, where my father took us when I was about six or seven. It was so evocative I seemed transported to my childhood for a moment. Having grown up in the rural America of the fifties and sixties, I ate my share of junk. I'll even confess to having sipped soft drinks through a strawberry licorice straw!! Somehow, the tumult and insult I inflicted on my palate did not destroy me. I think childhood indulgences and cravings for flavors are most evident in our approach to desserts. Here adults, willingly and wantonly, lay down restraint and subtlety and plunge with giddy abandon into the treasures of chocolate, sugar, vanilla, meringue, and richly flavored creams. It is not unusual to see people blush with desire when they order something sweet and sinfully delicious from the menu! The talented Ms. Susan Porter, who has worked with me over the years, has made the major contributions to this chapter. To say she knows how to cook is like saying Gene Kelly knows how to dance. She is a natural, self-taught, and gifted baker. We put in long hours in the kitchen, and the holidays mean even more work, yet Sue has the ability to make it look nearly effortless. But I've seen others work her position, myself included, so I know how truly good she is. The most amazing thing to me is her gift with puff pastry. You are often warned not to attempt this dough on a humid day. Well, in the tropics, they're impossible to avoid! I think she may be like one of those Indian swamis, and can lower the temperature of her hands at will.

I feel the dessert course is best when it is almost miniature, but dangerously intense, or has some savory element worked into it. Sue offers some alternatives to the overkill that sweet desserts can sometimes be. I might like to end a good meal with a thin slice of cheesecake with strawberries, but Sue adds a dimension by soaking the berries in twenty-five-year-old Italian balsamic vinegar. I call such offerings "adult desserts." I like the menus to have a balance of desserts, with choices for the adult *or* the child within.

Although we normally associate desserts with the end of a meal, sometimes I like to have an apple tart with ginger caramel and some strong coffee before work on a Saturday morning . . . or a vanilla and hazelnut cookie with some Chardonnay as a snack while playing cards on a stormy Sunday afternoon. Desserts need not necessarily be confined to the final scene. Sue's magic will be revealed in this chapter, and I hope you will view this category more broadly.

CUBAN BANANA RUM CUSTARD TART

Here in Key West we use the short, plump, sweet Cuban bananas, but you can substitute ordinary bananas.

Serves 8 to 10

CRUST

5	ounces cashews, finely chopped	1½	cups flour
¼	pound (1 stick) soft butter	1	egg, lightly beaten
2	tablespoons sugar	½	teaspoon vanilla extract

CUSTARD

2	eggs	¾	cup heavy cream
⅓	cup sugar	¼	cup dark rum
2	tablespoons flour		

6 to 8 Cuban bananas or 4 or 5 ordinary bananas

½ cup apricot preserves
Juice of 1 orange

1. Combine all crust ingredients in a mixing bowl, using either an electric mixer or a wooden spoon. This crust is difficult to roll out with a rolling pin so press the dough into an 11-inch tart shell using your fingertips. Try to keep the dough an even thickness. Chill the shell for at least 30 minutes.

2. Preheat the oven to 350 degrees. Line the tart shell with aluminum foil and fill the foil with dried beans or rice. (This weight will prevent the dough from rising while baking.) Bake the shell for 15 minutes, then remove the foil and beans and bake the shell 5 minutes more. Leave oven on but remove shell to cool slightly while you prepare custard.

3. Make the custard: Beat eggs and sugar until light and frothy. Mix in flour and stir until smooth. Add cream and rum. Pour into partially baked crust and bake approximately 20 minutes, or until custard is set.

4. After the baked custard is removed from the oven and allowed to cool slightly, top it with sliced bananas. Start at the outside edge of the tart and work your way toward the center, creating a neat pattern.

5. Warm the preserves and orange juice, stirring until the preserves have melted. Pour through a fine strainer and then brush on the bananas to protect them from turning brown and to add a shine to the tart.

COUNTRY APPLE TART
with Warm Ginger Caramel

The ginger adds a refreshing note to the sauce and the apples.

Serves 8 to 10

½ recipe Pâte Brisée (page 282)	¼ teaspoon freshly grated nutmeg
4 Granny Smith apples	2 teaspoons all-purpose flour
4 McIntosh apples	2 tablespoons butter
3 tablespoons sugar	2 cups Ginger Caramel Sauce (page 277)
¾ teaspoon ground cinnamon	

TOPPING

½ cup firmly packed brown sugar	4 tablespoons (½ stick) chilled butter
½ cup all-purpose flour	1 cup coarsely chopped pecans

1. Preheat oven to 350 degrees. Roll out pastry for an 11-inch tart pan. Fit it loosely into the pan and up the sides. Trim, leaving about ¾ inch overhang. Pinch the overhanging pastry into a rim, and flute it decoratively. Chill the shell while you prepare the filling.

2. Peel, core, and slice apples into ½-inch slices and place in a large bowl.

3. In a small bowl, combine sugar, cinnamon, nutmeg, and flour. Toss lightly with the apples.

4. Place apples in crust and arrange as evenly as possible. Dot with butter and bake for 20 minutes.

5. While tart is baking, prepare topping: Combine brown sugar and flour in a bowl. Cut in chilled butter until mixture resembles coarse meal. Mix in nuts lightly.

(recipe continues)

6. After tart has baked 20 minutes, sprinkle topping evenly over apples. Continue baking for 20 minutes more, or until nicely browned and slightly bubbly. Remove from the oven and cool slightly.

7. Cut and serve the tart warm on a pool of warm ginger caramel sauce.

Babas au Louies

Modeled after the classic babas au rhum, babas au Louies received its somewhat comical name after a short deliberation about whether or not we felt it was serious enough for the restaurant. Mercifully we came to our senses and determined that fun is just as important as seriousness.

If you like, you can make the mango butter ahead of time and rewarm it over barely simmering water just before serving.

Serves 12

2 packages active dry yeast	½ cup clarified butter
2 tablespoons sugar	½ medium mango, cut into chunks
3 eggs, at room temperature	Pouring Cream (page 280) made with 1½
Warm water	cups heavy cream, 1½ teaspoons confectioner's
1¾ cups all-purpose flour	sugar, and ¾ teaspoon flavoring
¾ teaspoon salt	

SYRUP

1½ cups water
¾ cup sugar
½ cup passion fruit or mango liqueur

MANGO BUTTER

1 mango	3 tablespoons passion fruit or mango liqueur
½ cup simple (sugar) syrup	4 tablespoons (½ stick) softened butter

1. Butter a muffin pan. Set aside. Combine yeast, sugar, and salt with ¼ cup warm water in the large bowl of an electric mixer. Let stand 5 to 10 minutes, or until bubbly.

2. Using the paddle attachment, set the mixer on low speed and add the flour all at once. With the machine on medium speed, add the eggs, one at a time, allowing for total incorporation after each egg.

3. Add warm water a tablespoon at a time until the dough is runny and elastic. It will take 4 or 5 tablespoons. Drizzle the clarified butter into the dough. Continue beating until all the butter is absorbed. The dough will be very liquid.

4. Pour the dough into a bowl, cover the bowl loosely with a tea towel, and allow dough to rise at room temperature until doubled in bulk. (Be careful not to put the bowl in too warm a place or the butter will separate from the dough.)

5. When dough has doubled, stir it down with a wooden spoon and mix in the mango chunks. Spoon the dough into the prepared muffin pan, filling each cup just over half full. Allow to rise at room temperature to within ¼ inch of the top of the pan. While it is rising, preheat the oven to 375 degrees.

6. Butter the bottom of a cookie sheet and place on top of babas. (This will create a flat "bottom.") Bake in the center of the oven for 20 to 25 minutes, or until babas are nicely browned and just spring back when touched in the center.

7. While the babas are baking, make the syrup by combining all ingredients and simmering gently until the sugar has dissolved.

8. Remove baked babas from the oven and pierce them several times with a fork before taking them out of the pan.

9. Remove babas from pan and arrange them in a 9- by 13-inch baking dish, pierced side down. Pour syrup over babas. Allow to sit 20 minutes and absorb syrup.

10. While babas are soaking, or earlier if you prefer, make mango butter: Peel the mango and remove the flesh from the pit over a bowl. Purée mango in a food processor using the steel blade.

11. Transfer the puréed mango to a heavy-bottomed saucepan and add simple syrup and liqueur. Heat slowly to a low simmer. Using a whisk, stir in butter 1 tablespoon at a time. When butter is incorporated, remove from heat and pour through a fine mesh strainer into a bowl.

12. Serve babas warm or at room temperature with pouring cream and mango butter.

PISTACHIO, CHOCOLATE, VANILLA CHEESECAKE

Serves 12 to 14

PISTACHIO PRALINE

1	teaspoon cooking oil	¾	cup sugar
1	cup shelled unsalted pistachio nuts	⅓	cup water

6	ounces semisweet chocolate	5	eggs, at room temperature
2¼	pounds cream cheese at room temperature	⅓	cup sugar
1	cup sour cream	1½	teaspoons vanilla

1. Prepare the praline: Preheat the oven to 325 degrees. Spread the cooking oil on a baking sheet and set aside.

2. Toast pistachios in the oven on another baking sheet for approximately 10 minutes, or until they are crunchy.

3. Place sugar and water in a heavy-bottomed pan over medium heat and bring to a boil. Boil the mixture until it starts to brown slightly. Reduce heat and continue to cook until the sugar caramelizes and the mixture is a rich brown color. Immediately pour the nuts into the caramelized sugar, stir to coat the nuts, and quickly pour the mixture onto the oiled baking sheet pan. Spread the nuts with the back of a wooden spoon. Cool completely. Break into small pieces.

4. Place the praline in the bowl of a food processor with the steel blade attached. Process until almost powdered, about 15 to 20 seconds.

5. Prepare the cheesecake: Lower oven temperature to 300 degrees. Butter a 10-inch springform pan and set aside. Chop the chocolate into small, uniform pieces and place in a heatproof bowl or the top of a double boiler. Place over (not in) barely simmering water. Stir occasionally while chocolate is melting. When it is completely melted, remove from heat and set aside.

6. Place the cream cheese in a mixer bowl. Using the paddle attachment, beat the cheese on medium speed until very creamy. Add the sour cream and beat until incorporated. Add the eggs, one at a time.

7. Divide the batter equally among 3 bowls, using the mixer bowl as one. To one, add the praline; stir the chocolate into another. To the third, add the ⅓ cup sugar and the vanilla.

8. Pour the chocolate mixture into prepared pan. Place in the freezer for 15 minutes. Carefully pour the pistachio layer on top of the chocolate layer, smoothing evenly. Freeze for 15 minutes. Top with the vanilla layer, smoothing the top. Bake for 1¼ hours. Cool to room temperature on a wire rack. Chill at least 3 hours before serving.

CHOCULIS EXTREMIS

I get a kick out of chefs giving their chocolate desserts names like "passion blackout gateau" or "decadence killer cake," so we decided to call this "choculis extremis" as our contribution to that trend.

Serves 12 to 14

2	cups all-purpose flour	⅔	cup butter
1½	teaspoons baking soda	1	cup sugar
½	teaspoon salt	2	eggs
½	cup freshly brewed espresso	1	cup buttermilk
½	cup cocoa	1	teaspoon vanilla

1. Preheat oven to 350 degrees. Butter a 10-inch cake pan and dust with flour. Set aside.

2. Sift the flour, baking soda, and salt together. Set aside.

3. In a small bowl mix espresso and cocoa to a smooth paste. Set aside.

4. In mixer bowl cream the butter and sugar on medium speed until light and fluffy. Add the eggs, one at a time, beating well after each addition. Turn mixer to low speed. Add the flour mixture in thirds, alternating with the buttermilk. Mix just until blended, scraping down the sides of the bowl with a rubber spatula as needed. Add the cocoa mixture and vanilla. Blend just until incorporated.

5. Remove mixer bowl from machine. Using a rubber spatula, fold the cake mixture several times to be sure all the cocoa is distributed and no white shows. Pour the mixture into the prepared pan and level the top with the spatula. Bake in the center of the oven for 25 to 35 minutes, or until a toothpick inserted in the center comes out clean.

6. Cool for 10 minutes, in the pan, on a wire rack. Then invert the cake onto the wire rack to finish cooling.

(recipe continues)

7. Place the cooled cake on a flat pan or cardboard round the same size as the cake. Using a knife, trace a 5-inch circle in the center of the cake. Carefully scoop out the top of this circle, using a spoon, being careful to leave at least a ½-inch layer of cake at the bottom. Reserve the cake crumbs.

FILLING

5 ounces bittersweet chocolate, coarsely chopped
⅓ cup heavy cream
1½ cups reserved cake crumbs

¼ cup coffee-flavored liqueur
¼ pound dried figs, cut into ½-inch pieces
½ cup pistachio nuts, toasted and coarsely chopped

1. Place the chocolate in the bowl of a food processor and pulse until finely chopped.

2. Scald the cream. With the machine running, slowly add the cream to the chocolate and process until smooth. Add the reserved cake crumbs and liqueur and continue processing until very smooth. (A bit more cream may be added if the mixture appears too thick or lumpy.)

3. Transfer the mixture to a bowl and stir in the figs and nuts. Pour this into the center of the cake. Smooth the top. Carefully wrap with plastic. Refrigerate until set, 2 to 3 hours or overnight.

GLAZE

½ pound bittersweet chocolate, coarsely chopped
2 to 3 tablespoons tasteless salad oil

1. Place the chocolate in a stainless bowl over (not in) a pot of barely simmering water. Heat until the chocolate is just melted, stirring often. Remove from heat and whisk in the oil; blend well.

2. Place the cake on a wire rack set over parchment or foil. Pour the glaze directly in the center of the cake. Using a spatula, quickly smooth the glaze toward the edges. Allow the glaze to drip down the sides. Smooth the top and the sides.

3. Chill the cake to set the glaze, but remove from refrigerator 15 minutes before serving.

CHÈVRE AND GINGER TART

A mild Californian goat cheese makes a much nicer cheesecake than cream cheese. Again, we use ginger to add zest to this dessert.

Serves 12 to 14

½   recipe Pâte Sucre (page 281)
12   ounces chèvre goat cheese
½   cup sugar
2   egg yolks
1   whole egg

1   cup heavy cream
2   tablespoons finely grated fresh gingerroot
1   teaspoon ground ginger
⅔   cup chopped candied ginger

1. Preheat oven to 350 degrees. Roll the pâte sucre to a 14-inch circle approximately ⅛ inch thick. Place the dough in an 11-inch tart pan with a removable bottom. Chill 30 minutes and then line with parchment paper or foil and weight down with pie weights, raw beans, or rice.

2. Bake for 10 to 15 minutes, then remove the weights and continue baking another 5 minutes. Remove and cool slightly on a wire rack. Lower oven temperature to 325 degrees.

3. In a mixer bowl using the paddle attachment at medium speed, beat goat cheese just until smooth. Add the sugar, egg yolks, and egg and mix until very smooth. Reduce speed to low and beat in remaining ingredients except the candied ginger, scraping down sides of bowl as necessary.

4. Pour the filling into tart shell. Sprinkle evenly with the reserved chopped candied ginger. Bake for 20 to 25 minutes, or until filling is set and lightly browned. Allow to cool on a wire rack at least half an hour before unmolding the tart from the pan. Serve at room temperature or slightly chilled.

LINZERTORTE
with Rhubarb, Apple, and Orange

This is heaven. Linzers are often made too sweet, but Sue's is just sweet enough.

Serves 8 to 10

DOUGH

2½ cups all-purpose flour
½ cup powdered sugar
6 tablespoons ground, toasted almonds

3 hard-cooked egg yolks, sieved
¾ pound (3 sticks) chilled butter, cut into ½-inch cubes
1 teaspoon vanilla extract

1. Place the flour, sugar, almonds, and egg yolks in mixer bowl. Using the paddle with the machine on low speed, mix the ingredients until blended, about 30 seconds.

2. With the machine running on low speed, add the butter cubes in three stages, mixing briefly between stages. Continue mixing until all of the butter is incorporated and no lumps of butter are visible. Add the vanilla and mix just until blended.

3. Gather the dough into two separate balls, wrap them in plastic, and chill for at least 1 hour, or overnight, before rolling.

FILLING

1 pound rhubarb, washed and cut into 1-inch pieces
2 apples, preferably Granny Smith, cored, peeled, and diced

¾ cup sugar
1½ cups orange Muscat wine, such as Essencia, or French Sauternes
2 oranges

1. Place the rhubarb, apples, sugar, and wine in a heavy-bottomed 2-quart stainless steel saucepan. Using a hand grater, grate the oranges' rind only (avoid the white pith) into the rhubarb apple mixture.

2. Cook the mixture over medium heat about 20 minutes, or until the rhubarb is cooked and the apples are tender, stirring occasionally to make sure it doesn't stick to the bottom of the pan. The mixture will reduce by almost half and be fairly thick. Remove from heat.

3. While fruit is cooking, trim the white pith from the oranges and divide them into sections. (Discard seeds and skin.) Coarsely chop the orange sections and stir the pieces into the rhubarb apple mixture.

4. Transfer the mixture to a bowl and set aside to cool.

ASSEMBLING AND BAKING

1. Preheat oven to 350 degrees. Remove one of the balls of dough from the refrigerator and, working on a lightly floured surface, roll it into a 13-inch circle, sprinkling lightly with extra flour as necessary. (Because of the large quantity of butter in this dough, it will seem sticky. This is normal, but *do* work quickly.)

2. Line an 11-inch tart pan (with a removable bottom) with the dough. Pour the cooled filling into the tart shell and smooth evenly. Refrigerate while rolling the remaining dough.

3. Roll the other half of the dough into a rectangle approximately 12 inches by 14 inches, and ⅛ inch thick. Cut into ½-inch by 12-inch strips, once again adding extra flour sparingly as necessary.

4. Start in the center of the tart and place the strips of dough ½ inch apart until the top is covered. Place another layer of strips crossing the first layer to create a diamond lattice, again starting in the center and working outward to the sides of the pan. Press the strips to the edges of the tart pan, pinching off and discarding any excess overlapping dough.

5. Bake for 30 minutes, or until the filling begins to bubble and the crust is golden brown. Cool on a wire rack to room temperature before slicing. (This can also be served chilled, but is best warm, perhaps with a rich vanilla ice cream.) Any leftovers keep well in the refrigerator.

FROZEN LIME SOUFFLÉ
with Fruit Coulis

People come to Key West wanting to taste Key lime pie. To my taste, the traditional recipe yields a dessert that is much too sweet to follow a fine meal. So, instead of merely reworking Key lime pie, we have devised a very light and refreshing soufflé utilizing the tart juice of Key limes.

Serves 6

6 egg yolks
Finely grated zest of 1 Key lime (or other lime, as available)
6 tablespoons freshly squeezed Key lime juice (or other lime juice, as available)

1 cup sugar
¾ cup water
2 teaspoons light corn syrup
¾ cup heavy cream

1. Prepare collars for six 4-ounce ramekins or individual soufflé dishes: Cut strips of aluminum foil or parchment paper and secure them to the dishes with tape to make collars that extend 1½ inches above the rims.

2. In a mixer bowl, combine the egg yolks and lime zest. Beat on high speed until very thick and pale. Slowly add the juice and continue beating on high speed for 3 or 4 minutes.

3. While the yolk mixture is beating, combine the sugar, water, and corn syrup in a small pan and heat to boiling.

4. Add the boiling syrup to the yolk mixture and continue beating until cool. While this is mixing, beat the cream to stiff peaks, by hand, in a large bowl. Refrigerate.

5. Fold the lime mixture into the cream until thoroughly incorporated. Pour the mixture into the prepared dishes and freeze at least 4 hours. Serve with a fresh fruit coulis.

COULIS

A mixture of tropical fruits such as kiwi, pineapple, and mango go nicely with this dessert.

Finely dice enough of the fruit (¼-inch dice) to yield one cup total. Lightly marinate the fruit in 2 tablespoons of a liqueur, such as Midori, to enhance the flavor. Cover and refrigerate.

The coulis should not be made more than 3 hours before serving.

CHOCOLATE FRITTERS
with Blueberry Sauce

Who could deny the pleasure of a crisp, hot, fried crêpe wrapped around a molten channel of first-class chocolate? Not I.

While the recipe looks complex, much of the work can be done several hours in advance, so you need only deep-fry the fritters at the last moment.

Serves 12

FILLING

10 ounces cream cheese, at room temperature

6 ounces bittersweet chocolate, cut into ½-inch pieces
¼ cup coffee liqueur

Double recipe Blueberry Sauce (page 280)

CRÊPE BATTER

1 cup flour
1 tablespoon sugar
3 tablespoons cocoa powder
1 teaspoon baking powder

1 whole egg
1 egg yolk
Grated rind of 1 orange
2 cups half and half

FRITTER BATTER

3 eggs, separated
1 cup half and half
3 tablespoons clarified butter

3 tablespoons orange juice
1½ cups flour
¾ teaspoon salt

3 tablespoons clarified butter
1 egg
1 teaspoon water

Enough oil for deep-frying the fritters (oil should completely cover the fritters)

1. First, make the filling: Melt the chocolate in a heatproof bowl over barely simmering water. Set aside to cool.

(recipe continues)

2. In the mixer bowl, using the paddle attachment, beat the cream cheese on medium speed until smooth. Add the melted chocolate and the liqueur and continue beating until all ingredients are blended. Cover and refrigerate until ready to assemble fritters.

3. Prepare the blueberry sauce and refrigerate.

4. Next, make the crêpe batter: Stir the flour, sugar, cocoa, and baking powder together in a bowl. Make a well in the center of the mixture.

5. Whisk the egg, egg yolk, and orange rind briefly in another bowl. Pour this mixture into the well. Gently whisk the dry ingredients into the egg mixture until moistened.

6. Pour the half and half into the batter and whisk until smooth. Cover and refrigerate the batter for 1 hour. Remove from refrigerator and strain through a fine-mesh strainer before continuing.

7. The fritter batter can be made up to 4 hours in advance: Whisk the egg yolks in a medium-sized bowl until light and lemon-colored. Add the half and half, butter, and orange juice. Blend well.

8. Stir the flour and salt together and slowly add to the yolk mixture.

9. Beat the egg whites until stiff but not dry. Gently fold them into the yolk mixture. Cover and refrigerate.

MAKING CRÊPES

1. Heat a 7-inch sauté pan over medium heat. Using a paper towel, lightly grease the pan with the clarified butter. When the pan is just starting to smoke, remove it from the burner and ladle about 2 tablespoons (⅛ cup) of the batter into the center of the pan. Immediately tilt the pan in all directions to even out the crêpe. You will want a crêpe about 4 inches in diameter. Remember the first crêpe is always a "test crêpe" to gauge the thickness of the batter (you don't want it too thick) and the heat of the pan. (If the crêpe bubbles and separates on the edges and sets immediately, the pan is too hot.) Turn the crêpe, using a spatula, after it has browned on the first side, in about 45 to 60 seconds. Cook the second side about half as long as the first. Turn the crêpe out by inverting the pan onto a clean surface.

2. Repeat until you have used up all the batter. Crêpes may be stacked after they have cooled. You should have 24 crêpes.

ASSEMBLING FRITTERS

1. Beat 1 egg with 1 teaspoon water.

2. Spoon one heaping tablespoon of filling into the center of each crêpe. Fold the bottom

edge of the crêpe over the filling. Fold in the side edges. Brush the top edge with the egg wash and fold the crêpe over. Place, egg-washed side down, on a platter. Continue until all crêpes are filled. Cover with plastic wrap and refrigerate. These can be assembled several hours before serving.

FRYING AND SERVING

1. In a deep pan heat the oil to 370 degrees. Dip the crêpes into the fritter batter. Let any excess batter drip off and deep-fry until golden, turning once. Drain on paper towels.
2. Serve the fritters hot with blueberry sauce poured over them.

Variation: The fritters also may be served with Cherry Sauce (page 279).

Frozen Tropical Marjolaine,
Mango and Bittersweet Chocolate Ice Creams

I believe the legendary Fernand Point created the original marjolaine. I have seen a number of reinterpretations of the master's work over the years, and I think it is appropriate that our version includes the tropics' mango fruit between the classic dacquoise layers. Furthermore, serving it frozen makes for a very refreshing respite from our island's famous heat. The ice creams may be made a day in advance.

Serves 10 to 12

BITTERSWEET CHOCOLATE ICE CREAM

½ pound bittersweet chocolate	6 egg yolks
1½ cups heavy cream	¼ cup sugar
1½ cups half and half	

1. Chop the chocolate into small, even pieces and place in a heatproof bowl. Melt over barely simmering water. Set aside.
2. In a large saucepan combine the heavy cream and half and half. Place on low heat.
3. Combine the egg yolks and sugar in a small bowl.

(recipe continues)

4. When the cream is hot remove from heat and whisk a small amount into the egg yolks. Stir the egg yolks into the remaining cream and return to the heat. Cook the mixture, stirring constantly, until it is very thick and heavily coats a wooden spoon, about 8 to 10 minutes. Remove from heat and strain through a fine-mesh strainer. Whisk the chocolate into the hot cream mixture. Chill.

5. Freeze in an ice cream maker according to manufacturer's directions. When frozen, place on a cookie sheet with sides and shape into a rectangular slab the same approximate dimensions as one of the dacquoise layers and about ¾ to 1 inch thick. Freeze until solid.

MANGO ICE CREAM

<table>
<tr><td>1</td><td>cup heavy cream</td><td>1</td><td>vanilla bean, split and scraped</td></tr>
<tr><td>1</td><td>cup half and half</td><td>1</td><td>medium-sized mango, peeled and</td></tr>
<tr><td>5</td><td>egg yolks</td><td></td><td>coarsely chopped</td></tr>
<tr><td>½</td><td>cup sugar</td><td></td><td></td></tr>
</table>

1. In a large saucepan, combine the heavy cream and half and half. Place on low heat.

2. Combine the egg yolks, sugar, and vanilla in a small bowl.

3. When the cream is hot, remove from heat and whisk a small amount into the egg yolk mixture. Stir the egg yolks into the remaining cream and return to the heat. Cook the mixture, stirring constantly, about 8 to 10 minutes until it is very thick and heavily coats a wooden spoon. Remove from heat and strain through a fine-mesh strainer. Chill.

4. Freeze in an ice cream maker according to manufacturer's directions. In the last 15 minutes of freezing, add the chopped mango to the ice cream. Shape the ice cream in the same manner as the chocolate ice cream and freeze solid.

DACQUOISE

<table>
<tr><td>3</td><td>ounces macadamia nuts</td><td>1</td><td>tablespoon flour</td></tr>
<tr><td>3</td><td>ounces grated unsweetened coconut, fresh or dried</td><td>4</td><td>egg whites (save the yolks for the ice cream)</td></tr>
<tr><td colspan="2">½ cup plus 2 tablespoons sugar</td><td></td><td></td></tr>
</table>

1. Preheat the oven to 350 degrees. Butter a 12- by 10½-inch baking sheet with sides. Cover with a sheet of parchment paper and butter the paper. Set aside.

2. Toast the macadamia nuts and the coconut in separate pans for approximately 10 minutes. The coconut should be evenly browned and dry. Remove from the oven and cool. Lower the oven temperature to 300 degrees.

3. Place the cooled coconut in the bowl of a processor. Using the steel blade, pulse until the coconut is finely chopped. Place in a small bowl. Repeat this procedure for the macadamia nuts. Combine with the coconut. Add ½ cup of sugar and the flour to the coconut and macadamias and stir well.

4. In the mixer bowl, beat the egg whites on medium speed until frothy. Slowly add the remaining 2 tablespoons sugar and continue beating until very stiff but not dry.

5. Pour the coconut mixture all at once into the egg whites. Using a rubber spatula, fold gently until evenly distributed.

6. Pour the mixture onto the parchment-lined pan. Spread evenly. (This is very important, since the batter will not spread during baking.)

7. Bake for 30 minutes or until set and lightly browned all over.

8. Remove from the oven. Quickly lift the dacquoise from the pan, still on the parchment. Immediately trim the edges and cut lengthwise into 3 even strips. Carefully peel off the parchment and cool the dacquoise. It should be crisp when cool. If it isn't, it may be returned to the oven for further baking.

ASSEMBLING THE MARJOLAINE

1. On a serving plate, place one layer of the dacquoise. Using a long spatula, carefully lift the chocolate ice cream slab from its pan and place on the dacquoise. Trim any excess ice cream or dacquoise. Top with another dacquoise layer and the mango ice cream. Again trim any excess. Finally, top with the final dacquoise layer and trim.

2. Store, well wrapped, in the freezer. Slice the marjolaine in ½-inch slices to serve.

APRICOT AND ALMOND "RAVIOLI"
with Toasted Almond Anglaise

These "ravioli" are warm, crisp, fruit-filled dough, lightly coated with cinnamon and sugar and marvelously paired with almond.

Serves 6

DOUGH

1½ cups all-purpose flour
2 tablespoons sugar
½ teaspoon baking powder

½ vanilla bean, split and scraped
1 tablespoon plus 1 teaspoon salad oil
½ cup lukewarm water

FILLING

3 ounces dried apricots (approximately 8 to 10 large halves)
1½ ounces toasted almonds

¼ cup (½ stick) butter
¼ teaspoon almond extract

1 egg
1 tablespoon water
½ cup sugar

½ teaspoon cinnamon
Enough oil for deep-frying ravioli
Nut Anglaise (page 278), made with almonds

1. Make the dough: In a bowl mix the flour, sugar, and baking powder. Add the scraped vanilla and, using your fingertips, mix the seeds throughout. Make a well in the center of the flour.

2. Pour the oil and water into the well. Using a fork, gently mix the flour into the oil and water. The mixture may seem dry, but don't add any more liquid. When the dry ingredients have been moistened, turn the dough out onto a clean surface and knead for 5 minutes. The dough should be very smooth. Cover with plastic wrap and allow to relax for 30 minutes at room temperature.

3. While the dough is relaxing, make the filling: Chop the apricots to ¼-inch dice, place in a bowl, and set aside.

4. Place the almonds in a food processor and pulse until finely chopped. Add to the apricots.

5. In a mixer bowl, using the paddle attachment, beat the butter until very smooth. Add the almond extract and the dried fruit and nuts. Blend well. Chill until ready to assemble.

ASSEMBLING RAVIOLI

1. Roll the dough on a very lightly floured surface to a rectangle measuring approximately 6 inches by 18 inches. Cut the dough into 1½- by 2-inch rectangles.

2. Prepare the egg wash by beating the egg and the tablespoon of water together in a small bowl.

3. Place a teaspoon of filling in the center of half the dough rectangles. Brush all edges with egg wash and top with another rectangle. Press firmly all around the edges to seal. Refrigerate until ready to serve.

FRYING AND SERVING

1. Mix the sugar and cinnamon in a small bowl.

2. Heat oil in a deep pan to 370 degrees. Drop the ravioli into the oil a few at a time and fry until puffed and crisp, turning once. Drain on paper toweling.

3. Roll quickly in sugar/cinnamon mixture and serve the ravioli atop the nut anglaise.

HAZELNUT CHOCOLATE COOKIES

As the conclusion to a particularly involved winery dinner, I chose these delicate and dreamy cookies Sue conjures up. The reaction was almost embarrassing. I was afraid the chateau we were hosting was going to hire her away from me so they would have a steady supply of these cookies! In the end, I just agreed to ship them a box periodically.

Makes 2 dozen cookies

1 cup hazelnuts	1 egg yolk
½ pound (2 sticks) plus 1 tablespoon butter	2 cups flour
	4 ounces bittersweet chocolate
¾ cup sugar	3 tablespoons cream
2 tablespoons hazelnut oil or salad oil	

1. Toast the hazelnuts in a 325-degree oven until crunchy and lightly browned. Place the hot nuts on a clean towel and gently roll them in the towel to remove the skins. When the nuts have cooled, place them in a food processor and pulse until finely chopped.

(recipe continues)

2. In a mixer bowl using the paddle attachment, cream ½ pound butter and the sugar on medium speed until light and fluffy. Add the oil and egg yolk and mix well. Add the flour and the chopped hazelnuts. Mix just until blended.

3. Place the dough on a piece of parchment paper and form a 2-inch-wide log, using the paper to shape the dough. Freeze. To ensure a perfectly round cookie, remove the dough after half an hour and roll the parchment-wrapped log on a hard surface, thus eliminating the flat side that develops as the dough is chilling. Return the dough to the freezer for half an hour more.

4. When ready to bake the cookies, preheat oven to 350 degrees. Slice the frozen dough into ¼-inch-thick slices. Place 1 inch apart on a parchment-lined baking sheet. Bake for 10 to 15 minutes, or until slightly brown around the edges. Cool on wire racks.

5. Chop the chocolate evenly into ½-inch pieces and place in a heatproof bowl with 1 tablespoon butter and the cream. Place the bowl over barely simmering water and stir occasionally until the chocolate is melted and the mixture is quite smooth. Remove from heat and allow to cool.

6. Using a small spatula, carefully spread the chocolate on the flat bottom of a cookie. Top with another cookie. Repeat until you have paired all the cookies.

CALVADOS APPLE TURNOVERS
with Black Pepper Feuilleté

We automatically think that pepper belongs only in a savory category. Good Tellicherry black pepper possesses a floral cinnamon/clove property that belongs with apples. In addition, the spark of the pepper offers a pleasant counterpoint to the mellow heat of the calvados and the buttery delicacy of the pastry.

Makes 8 turnovers

3 Granny Smith apples	Black Pepper Feuilleté (page 275)
3 tablespoons butter	1 egg
1 tablespoon sugar	1 teaspoon water
¼ cup calvados	

1. Peel, core, and slice apples into ¼-inch slices.

2. Melt the butter in a 10-inch sauté pan over medium-high heat until bubbly.

3. In a bowl, toss the apples with the sugar and add to the heated butter. Cook the apples, stirring frequently, for 3 or 4 minutes.

4. Add the calvados and ignite by tilting the pan toward the flame or using a match. Allow flame to go out on its own.

5. Transfer to a bowl and allow to cool completely.

ASSEMBLING TURNOVERS

1. Roll the puff pastry in a rectangular shape approximately 4½ by 32 inches, and ⅛ inch thick. Trim all edges with a long, sharp knife. (Cut straight down on the dough, don't drag the knife.) Cut the dough into 4-inch squares. Chill for 30 minutes.

2. Prepare an egg wash by beating an egg with 1 teaspoon cold water.

3. Place 6 to 8 slices of apple in the center of each puff pastry square. Brush 2 right-angle sides of the square with the egg wash, being careful not to let the wash drip down the edges of the dough at any time, as this will inhibit its rising.

4. Turn up the other two sides of the square to form a triangle shape, and press the edges firmly to seal. Brush the entire outside of the turnover with egg wash, again being careful not to let the egg wash drip down the edges of the pastry. Refrigerate for 30 minutes. (If you live in a warm climate or your kitchen is hot, it is best to assemble these one at a time, leaving the remainder of the dough squares in the refrigerator.)

5. Preheat oven to 425 degrees.

6. Place all turnovers on an ungreased baking sheet lined with parchment paper. Bake for 10 minutes, then reduce oven temperature to 375 degrees and bake for 15 to 20 minutes more, or until firm and uniformly browned.

COCONUT FLAN WITH MANGO
in Sauternes and Coconut Chips

Serves 6

1 large fresh coconut	½ cup water
3 cups milk	6 eggs
2 cups plus 1 tablespoon sugar	1 large mango
	1 cup Sauternes

1. Preheat oven to 325 degrees. Place coconut in the oven for 10 minutes.

2. Remove and wrap with a towel. Place on a hard surface and whack with a hammer or the back of a cleaver to crack the shell. Remove the meat from the shell. (It is best to try to get large pieces of the meat for ease in grating. If the meat does not pull away from the shell, place the point of a knife just between the meat and shell at any edge and gently pry the meat away.)

3. From one of the larger chunks of coconut, cut 18 very thin slices. Wrap and refrigerate.

4. Grate the remaining coconut, using a cheese grater. Place the grated coconut on a cookie sheet and toast in the oven until golden brown. Meanwhile, heat the milk to just hot (approximately 110 degrees). Stir the toasted coconut into the milk. Set aside for several hours, or overnight. (If steeping overnight, refrigerate the mixture when it reaches room temperature.)

5. In a heavy 2-quart pan, place 1¼ cups of the sugar and ½ cup water. Cover with a lid and place over high heat. When the mixture is boiling, remove the lid and reduce heat to medium-high. As this mixture boils, sugar may be caught against the side of the pan and crystallize. If this happens, brush the crystals down with a wet pastry brush. Continue cooking until thick and golden brown (approximately 340 degrees on a candy thermometer). Pour the caramel into 6 porcelain soufflé cups.

6. Preheat oven to 300 degrees. Strain the coconut and milk through a fine-mesh strainer into a medium saucepan. Heat to just warm. Beat the eggs in a bowl with ¾ cup sugar. Whisk the milk into the eggs. Pour this mixture through a fine-mesh strainer and ladle off any foam. Pour the custard into the prepared soufflé molds. Place the molds in a roasting pan with a thick dishtowel lining the base of the pan. Pour very hot water into the pan so that it comes halfway up the sides of the soufflé dishes. Cover the pan with aluminum foil and place in oven. Bake 30 to 40 minutes, or until custard is set and a knife inserted in the center comes out clean.

7. While the flans are baking, toss the reserved coconut chips with remaining 1 tablespoon sugar and place them on a cookie sheet. Toast the chips in the oven until crisp and golden brown all over, stirring them around occasionally. This takes approximately 20 to 30 minutes.

8. Remove the baking pan from the oven; take the soufflé molds out of the water and place them on a wire rack. Cool at room temperature for ½ hour and then refrigerate them for at least 1 hour before serving.

9. Peel and slice the mango, and dice into ½-inch chunks. Place in a bowl with the Sauternes. Refrigerate until needed.

TO SERVE:

1. Dip each soufflé mold into a pan of very hot water. Place a serving plate on top of each mold and invert to release the flan.

2. Spoon the mango around the flan and garnish with coconut chips.

BLACK PEPPER FEUILLETÉ

Each time puff pastry dough is rolled out and folded is called a "turn." Puff pastry should have six turns in all to attain maximum baked height. Classically, the dough is rolled out and folded into thirds to accomplish one turn. Here I have simplified the process by doing three folds followed by four folds in a series of turns, thereby cutting down the time required to make the dough.

Yields 18 to 20 4-inch by 4-inch squares.

3¾ cups all-purpose flour	1¼ cups heavy cream
1 teaspoon salt	1 pound chilled unsalted butter, cut into ½-inch cubes
2 tablespoons coarsely ground black pepper	

1. Combine 3¼ cups flour with all of the salt and pepper in mixer bowl. Using the paddle attachment on low speed, slowly stream the cream into the bowl, mixing until the dough just comes together. (It should be smooth, not too dry or sticky.)

(recipe continues)

2. Remove dough from bowl and pat with the heel of your hand into a rectangle about 5 inches by 8 inches. Wrap in plastic wrap and refrigerate for 30 minutes.

3. Place butter and remaining ½ cup flour in mixing bowl. Using paddle attachment, mix on low speed until well blended and only small lumps of butter appear. Remove from bowl and pat to a 5- by 8-inch rectangle on plastic wrap. Seal with the wrap and refrigerate for 30 minutes.

4. On a very lightly floured surface, roll dough into a rectangle large enough to envelop the butter. Place butter in the center of the dough. Fold the 2 ends of the dough over the butter and press the ends together; press also along the sides. The butter should not show through anywhere. Brush off any excess flour, wrap in plastic, and refrigerate for 30 minutes.

5. Remove the dough from the refrigerator and allow to soften a few minutes at room temperature.

6. On a lightly floured surface, roll the dough to a rectangle approximately 9 inches by 15 inches. Reposition the dough if necessary to flour lightly underneath it and to keep the corners squared off. If at any time the butter cracks through the dough, lightly flour the area where it came through and let the dough rest a few minutes to soften the butter. If the butter is oozing out at any point, it is too soft and the entire piece should be wrapped in plastic and refrigerated 15 to 20 minutes to harden the butter before continuing. When you have rolled out the rectangle, fold the dough into thirds, like a business letter. Brush off any excess flour with a pastry brush. Wrap in plastic and refrigerate for 30 minutes.

7. Remove the dough from the refrigerator and allow to soften a few minutes at room temperature.

8. On a lightly floured surface, roll the dough to a 9- by 18-inch rectangle, being careful to maintain square corners and avoid rolling over the ends of the dough. Fold the entire piece in half widthwise, to make a 9-inch square, then open out flat. This will give you a crease mark where the center of the dough is. Fold the outer edges toward the center so that they are about ½ inch from the center crease. Now fold the entire piece in half again (this accomplishes two turns). Brush off any excess flour. Wrap in plastic and refrigerate at least 1 hour.

9. Repeat steps 5 through 8.

10. The dough is now ready for use. Any unused portion of dough may be well wrapped and refrigerated for 2 to 3 days or kept in the freezer for up to 2 months. Scraps of dough can be pressed together at the edges and frozen for later use as the lining for a tart shell or for small items such as hot hors d'oeuvre. If the dough is kept in the freezer, thaw in the refrigerator a day in advance of use.

GINGER CARAMEL SAUCE

This is tremendous with ice cream and with an apple tart. This sauce keeps in the refrigerator for 1 week and can be reheated slowly in a double boiler.

Makes approximately 3 cups

2 cups heavy cream	1½ cups sugar
A 2-inch piece fresh gingerroot, peeled and sliced into ½-inch pieces	2 cups water

1. Scald cream and add ginger. Remove from heat and allow to steep 30 minutes.

2. Place sugar and water in a 2-quart, heavy-bottomed pan and bring to a boil. Cover and continue boiling for 10 minutes. Remove lid and reduce heat to medium. Continue cooking until the mixture gets thick and starts to brown.

3. At this point, strain the ginger from the cream and reheat the cream until it is hot.

4. When the sugar mixture has become a deep brown, whisk in the cream, pouring the cream slowly and whisking vigorously; the mixture will foam up rapidly at first and will settle down more as you add cream. Whisk until all the caramel is blended with the cream.

Variations:

Plain Caramel: Omit the ginger. Proceed with recipe as directed.

Orange Caramel: Using a vegetable peeler or sharp knife, peel 2 oranges, avoiding the bitter white pith. Steep the orange peels in the cream (as with the ginger) and proceed as directed.

CRÈME ANGLAISE

This is a basic dessert sauce and can accompany warm fruit tarts, chocolate desserts, or simple fresh fruit.

Makes 3 cups

2 cups milk	6 egg yolks
⅔ cups sugar	½ vanilla bean, split and scraped

1. In a heavy-bottomed 1-quart pan, heat the milk over low heat until hot. While the milk is heating, combine the other ingredients in a bowl.

2. When the milk is very hot, ladle about ½ cup into the egg mixture, whisking rapidly.

3. Return this mixture to the rest of the milk and stir constantly with a wooden spoon over low heat until it thickens and just coats the spoon, about 7 to 10 minutes.

4. Pour the anglaise through a fine-mesh strainer into a bowl. Cool and refrigerate.

Variations:

Nut Anglaise: Place 1 cup of nuts (almonds, hazelnuts, or cashews) on a baking sheet and toast in a 325-degree oven for approximately 10 minutes. Add the toasted nuts to the heated milk in Step 1 and allow to steep for 30 minutes. Strain the milk and reheat before proceeding with the recipe.

Orange Anglaise: Using a vegetable peeler, cut only the skin from 2 oranges. Add to the heated milk in Step 1 and allow to stand for 30 minutes. Strain the milk and reheat before proceeding with the recipe.

CHOCOLATE SAUCE

This is a basic chocolate sauce. It can be served over ice cream or with anything else you feel deserves a chocolate flavor. It will keep two weeks in the refrigerator.

Makes 3 cups

1   cup cocoa powder
1   cup (2 sticks) butter, cut in pieces
1   cup heavy cream
⅔ cup sugar

¾ teaspoon vanilla
2   tablespoons black raspberry liqueur or other liqueur of your choice

1. Place the cocoa powder, butter, cream, and sugar in a heatproof bowl. Place the bowl over, not in, a pan of simmering water. When the butter has melted, whisk the mixture until smooth. Taste to make sure the sugar has melted. If it has not, continue whisking until it has.

2. Remove from heat and whisk in vanilla and liqueur.

CHERRY SAUCE

Makes 3 cups

2   cups Black Muscat wine (Elysium by Andrew Quady), or substitute a good port
½ cup sugar

1   cinnamon stick
1   cup bing cherries, halved and pitted

1. Place all the ingredients except the cherries in a saucepan and heat to boiling. Reduce heat and simmer 20 minutes. Add cherries and continue cooking 5 minutes more. Remove from heat and discard cinnamon stick. This sauce may be served hot or cold.

BLUEBERRY SAUCE

Makes 2 cups

    2 *cups fresh blueberries, picked over and*
        washed
   ½ *cup crème de cassis*

1. Purée 1½ cups blueberries in a food processor or blender.
2. In a small saucepan bring the purée and cassis to a boil. Lower heat and simmer for 10 minutes. Remove from heat and strain through a fine-mesh strainer. Stir in remaining ½ cup of blueberries. Serve chilled. If sauce seems too thick, it can be thinned with additional cassis.

POURING CREAM

Makes about 3 cups

    2 *cups heavy cream, well chilled*   1 *teaspoon vanilla extract, or any liqueur*
    2 *teaspoons confectioner's sugar*

1. Pour cream and sugar into a medium bowl. Whisk the cream until barely whipped (it should be pourable).
2. Gently whisk in vanilla or other flavoring.

PÂTE SUCRE

This is a basic sweet almond pie dough.

**Makes enough dough
for two 11-inch tart shells**

2 cups all-purpose flour
3 tablespoons sugar
¼ teaspoon salt
½ cup ground almonds

⅞ cup (1¾ sticks) chilled butter, cut into
    ½-inch cubes
1 egg
½ teaspoon vanilla

1. Combine flour, sugar, salt, and almonds in mixer bowl. Using the paddle attachment with the machine on low speed, mix these ingredients briefly.

2. Add butter and continue beating on low speed until the mixture resembles coarse meal. This will take several minutes. There should be no lumps of butter visible. If there are, stop the machine and break them up with your fingertips. Then continue mixing.

3. Beat egg with vanilla in a bowl and slowly stream into flour mixture. Mix just until the beaten egg is incorporated.

4. Wrap the dough in plastic wrap and chill at least 3 hours. (This dough is easiest to work with if allowed to rest overnight.) Any unused portion can be frozen. Thaw in the refrigerator overnight before rolling.

PÂTE BRISÉE

A basic pie dough.

**Makes enough dough
for two 11-inch pie shells**

2 cups flour
½ teaspoon salt

1 cup (2 sticks) chilled butter, cut into ½-
inch cubes
3 to 4 tablespoons ice water, more if needed

1. Place the flour and salt in the bowl of a food processor. Using the steel blade, pulse for 10 seconds.

2. Stop the machine, add the butter, pulse at 15-second intervals until the mixture resembles coarse meal. (This can also be done with a pastry blender or two table knives.)

3. Transfer the mixture to a bowl and make a well in the center. Add the ice water, 1 tablespoon at a time, tossing gently with a fork, until the dough starts to hold together.

4. Gather the dough into a ball, wrap in plastic wrap, and chill for 30 minutes before rolling.

RECOMMENDED READING

The following is a list of books I have enjoyed very much over the years; perhaps you will too.

•

BEARD, JAMES
James Beard's Theory and Practice of Good Cooking.
New York: Alfred A. Knopf, 1977.

The New James Beard.
New York: Alfred A. Knopf, 1981.

•

BLANC, GEORGES
The Natural Cuisine of Georges Blanc.
New York: Stewart, Tabori & Chang, 1987.

•

BRILLAT-SAVARIN
The Physiology of Taste.
San Francisco: North Point Press, 1986.

•

BUGIALLI, GUILIANO
Guiliano Bugialli's Foods of Italy.
New York: Stewart, Tabori & Chang, 1984.

•

CASAS, PENELOPE
Foods & Wines of Spain.
New York: Alfred A. Knopf, 1982.

•

DAVID, ELIZABETH
Elizabeth David Classics:
Mediterranean Food, French Country Cooking,
Summer Cooking.
New York: Alfred A. Knopf, 1980.

•

DEGROOT, ROY A.
The Auberge of the Flowering Hearth.
New York: Ballantine Books, 1984.

•

FISHER, M.F.K.
The Art of Eating.
New York: Random House, 1976.

•

GIRARDET, FREDY
Cuisine of Fredy Girardet.
New York: William Morrow, 1984.

•

GUERAD, MICHEL
Michel Guerad's Cuisine Gourmande.
New York: William Morrow, 1979.

•

HAZAN, MARCELLA
Marcella's Italian Kitchen.
New York: Alfred A. Knopf, 1986.

•

HOM, KEN
Ken Hom's East Meets West Cuisine.
New York: Simon & Schuster, 1987.

•

KENNEDY, DIANA
The Cuisines of Mexico.
New York: Harper & Row, 1972.

•

RECOMMENDED READING

LENOTRE, GASTON
Lenotre's Desserts & Pastries.
New York: Barron, 1977.

•

MCCLANE, A.J., ED.
The Encyclopedia of Fish Cookery.
Toronto: Holt, Rinehart & Winston, 1977.

•

MONTAGNE, PROSPER
The New Larousse Gastronomique:
The Encyclopedia of Food, Wine, & Cooking.
New York: Crown, 1977.

•

OLNEY, RICHARD
The French Menu Cookbook.
Boston: Godine, 1985.

•

POINT, FERDNAND
Ma Gastronomie.
Wilton, Conn.: Lyceum Books, 1969.

•

PRUDHOMME, PAUL
Chef Paul Prudhomme's Louisiana Kitchen.
New York: William Morrow, 1984.

•

ROOT, WAVERLY
Food.
New York: Simon & Schuster, 1980.

•

SENDERENS, ALAN
The Three-Star Recipes of Alan Senderens.
New York: William Morrow, 1982.

•

SHERE, LINDSEY R.
Chez Panisse Desserts.
New York: Random House, 1985.

•

SILVERTON, NANCY
Desserts.
New York: Harper & Row, 1986.

•

TOWER, JEREMIAH
Jeremiah Tower's New American Classics.
New York: Harper & Row, 1986.

•

TROISGROS, JEAN,
AND TROISGROS, PIERRE
The Nouvelle Cuisine of
Jean & Pierre Troisgros.
New York, William Morrow, 1978.

•

TSUJI, SHIZUO
Japanese Cooking:
A Simple Art.
Tokyo: Kodansha, 1980.

•

VERGE, ROGER
Roger Verge's Cuisine of South France.
New York: William Morrow, 1980.

•

WATERS, ALICE
The Chez Panisse Menu Cookbook.
New York: Random House, 1982.

•

CURTAN, PATRICIA,
AND LABRO, MARTIN
*The Chez Panisse
Pasta, Pizza & Calzone.*
New York: Random House, 1982.

•

WOLFERT, PAULA
Mediterranean Cooking.
New York: Times Books, 1977.

The Cooking of South-West France.
New York: (Dial) Doubleday, 1983.

INDEX

Achiote-marinated skewered quail with torn greens and papaya-chile vinaigrette, 109–10

Acorn squash. *See* Squash

Aigrelette sauce, 231

Aioli, 233–34
stuffed baked mussels with shellfish béarnaise and, 76–77

Almonds
anglaise, 278; and apricot "ravioli" with toasted almond anglaise, 270–71; in linzertorte with rhubarb, apple, and orange, 262; in pâte sucre, 281

American Spoonfood Company, 156

Ancho chile peppers. *See* Peppers, chile

Anchovies
in dressing for Caesar salad, 97; in steak tartare, 96–97; in tapenade, 225; in tonnato, 235

Andouille sausage. *See* Sausage

Anise, star
creamy mussel soup with saffron, orange, and, 32

Annatto seeds. *See* Achiote

Appetizers, cold, 44–58
about, 43; charred "raw" tuna with wasabi, and pickled onions, 52; chipotle chile and shrimp terrine, 54; kumamoto oysters on the half shell with smoked salmon, slaw and

sauce mignonette, 53; lobster terrine with caviars and citrus on a champagne yogurt dressing, 48–50; pepper-charred tenderloin, chile mayonnaise, and grilled tortillas, 50; salmon carpaccio with caviar, hard-cooked eggs, and brioche, 57–58; shellfish seviche on a creole vinaigrette with Southern slaw, 46–47; stone crab claws with mustard sauce and vegetable chowchow, 55–56; Texas Gulf shrimp steamed in Dixie beer with Southern slaw and creole rémoulade, 44–45; tortilla paisana, 56–57; wild mushroom terrine, 51; *see also* Appetizers, hot

Appetizers, hot, 59–89
about, 43; artichoke and gorgonzola torta with red beet purée, 81–82; bruschetta with Roquefort and tapenade, 86–87; carnitas in red chili cakes with black beans, sour cream, and salsa, 87–89; crisp potato cakes with sour cream and caviar, 82–83; fisherman's pan stew with fettuccine and white wine cream, 71–72; foie gras, parsnip pancakes, and savory caramel sauce, 62–63; game bird ravioli, citrus pasta, sauce adobado, 80–81; ginger ravioli with smoked capon and chut-

ney, port mustard cream, 68–69; grilled marinated shrimp and chorizo with Spanish sherry vinegar, 59–60; grilled sweetbreads in corn cakes with kumquat jelly, 72–73; lasagnetta with Gulf shrimp and California escargots in a lemon-mustard cream, 84–85; lobster fritters with conch tartar sauce, 67–68; lobster and pasta with mango, avocado, and Chardonnay butter, 66–67; Manila clams in Rioja with Spanish sausage, 85; my "short stack"—foie gras, parsnip pancakes, and savory caramel sauce, 62–63; pan-fried buffalo mozzarella with smoked plum tomato cream, 67–71; pan-fried Gulf crab cakes with mustard béarnaise, 74–75; pan-seared spiced shrimp with gumbo sauce, 143–44; pork Havana "nueva," 60–62; scallop chartreuse with sun-dried tomato pesto and a rosé butter sauce, 78–79; stuffed baked mussels with shellfish béarnaise and aioli, 76–77; veal ragout in poblano peppers with ricotta cream, 64–65; *see also* Appetizers, cold

Apples
chutney, 204; and coconut; curried carrot and chicken

Apples (*continued*)
soup with, 38; linzertorte with rhubarb, orange, and, 262–63; in mango chutney, 203; tart with warm ginger caramel; country, 255–56; turnovers with black pepper feuilleté; calvados, 272–73

Apricot and almond "ravioli" with toasted almond anglaise, 270–71

Artichokes
about, 99; and gorgonzola torta with red beet purée, 81–82; hearts; poached, 100

Asparagus spears, steamed, with black pepper pesto vinaigrette, 108–9

Avocados
bell pepper, endive, jicama salad with a salsa vinaigrette, 106; buttermilk, and grilled eggplant soup; cold, 33; crabmeat, and mango with olive oil and lime vinaigrette, 101; mango, and Chardonnay butter; lobster and pasta with, 66–67; poblano chiles relleños with lobster, pepitas, and, 144–45; in spinach salad, 98–99; and tomato béarnaise, 124–25; and tomato salad with smoked trout-buttermilk dressing, 110–11

Babas au Louies, 256–57

Bacon
applejack brandy, and green onions; sautéed calf's liver with, 169–70; in brown sauce, 248–49; dressing; warm, 229; herbs, and red wine butter; roasted swordfish with, 129–30; peanuts, and green onions pan butter; catfish with, 148–49; wild mushrooms, pearl on-

ions, and a red wine vinegar sauce; roasted chicken with, 179–80;

Bahamian conch chowder, 22–23

Banana chile peppers. *See* Peppers, chile

Bananas
rum custard tart; Cuban, 254–55; *see also* Plantains

Basic all-purpose flour pasta, 206

Basic homemade mayonnaise, 232

Basic vinaigrette, 227

Basic white butter sauce (Beurre Blanc), 237

Basil
and Key lime butter sauce, 142; in pesto, 224–25

Bass. *See* Striped bass

Beans, dried
black, 134–35
ginger, scallion, and citrus relish, 134–35; sauce, 61–62; soup, with jalapeño sour cream and cilantro salsa, 27–28
black turtle, 88
soup with jalapeño sour cream and cilantro salsa, 27–28
white
salad with cracklings, duck livers, and greens, sherry vinaigrette; warm, 103–4
see also Lentils

Beans, green. *See* Haricots verts

Beard, James, 206, 210

Béarnaise sauce, 238
avocado and tomato, 124–25; mustard, 75; and salmon caviar; grilled Norwegian salmon with a sour cream, 146; shellfish, 76–77

Béchamel, 29–30

Beef
filet mignon
tartare, 96–97

liver, calf's
roasted, with Madeira, country ham, and sweet melon, 170–71; sautéed, with slab bacon, applejack brandy, and green onions, 169–70
prime rib of
for Cajun rib steak, sweet peppers, and hot chiles, 167–69
steak tartare, 96–97; steaks grilled, with gorgonzola butter and marinated deep-fried red onions, 177–78
tenderloin
pepper-charred, chile mayonnaise, and grilled tortillas, 50
see also Veal

Beer
cheese soup with rye croutons, 39–40; court bouillon, 239
Texas Gulf shrimp steamed in, 44–45

Beets
purée, 81–82; in vegetable chowchow, 55–56

Bell peppers. *See* Peppers, bell

Beurre Blanc. *See* Basic white butter sauce

Bittersweet chocolate ice cream, 267–68

Black beans. *See* Beans, dried

Black pepper
brioche; cracked, 209–10; feuilleté, 275–76
calvados apple turnovers with, 272–73
pesto, 108–9
vinaigrette, 108–9

Blanc, Georges, 231

Blue cheese
and Tuscan vinegar; hearts of romaine and tiny green beans with, 113; *see also* Gorgonzola cheese

Blue corn cakes, 195

Blueberry sauce, 280
  chocolate fritters with, 265–67
Body analogy, 6–7
Braided sashimi of red snapper
  and yellowfin tuna with tart
  herbal dressing and mixed lettuces, 102
Braised breast of chicken with
  "salt and pepper," 174–76
Braised fennel with proscuitto
  and parmesan, 191–92
Braised striped bass in Chardonnay with a chiffonade of lettuces, 122–23
Bread
  cracked black pepper brioche,
  209–10; grilled, with soft
  cheese, 104; salad; Mediterranean, 95–96; see also Bread
  crumbs; Cornbread; Croutons
Bread crumbs
  making, 70
Brioche, cracked black pepper,
  209–10
  caviar, and hard-cooked eggs;
  salmon carpaccio with, 57–58;
  and wild mushrooms stuffing,
  for quail, 156–57
Broccoli
  in little vegetable pancakes,
  196
Broths. See Soups
Brown sauce, 248–49
Bruschetta with Roquefort and
  tapenade, 86–87
Butter
  gorgonzola, 177–78; herb,
  236–37; lemon, 132; mango,
  256–57
Butter sauces. See Sauces
Buttermilk
  avocado, and grilled eggplant
  soup; cold, 33; in homemade
  ricotta, 211–12; smoked trout
  dressing, 110; in Southern slaw
  dressing, 236

Cabbages
  in Southern slaw, 44
Caesar salad steak "tartare," 96–
  97
Café at Louie's Backyard, 4, 84
Cajun rib steak, sweet peppers,
  and hot chiles, 167–69
Calvados apple turnovers with
  black pepper feuilleté, 272–73
Cantaloupe. See Melon
Capon, smoked
  and chutney filling, for ginger
  ravioli, 68–69
Caramel sauce
  ginger, 277; orange, 277; plain,
  277 savory, 246
    foie gras, parsnip pancakes,
    and, 62–63
Carnitas in red chili cakes with
  black beans, sour cream, and
  salsa, 87–89
Carrots
  in brown sauce, 248–49; and
  chicken soup; curried, with
  apples and coconut, 38; in little
  vegetable pancakes, 196; in
  sauce creole, 226–27; in
  Southern slaw, 44; in vegetable
  chowchow, 55–56
Cashews
  anglaise, 278; in Cuban banana rum custard tart, 254–55
Catfish with peanuts, green onions, and bacon pan butter,
  148–49
Caviars
  and citrus, for cold lobster terrine, 49; as garnish for grilled
  Norwegian salmon, 146; hard-
  cooked eggs, and brioche;
  salmon carpaccio with, 57–58;
  and sour cream; crisp potato
  cakes with, 82–83
Celery
  in brown sauce, 248–49; in
  creole rémoulade, 45; in sauce
  creole, 226–27; in Southern

slaw, 44
Chanterelles. See Mushrooms
Chardonnay. See Wine
Chardonnay-hazelnut vinaigrette,
  228
Char-grilled vegetable soup with
  summer salsa, 34–35
Charred "raw" tuna with wasabi
  and pickled onions, 52
Chartreuse
  lining, 78–79; scallop, with
  sun-dried tomato pesto and a
  rosé butter sauce, 78–79
Chase, Dooky, 226
Chateau Montelena, 153
Cheddar cheese beer soup, 39
Cheese
  beer soup with rye croutons,
  39–40; for a savory flan, 193;
  see also individual names
Cheesecake. See Desserts
Cherries
  in apple chutney, 204; sauce,
  279
    chocolate fritters with (varia-
    tion), 267
Chèvre and ginger tart, 261
Chicken
  breasts
    braised, with "salt and pep-
    per," 174–76; and carrot
    soup; curried with apples
    and coconut, 38; salad with
    honey-mustard dressing;
    hot-fried, 94–95;
  carcasses
    in stock, 240–41
  and carrot soup; curried, with
  apples and coconut, 38; fricassee of, with corn cakes, root
  vegetables, and bell pepper
  cream (substitute), 164–65;
  pan-cooked young, with corn-
  bread-chorizo stuffing and
  port-ginger sauce, 158–59;
  poussin
    pan-cooked, with cornbread-

Chicken (*continued*)
  chorizo stuffing and port-
  ginger sauce, 158–59
  roasted, with lardoons, wild
  mushrooms; pearl onions, and
  a red wine vinegar sauce, 179–
  80; salad with honey-mustard
  dressing; hot fried, 94–95;
  smoked
    and chutney filling, for gin-
    ger ravioli (substitute), 68–
    69; in hot sausage and shell-
    fish gumbo (variation), 27
  smoked bones
    in smoked stock, 241
  stock, 240–41; whole
    roasted, with lardoons, wild
    mushrooms, pearl onions,
    and a red wine vinegar
    sauce, 179–80
Chiffonade of lettuces, 122
Chile mayonnaise, 233
Chile peppers. *See* Peppers, chile
Chilled fennel soup with grilled
  shrimp, 36
Chinese parsley. *See* Cilantro
Chipotle chile peppers. *See* Peppers, chile
Chocolate
  in choculis extremis, 259–60;
  fritters with blueberry sauce,
  265–67; hazelnut cookies,
  271–72; ice cream; bittersweet,
  267–68; pistachio, vanilla
  cheesecake, 258–59; sauce,
  279
Choculis extremis, 259–60
Chorizo sausage. *See* Sausage
Chowchow, vegetable, 55–56
Chowders. *See* Soups
Chutney
  apple, 204; mango, 203
Cilantro
  and chile broth, 23–24; and jalapeño sour cream salsa, 28;
  and sesame seed sauce, 133
Citrus butter sauce, 145

Citrus marinade
  for grilled fish, 134–35
Clams
  and corn chowder with roast
  chiles, 28–30; Manila
    in Rioja with Spanish sau-
    sage, 85
  preparing for use, 11
Coach House Restaurant, 27
Coconut
  and apples; curried carrot and
  chicken soup with, 38; in dacquoise, 268–69; flan with
  mango in Sauternes and coconut chips, 274–75; meat, removing, 274
Cold avocado, buttermilk, and
  grilled eggplant soup, 33
Cold lobster terrine with caviars
  and citrus on a champagne yogurt dressing, 48–50
Compote
  Black Muscat, f181–2; mango,
  183
Conch
  about, 23; butter sauce, 136–
  37; chowder, Bahamian, 22–
  23
    in conch butter sauce, 136–
    37; in tartar sauce, 67–68
  lasagne, 118–20; tartar sauce,
  67–68
Cookies. *See* Desserts
Cooking advice and techniques,
  12–13
Cooking tools, 14–15
  food mill, 14; meat grinder, 14;
  pasta machine, 14; smoker, 14;
  soufflé molds, 15; tart pans,
  14; terrine molds, 15
Cook's Magazine, 34
Corn
  cakes, 73–74, 194; and clam
  chowder, with roast chiles, 28–
  30; in cornbread, 210–11
Corn cakes, 194
  blue, 195

pan-cooked scallops with red
  pepper purée and, 130–31
grilled sweetbreads in, 72–74;
root vegetables, and bell pepper cream; fricassee of rabbit
with, 164–65
Cornbread, 210–11
  chorizo stuffing, 158–59
Cornmeal
  blue
    in corn cakes, 195
  in corn cakes, 73–74, 194; in
  cornbread, 210–11; in polenta,
  grilled parmesan, 98–99
Coulis, fruit, 264
Country apple tart with warm
  ginger caramel, 255–56
Court bouillon, 172–73
  beer, 239
Crabs and crabmeat
  blue
    cakes, pan-fried, with mus-
    tard béarnaise, 74–75
  mango, and avocado with olive
  oil and lime vinaigrette, 101;
  soft-shell
    pan-cooked, with papaya
    and lime, 147
  stone
    claws with mustard sauce
    and vegetable chowchow,
    55–56
  stone, Florida
    and lobster with acorn
    squash, garlic, and ginger
    butter sauce, 127–28
Cracked black pepper brioche,
  209–10
Cracklings, 10–11
  duck livers, and greens, sherry
  vinaigrette; warm white bean
  salad with, 103–104
Cream
  in béchamel, 29–30; in crème
  fraîche, 37, 211; creole mustard, 166; lemon-mustard, 84;
  plum tomato, 70–71; port

Feast of Santa Fe (Dent), 11

Fennel
braised, with proscuitto and parmesan, 191–92; mayonnaise, 232; soup with grilled shrimp; chilled, 36 in stuffing for baked mussels, 76–77

Fettuccine
and hot sausages with chèvre and ratatouille, 178–79; and lobster with mango, avocado, and Chardonnay butter, 66–67; sweetbreads with Barsac, glazed pearl onions, and, 172–74; and white wine cream; fisherman's pan stew with, 71–72

Figs, dried
in choculis extremis, 259–60; roast garlic, mint, and pine nuts; roasted leg of lamb with, 162–63

Fish
anchovies
in dressing for Caesar salad, 97; in steak tartare, 96–97; in tapenade, 225; in tonnato, 235
catfish
with peanuts, green onions, and bacon pan butter, 148–49
in fisherman's pan stew with fettuccine and white wine cream, 71–72; freshness, checking for, 244; grouper with Asian vegetables, 120–21; herb-crusted, char-grilled, with lemon butter (substitute), 132; pan-cooked, over ancho butter sauce with avocado and tomato béarnaise, 124–25; panéed, with Alabama oysters and conch butter sauce, 136–37; soy- and sesame-grilled, with a tropical fruit salsa, 126

heads and frames for stock, 244–45
salmon
carpaccio with caviar, hard-cooked eggs, and brioche, 57–58; in cold lobster terrine with caviars and citrus on a champagne yogurt dressing, 48–50; grilled, with a sour cream béarnaise and salmon caviar, 146; herb-crusted, char-grilled with lemon butter (substitute), 132; herb-cured, 213–14; slaw; smoked, 53
snapper
braised in Chardonnay with a chiffonade of lettuces (substitute), 123; pan-cooked whole, with Key lime butter and basil (substitute), 141–42; in shellfish seviche on a creole vinaigrette with Southern slaw, 46–47; and yellowfin tuna with tart herbal dressing and mixed lettuces; braided sashimi of, 102
stock, 244–45
in seafood mornay, 119
striped bass
braised in Chardonnay with a chiffonade of lettuces, 122–23
swordfish
herb-crusted, char-grilled, with lemon butter, 132; roasted with herbs, smoked bacon, and red wine butter, 129–30
trout
buttermilk dressing; smoked; 110
tuna
charred "raw," with wasabi and pickled onions, 52; grilled, with ginger, scallion,

citrus, and black bean relish, 134–45; herb-crusted, char-grilled, with lemon butter (substitute), 132; and red snapper with tart herbal dressing and mixed lettuces; braided sashimi of, 102; in tonnato, 235
yellowtail
pan-cooked whole, with Key lime butter and basil, 141–42
see also Shellfish; individual names

Fisherman's pan stew with fettuccine and white wine cream, 71–72

Flan, a savory, 192–93

Flavor, 6–7

Florida lobster tortellini in chile and cilantro broth, 23–25

Florida stone crabs and lobster with acorn squash, garlic, and ginger butter sauce, 127–28

Foie gras, parsnip pancakes, and savory caramel sauce, 62–63

Food mill, 14

Four Seasons restaurant, 59

Fricassee of rabbit with corn cakes, root vegetables, and bell pepper cream, 164–65

Fritters, 265–67
chocolate, with blueberry sauce, 265–67; lobster, 67–68

Frozen lime soufflé with fruit coulis, 264

Frozen tropical marjolaine, mango and bittersweet chocolate ice creams, 267–69

Fruit
coulis, 264; *see also* individual names

Game birds
quail
anchiote-marinated skew-

Shellfish (*continued*)
  with saffron, orange, and star anise; creamy, 32; stuffed baked, with shellfish béarnaise and aioli, 76–77
oysters
  about, 228; with grouper and conch butter sauce; panéed, 136–37; in hot sausage and shellfish gumbo, 25–27; on the half shell with smoked salmon slaw and sauce mignonette, 53
scallops
  chartreuse with sun-dried tomato pesto and a rosé butter sauce, 78–79; grilled ginger-studded, with Chinese parsley and sesame seed sauce, 133; mousse, 78–79; pan-cooked, with red pepper purée and blue corn cakes, 130–31
seviche on a creole vinaigrette with Southern slaw, 46–47;
shells
  in stock, 245
shrimp
  with anchos, tequila, and red onion salsa; sautéed, 138–39; in beer court bouillon, 239; and California escargots in a lemon-mustard cream; lasagnetta with, 84–85; and chipotle chile terrine, 54; with citrus, wild mushrooms, and roasted peppers in a Sauternes butter sauce; sautéed (substitute), 140–41; grilled, 36; grilled marinated, and chorizo with Spanish sherry vinegar, 59–60; pan-seared spiced, with gumbo sauce, 143–44; in seviche on a creole vinaigrette with Southern slaw, 46–47; Texas Gulf, steamed

in Dixie beer with Southern slaw and creole rémoulade, 44–45
stock, 245
  for crabs and lobster, 127–28
Shiitakes. *See* Mushrooms
Shock and seduction, 7–8
Shrimp
  with anchos, tequila, and red onion salsa; sautéed, 138–39; in beer court bouillon, 239; and California escargots in a lemon-mustard cream; lasagnetta with, 84–85; and chipotle chile terrine, 54; with citrus, wild mushrooms, and roasted peppers in a Sauternes butter sauce; sautéed (substitute), 140–41; grilled, 36; grilled marinated, and chorizo with Spanish sherry vinegar, 59–60; pan-seared spiced, with gumbo sauce, 143–44; in shellfish seviche on a creole vinaigrette with Southern slaw, 46–47;
shells
  for fish stock, 245
Texas Gulf, steamed in Dixie beer with Southern slaw and creole rémoulade, 44–45
Simonton, John, 117
Sinclair, Gordon, 216
Sinclair's restaurant, 216
Smoked duck salad Szechuan
  with somen noodles and Oriental vegetables, 107–8
Smoked stock, 241
Smoked tomatoes, 69–70
Smoker, 14
Snapper
  braised in Chardonnay with a chiffonade of lettuces (substitute), 123; pan-cooked whole, with Key lime butter and basil (substitute), 141–42; red
  and yellowfin tuna with tart

herbal dressing and mixed lettuces; braided sashimi of, 102
  in shellfish seviche on a creole vinaigrette with Southern slaw, 46–47
Somen noodles
  and Oriental vegetables; smoked duck salad Szechuan with, 107–8
Soufflé molds, 15
Soufflé, frozen lime, with fruit coulis, 264
Soups, 22–40
  acorn squash, with smoked duck, 40; avocado, buttermilk, and grilled eggplant, cold, 33; beer-cheese, with rye croutons, 39–40; black bean, with jalapeño sour cream and cilantro salsa, 27–28; broth
    chile and cilantro, 23–24
  carrot and chicken, curried, with apples and coconut, 38; chowder
    Bahamian conch, 22–23; clam and corn, with roast chiles, 28–30
  fennel, with grilled shrimp, chilled, 36; garlic, with sausage and St. André croutons, poached, 30–31; gumbo, hot sausage and shellfish, 25–27; lobster tortellini in chile and cilantro broth, Florida, 23–25; mussel, with saffron, orange, and star anise, creamy, 32; tomato, with pesto crème fraîche, warm, 37; vegetable, with summer salsa, char-grilled, 34–35; *see also* Stocks
Sour cream
  béarnaise and salmon caviar; grilled Norwegian salmon with a, 146; and caviar; crisp potato cakes with, 82–83; in pistachio, chocolate, vanilla cheese-

About the Author

Norman Van Aken is a native of Diamond Lake, Illinois. From humble beginnings as a short-order cook at Tom and Jerry's Fireside Inn in Libertyville, Illinois, he has gone on to become one of the few truly self-taught master chefs in the U.S. and the winner of dozens of major culinary awards. He has presided over the kitchens at Sinclair's in Lake Forest, Illinois; Sinclair's American Grill in Jupiter, Florida; Louie's Backyard, the Café at Louie's, and MIRA, all in Key West; a Mano in Miami Beach; and Norman's in Coral Gables, where he is currently chef and co-owner. He was named a winner of the Robert Mondavi Culinary Award of Excellence in 1996 and was named Best Chef in the Southeast by the James Beard Foundation in 1997. He has also written *The Great Exotic Fruit Book.*